The
Vital Center

The Politics of Freedom

Books by Arthur M. Schlesinger, Jr.

The
Vital Center

The Politics of Freedom

By

Arthur M. Schlesinger, Jr.

With a new Introduction by the author

Houghton Mifflin Company Boston

Sixth Printing, C

Printed in the U.S.A.

for

Stephen

Katharine Christina

Andrew

Turning and turning in the widening gyre
The falcon cannot hear the falconer;
Things fall apart; the centre cannot hold;
Mere anarchy is loosed upon the world,
The blood-dimmed tide is loosed, and everywhere
The ceremony of innocence is drowned;
The best lack all conviction, while the worst
Are full of passionate intensity . . .
And what rough beast, its hour come round at last,
Slouches toward Bethlehem to be born?

W. B. YEATS

Introduction

THE VITAL CENTER was written in the autumn and winter of 1948–49. This was a moment of transition in the postwar history of American liberalism — a moment when the liberal community was engaged in the double task of redefining its attitude toward the phenomenon of Communism and, partly in consequence, of reconstructing the bases of liberal political philosophy.

In the years since, the process of redefinition has been completed: I believe that all American liberals recognize today that liberalism has nothing in common with Communism, either as to means or as to ends.

As for the process of reconstruction, this is by its nature continuous: if liberalism should ever harden into ideology, then, like all ideologies, it would be overwhelmed by the turbulence and unpredictability of history — especially in an age when science and technology have made the velocity of history so much greater than ever before. The continuing enterprise of reconstruction has consequently brought new phases of liberal thought to the forefront in the thirteen years since this book was published.

It may be worthwhile to note some of these later developments.

So far as Communism is concerned, in the confused years immediately after the end of the Second World War, and in spite of Stalin's notable record in the thirties of internal terror and international betrayal, the Soviet Union retained for some people traces of the idealistic fervor of the Russian Revolution. By 1962, it seems safe to say that postwar Soviet policy has extinguished any remaining elements of idealism in the Communist appeal. No one with any knowledge of history can believe in the Soviet Union on the supposition that Communist victory would usher in a generous and beneficent society. Where people believe in the Soviet Union today, it is on quite other grounds: it is basically because they are persuaded that, whether they like it or not, Communism is going to win, and that they had therefore better make their terms with a Communist world. The essence of contemporary Soviet policy is to enhance this impression of the inevitability of Communist triumph, to employ every resource of science and politics to identify Communism with the future and to convince people everywhere that they must accept the necessity of Communism or face the certainty of obliteration. They have addressed this policy especially to the southern half of the world where the awakening of underdeveloped countries from centuries of oblivion is discharging new and incalculable energies into human society.

The irony is that the very eagerness with which intellectuals in emergent nations often embrace Communism itself suggests that Communism is *not* the wave of the future and is, if it is anything, a passing stage to which some may temporarily turn in the quest for modernity. Where Marx portrayed Communism as the fulfillment of the process of modernization, history seems abundantly to show that, if the world avoids thermonuclear suicide, the modernization process, contrary to Marxist prophecy, will vindicate the mixed society and render Communism obsolete.

The Marxist contention has been (a) that capitalism is the predestined casualty of the modernization process, and (b) that Communism is its predestined culmination. In these terms Communism has boasted the certification of history. But history quite plainly refutes the Communist case. It shows (a) that the mixed society, as it modernizes itself, can overcome the internal contradictions which in Marx's view doomed it to destruction, and (b) that Communism is historically a function of the prefatory rather than the concluding stages of the modernization process.

Marx rested his case for the inevitability of Communist triumph on the theory that capitalism contained the seeds of its own destruction. He argued that the capitalist economy generated inexorable inner tendencies — "contradictions" — which would infallibly bring about its downfall. One inexorable tendency was the increasing wealth of the rich and the increasing poverty of the poor. Another was the increasing frequency and severity of economic crisis. Together these tendencies would infallibly carry society to a point of revolutionary "ripeness" when the proletariat would rise in its wrath, overthrow the possessing classes and install a classless society. Marx saw no way of denying this process, because he believed that the capitalist state could never be anything but the executive committee of the capitalist class.

This was Marx's fatal error. The capitalist state in developed societies, far from being the helpless instrument of the possessing class, has become the means by which other groups in society have redressed the balance of social power against those whom Hamilton called the "rich and well-born." This has been true in the United States, for example, since the age of Jackson. The liberal democratic state has accomplished two things in particular. It has brought about a redistribution of wealth which has defeated Marx's prediction of progressive immiseration; and it has brought about an economic stabilization which has defeated Marx's prediction of ever-worsening economic crisis. What the democratic parties of the developed nations have done, in short, has been to use the state to force capitalism to do what both the classical capitalists and the classical Marxists declared was impossible: to control the business cycle and to reapportion income in favor of those whom Jackson called the "humble members of society."

The champions of the affirmative state, in their determination to avert Marxist revolution, had to fight conservatism at every step along the way. Nonetheless, they persevered; and the twentieth century in America and Great Britain saw the rejection of laissez-faire, the subjugation of the business cycle, the drowning of revolution in a torrent of consumer goods, and the establishment of the "affluent society." The revolutionary fires within capitalism, lit by the great industrialists in the nineteenth century, were put out in the twentieth by the triumphs of industry — and by the liberal politicians, by Theodore Roosevelt and Woodrow Wilson and Franklin D. Roosevelt. Such men ignored the dogmatists, the philosophers of either/or, and created the mixed society. Both classical socialism and classical capitalism were products of the nineteenth century, and their day is over. As a result, capitalism can no longer be relied upon to dig its own grave; and Communism, if it ever comes to developed countries, will come, not as a consequence of social evolution, but only on the bayonets of the Red Army.

At the same time, history has thrown sharp light on the actual function of Communism. Marx, regarding Communism as the climax of the development process, prophesied that it would come first in the most developed nations. On the contrary, it has come to nations in the early phases of development, like Russia and China; and it has appealed to activists in such nations precisely because they see it as the means of rapid and effective modernization. Instead of being the culmination of the modernization effort, Communism would seem to be a form of social organization to which some countries aspiring to development have resorted in the hope of speeding the pace of modernization. We do not know what will happen to Communism in a Communist state which achieves full development; but, if it should then survive in anything like its present form, it would be because of the efficiency of its apparatus of control and terror, not because it is the natural organizational expression of the institutions of affluence.

History thus shows plainly that Communism is not the form of social organization toward which all societies are irresistibly evolving. Rather it is a phenomenon of the transition from stagnation to development, a "disease" (in Walt Rostow's phrase) of the modernization process. Democratic, regulated capitalism — the mixed society — will be far more capable of coping with the long-term consequences of modernization. "The wave of the future," Walter Lippmann has well said, "is not Communist domination of the world. The wave of the future is social reform and social revolution driving us toward the goal of national independence and equality of personal status."

If this is so, it emphasizes more than ever the need to keep abreast of history in our own social ideas and programs. We are all indebted to J. K. Galbraith for his demonstration that the affluent society compels a sweeping reconsideration of social and economic policies. The problems of the New Deal were essentially quantitative problems — problems of meeting stark human needs for food, clothing, shelter and employment. Most of these needs are now effectively met for most Americans; but a sense of spiritual disquietude remains nevertheless. A full dinner pail turns out to be something less than the promised land. The final lesson of the affluent society is surely that affluence is not enough — that solving the quantitative problems of living only increases the importance of the quality of the life lived. These qualitative problems seem next on the American agenda.

The qualitative aspects of life are only marginally within the reach of government. Yet public policy surely has its contribution to make to the elevation of American civilization. "The great object of the institution of civil government," said John Quincy Adams in his first message to Congress, "is the improvement of the condition of those who are parties to the social compact, and no government, in whatever form constituted, can accomplish the lawful end of its institution but in proportion as it improves the condition of those over whom it is established . . . Moral, political, intellectual improvement are duties assigned by the Author of Our Existence to social no less than to individual man. For the fulfillment of those duties governments are invested with power, and to the attainment of the end — the progressive improvement of the condition of the governed — the exercise of delegated powers is a duty as sacred and indispensable as the usurpation of powers not granted is criminal and odious."

A central issue of contemporary domestic polity is a variation on the question which concerned Adams — that is, the question of the balance between the amount of our national wealth we reserve for private satisfaction and the amount we dedicate to public need. In the thirties "recovery" was the catchword of our national economic philosophy; in the forties, "full employment"; in the fifties, "economic growth"; in the future, it is likely to become "allocation of resources." No one would argue that steering more resources into the public sector would cure the spiritual ailments of the affluent society; but it seems possible that the resulting improvements in opportunities in education, medical care, social welfare, community planning, culture and the arts will improve the chances for the individual to win his own spiritual fulfillment.

The impending shift from quantitative to qualitative liberalism emphasizes once again the hazards involved in the degeneration of liberalism into ideology. By tradition American liberalism is humane, experimental and pragmatic; it has no sense of messianic mission and no faith that all problems have final solutions. It assumes that freedom implies conflict. It agrees with Madison, in the Tenth Federalist, that the competition among economic interests is inherent in a free society. It also agrees with

George Bancroft, who wrote: "The feud between the capitalist and laborer, the house of Have and the house of Want, is as old as social union, and can never be entirely quieted; but he who will act with moderation, prefer fact to theory, and remember that everything in the world is relative and not absolute, will see that the violence of the contest may be stilled."

Its empirical temper means that American liberalism stands in sharp contrast to the millennial nostalgia which still characterizes both the American right and the European left — the notion that the day will come when all conflict will pass, when Satan will be cast into the lake of fire and brimstone, and mankind will behold a new heaven and a new earth. José Figueres, the Latin American patriot, calls his finca in the Costa Rican uplands "La Lucha San Fin" — the struggle without end. Freedom is inseparable from struggle; and freedom, as Brandeis said, is the great developer; it is both the means employed and the end attained. This, I believe, states the essence of the progressive hope — this and the understanding that the struggle itself offers not only better opportunities for others but a measure of fulfillment for oneself.

The text of this edition is reprinted substantially without change from 1949. I have omitted a few personal allusions, and I have clarified one or two passages where the meaning seemed unclear. But I have not tried to bring my views up to date. If I were writing the book today, I would give more emphasis to the reminder in the 1949 Foreword that American businessmen share with American liberals a basic faith in free society. I have more confidence now than then in the intelligence and responsibility of businessmen who have thought about problems of public policy; and I fear I allowed myself then to be beguiled to extreme conclusions by Joseph A. Schumpeter's brilliant but exaggerated argument that the processes of capitalism were inevitably destroying entrepreneurial initiative. With respect to such matters, I can only comfort myself with the remark of Lord Randolph Churchill, as recommended to future generations by his distinguished son: "I neither withdraw nor apologize for anything that I have said at any time, believing as I do that anything which I may have said at any time was perfectly justified by the special circumstances of that time, and by the amount of information I may have had in my possession." Though I would now diminish the polemical sharpness of occasional expressions, and though I regret allusions which, topical in 1949, must seem dated or obscure in 1962, I hope that the underlying faith in the vitality of the center may seem to some to have survived the passage of time.

ARTHUR M. SCHLESINGER, JR.

January 1962

Contents

Foreword

THIS WORK is not designed to set forth novel or startling political doctrines. It is intended rather as a report on the fundamental enterprise of re-examination and self-criticism which liberalism has undergone in the last decade. The leaders in this enterprise have been the wiser men of an older generation. But its chief beneficiaries have been my own contemporaries; and its main consequence, I believe, has been to create a new and distinct political generation.

This new generation can be briefly defined by a few historical — and biographical — notations. If I may use myself as a convenient example, I was born in 1917. I heard Franklin Roosevelt's first inaugural address as a boy at school, fifteen years old. Since that March day in 1933, one has been able to feel that liberal ideas had access to power in the United States, that liberal purposes, in general, were dominating our national policy. For one's own generation, then, American liberalism has had a positive and confident ring. It has stood for responsibility and for achievement, not for frustration and sentimentalism;

it has been the instrument of social change, not of private neurosis. During most of my political consciousness this has been a New Deal country. I expect that it will continue to be a New Deal country.

The experience of growing up under the New Deal meant too that Communism shone for few of one's generation with the same unearthly radiance that it apparently shone for other young men a decade earlier. It was partly the fact that we did not need so desperately to believe in the Soviet utopia. Franklin Roosevelt was showing that democracy was capable of taking care of its own; the New Deal was filling the vacuum of faith which we had inherited from the cynicism and complacency of the twenties, and from the breadlines of the early thirties. Partly too the Soviet Union itself was no longer the bright dream of the twenties — the land of hope encircled by capitalist aggressors and traduced by newspapermen sending lies out of Riga. What we saw in the Russia of the thirties was a land where industrialization was underwritten by mass starvation, where delusions of political infallibility led to the brutal extermination of dissent, and where the execution of heroes of the revolution testified to some deep inner contradiction in the system. This conclusion was not, for most of us, a process of disillusionment for which we had to pay the psychological price of a new extremism. We were simply the children of a new atmosphere: history had spared us any emotional involvement in the Soviet mirage.

The degeneration of the Soviet Union taught us a useful lesson, however. It broke the bubble of the false optimism of the nineteenth century. Official liberalism had long been almost inextricably identified with a picture of man as

perfectible, as endowed with sufficient wisdom and selflessness to endure power and to use it infallibly for the general
good. The Soviet experience, on top of the rise of fascism,
reminded my generation rather forcibly that man was,
indeed, imperfect, and that the corruptions of power
could unleash great evil in the world. We discovered a
new dimension of experience — the dimension of anxiety,
guilt and corruption. (Or it may well be, as Reinhold
Niebuhr has brilliantly suggested, that we were simply
rediscovering ancient truths which we should never have
forgotten.)

Mid-twentieth-century liberalism, I believe, has thus
been fundamentally reshaped by the hope of the New
Deal, by the exposure of the Soviet Union, and by the
deepening of our knowledge of man. The consequence of
this historical re-education has been an unconditional
rejection of totalitarianism and a reassertion of the ultimate integrity of the individual. This awakening constitutes the unique experience and fundamental faith of contemporary liberalism.

This faith has been and will continue to be under
attack from the far right and the far left. In this book I
have deliberately given more space to the problem of protecting the liberal faith from Communism than from
reaction, not because reaction is the lesser threat, but because it is the enemy we know, whose features are clearly
delineated for us, against whom our efforts have always
been oriented. It is perhaps our very absorption in this
age-old foe which has made us fatally slow to recognize
the danger on what we carelessly thought was our left —
forgetting in our enthusiasm that the totalitarian left and
the totalitarian right meet at last on the murky grounds

of tyranny and terror. I am persuaded that the restoration of business to political power in this country would have the calamitous results that have generally accompanied business control of the government; that this time we might be delivered through the incompetence of the right into the hands of the totalitarians of the left. But I am persuaded too that liberals have values in common with most members of the business community — in particular, a belief in free society —which they do not have in common with the totalitarians.

The experience with Communism has had one singularly healthy effect: it has made us reclaim democratic ideas which a decade ago we tended to regret and even to abandon. The defense of these ideas against both right and left will be a continuous and exacting commitment. But there lies in that commitment the possibility of recharging the faith in democracy with some of its old passion and principle. I am certain that history has equipped modern American liberalism with the ideas and the knowledge to construct a society where men will be both free and happy. Whether we have the moral vigor to do the job depends on ourselves.

ARTHUR M. SCHLESINGER, JR.

January 1949

The
Vital Center

The Politics of Freedom

I

Politics in an Age of Anxiety

Western man in the middle of the twentieth century is tense, uncertain, adrift. We look upon our epoch as a time of troubles, an age of anxiety. The grounds of our civilization, of our certitude, are breaking up under our feet, and familiar ideas and institutions vanish as we reach for them, like shadows in the falling dusk. Most of the world has reconciled itself to this half-light, to the reign of insecurity. Even those peoples who hastily traded their insecurities for a mirage of security are finding themselves no better off than the rest. Only the United States still has buffers between itself and the anxieties of our age: buffers of time, of distance, of natural wealth, of national ingenuity, of a stubborn tradition of hope.

A nation which has made a religion of success ought to find it hard to acclimate itself to the middle of the twentieth century. For frustration is increasingly the hallmark of this century — the frustration of triumphant science and rampant technology, the frustration of the most generous hopes and of the most splendid dreams. Nineteen hundred looked forward to the irresistible expansion of freedom, democracy and abundance; 1950 will look back to totalitarianism, to concentration camps, to mass starvation, to atomic war. Yet for the United States the world tragedy still has the flickering unreality of a motion picture. It grips us as we see it; but, lingering over the familiar milkshake in the bright drugstore, we forget the nightmare in the resurgence of warmth and comfort. Anxiety is something we hear about. It is not yet part of our lives — not of enough of our lives, anyway, to inform our national decisions.

The world tragedy, as it impinges upon Americans, strikes us in relatively simple terms. It is we or they; the United States or the Soviet Union; capitalism or Communism; let us resolve this conflict, and all problems will be solved. These choices are, indeed, the terms of the immediate problem; and it is only in these terms that steps can be taken toward enduring solutions. But let us not deceive ourselves into regarding the American-Russian rivalry as the source of world troubles.

Neither capitalism nor Communism is the cause of the contemporary upsurge of anxiety. Indeed, to a considerable degree, unhappy people have registered the same complaints against both. Each system is charged with having dehumanized the worker, fettered the lower classes and destroyed personal and political liberty. Before the First War, the case against Communism was generally made in terms of efficiency, the case against capitalism in terms of morality; that is, Communism was conceded to be enlightened in principle but was held not to work; capitalism was conceded to work but was held not to be enlightened in principle. After the Soviet experience, the Great Depression and the Second War, we see a reverse tendency — a disposition to admit the inefficiency of capitalism and justify it as providing the margin on which liberty and democracy subsist; a disposition to believe that the very completeness of Communist control necessarily squeezes out freedom.

In a sense, the arguments are interchangeable, the indictments cancel out. Does not this suggest that both sides have indulged in what Whitehead calls the "fallacy of misplaced concreteness" — the error of mistaking abstractions for concrete realities? We have seen identical criticisms lodged with heat and fervor against the abstractions "capitalism" and "Communism." But these criticisms may perhaps be lodged more profoundly, not against any particular system of ownership, but against industrial organization and the post-industrial state, whatever the system of ownership.

The human race in the last three centuries has been going through a global change-of-life. Science and technology have ushered man into a new cycle of civilization, and the consequence has been a terrifying problem of adjustment. In two centuries science and technology have narrowed the seas, ravaged the forests and irrigated the deserts. They have leveled national frontiers, undermined national self-sufficiencies and infinitely increased man's power to build and to destroy. The velocity of life has entered into a new phase. With it has come the imperative need for a social structure to contain that velocity — a social structure within which the individual can achieve some measure of self-fulfillment.

This new social structure must succeed where the ancient jurisdictions of the family, the clan, the guild and the nation-state have failed. It must solve the problems created by the speed-up of time, the reduction of space and the increase in tension. It must develop new equivalents for the sanctions once imposed by custom and by religion. The specifications for the new society cannot but strain to the utmost the emotional and moral resources of the individual and the community.

In retrospect, these demands seem to have been too severe and exhausting. Civilization has not met them, which is why today it is consumed by anxiety and fear. Failing to create a new social structure, it has become the victim rather than the master of industrialism. The liberation of the individual during the Renaissance and Reformation set the Industrial Revolution in motion; in its course, industrialism has given people new freedom and opportunity. Yet its ultimate tendency under whatever system of ownership — a tendency inherent in its very technical structure — is to impersonalize economic relationships. In the end industrialism drives the free individual to the wall.

A static and decentralized society, based on agriculture and handicraft, was a society dependent on personal ties and governed by a personal ethic. Industrialism shattered the ties and consequently the ethic. A new code arose to cope with the remote and statistical units of the modern economy; and the gap between economic practice and personal morality widened swiftly and alarmingly. The industrial manager dealt, not in familiar personal relationships, but in impersonal magnitudes over great stretches of time and distance. The corporation was almost as much a device to solve moral as economic problems. It gave the new impersonality an institutional embodiment; a corporation, as the saying went, had neither a body to be kicked nor a soul to be damned. "Corporations will do what individuals would not dare to do," the richest man in Boston wrote with candor a century ago. " — Where the dishonesty is the work of *all* the Members, every *one* can say with Macbeth in the murder of Banquo 'Thou canst not say I did it.' " [1]

The impersonality of the new economic system meant, in brief, that no one had to feel a direct responsibility for the obvious and terrible costs in human suffering. Doubtless there was a lurking sense of guilt; but the very mechanism of organization provided solace and remission. As organization became more elaborate and comprehensive, it became increasingly the instrumentality through which moral man could indulge his natural weakness for immoral deeds. All organization suffered from this internal tendency. What was true of the competitive corporation became all the more true of the monopoly; and what was true even to a degree of the democratic state (which, after all, was responsive to popular control as the corporation was not) became horribly true of the totalitarian state. "A crime which would press quite heavily on the conscience of one man, becomes quite endurable when divided among many." [2]

The impersonality of the system, in other words, brought out, not the best, but the worst in the men who operated it. Industrialism, at the same time that it released vast new energies, imposed on the world a sinister new structure of relationships. The result was to give potent weapons to the pride and the greed of man, the sadism and the masochism, the ecstasy in power and the ecstasy in submission; and it thereby increased man's sense of guilt. The result was to create problems of organization to which man has not risen and which threaten to engulf him; and it thereby multiplied man's anxieties. The result was to devitalize the old religions while producing nothing new capable of controlling pride and power; and it thereby heightened both guilt and anxiety.

Man today must organize beyond his moral and emotional means: this is the fundamental cause of our distempers. This basic dilemma projects itself to us in the middle of the twentieth century in terms of the conflict between the United States and the Soviet Union. But the USA and the USSR are not the alternatives today because either nation has solved the basic problem — because either nation has succeeded in squaring the temptations of power and the corruptions of organization with the weaknesses of man. They are centers of hope because they are centers of power; and they are centers of power, less because of political or social wisdom than because of natural endowments in population, in fertility of the soil and in treasures beneath it, in geographical size and geographical remoteness. Their power makes them the inevitable focus of the tensions of the age. But they are not the cause of the tensions. Nor does either nation have the secret of their solution. Nor will the destruction of one by the other usher in utopia.

The fact that the contest between the USA and the USSR is not the source of the contemporary crisis does not, however, alter the fact that the crisis must be met in terms of this contest. Enthusiasts have suggested other strategies. If organization is the basic trouble, for example, one can sympathize with the anarchist rejection of organization. One can dally with the distributist dream of decentralization and the restoration of feudalism. One can admire the serenity of those who follow Gandhi's faith in non-violence. But one must face the fact that none of these "solutions" solves very much except the complexes of the individual who adopts them. They raise questions which must be raised; they provide the basis perhaps for a searching moral criticism of the existing order; but they leave the main forces of social chaos untouched. A Thoreau or a Gandhi, who has gone himself through intense moral ordeals, has earned the most profound moral respect. But it is a far cry from Thoreau or Gandhi to the ineffectual escapists who in their name engage in such practices as conscientious objection in time of war.

You cannot flee from science and technology into a quietist dreamworld. The state and the factory are inexorable: bad men will run them if good abdicate the job. The USA, the USSR, the strength of industrialism and the weakness of man cannot be evaded; they make up the problem; and there is no point, in General Marshall's phrase, in "fighting the problem." We must understand that the terms of the problem do not exhaust the dilemma of history; but we must understand equally that men in the middle of the twentieth century can strike at the dilemma of history only in terms of the problem.

We can act, in consequence, only in terms of imperfect alternatives. But, though the choice the alternatives present may be imperfect, it is nonetheless a real choice. Even if capitalism and Communism are both the children of the Industrial Revolution, there remain crucial differences between the USA and the USSR. These can be defined as basically the differences between free society and totalitarianism. This is a choice we cannot escape.

The conception of the free society — a society committed to the protection of the liberties of conscience, expression and political opposition — is the crowning glory of western history. Centuries of struggle have drawn a ring of freedom around the individual, a ring secured by law, by custom and by institutions. Here is a classic statement of the tests of freedom:

1. Is there the right to free expression of opinion and of opposition and criticism of the Government of the day?
2. Have the people the right to turn out a Government of which they disapprove, and are constitutional means provided by which they can make their will apparent?
3. Are there courts of justice free from violence by the Executive and free of all threats of mob violence and all association with any particular political parties?
4. Will these courts administer open and well-established laws which are associated in the human mind with the broad principles of decency and justice?
5. Will there be fair play for poor as well as for rich, for private persons as well as Government officials?
6. Will the rights of the individual, subject to his duties to the state, be maintained and asserted and exalted?
7. Is the ordinary peasant or workman, earning a living by daily toil and striving to bring up his family, free from the fear that some grim police organization under the control of a single party, like the Gestapo, started by the Nazi and Fascist parties, will tap him on the shoulder and pack him off without fair or open trial to bondage or ill-treatment? [3]

A conception of unequaled grandeur (modern liberals will, I trust, forgive the fact that the quotation is from Winston Churchill) — yet this conception has broken down at vital points under the pressures of industrial organ-

ization. Its failure has created its totalitarian enemy —
which professes to meet these needs and moves to do so,
proudly and even flagrantly, at the expense of the liberties
which define free society.

Is there reason to believe that totalitarianism will be
any more effective a master of the pressures of industrial
society? The evidence suggests rather that the totalitarian
enterprise brings in its wake a whole series of new and
intolerable evils. Far from solving the problems of organization, totalitarianism raises them to a climax. A man
like Thoreau could find the liberal state of free society a
"semihuman tiger or ox, stalking over the earth, with its
heart taken out and the top of its brain shot away." [4] But
the liberal state acknowledged many limitations in its demands upon men: the total state acknowledges none. It
systematically annihilates the gaps and rivalries which
make for freedom in a more loosely organized society. It
dispenses with liberty without providing security. If organization corrupts, total organization corrupts totally.

Free society and totalitarianism today struggle for the
minds and hearts of men. If the USA and the USSR were
in entire ideological agreement, the imperatives of power
— of geography and of economic competition — would still
tend to create rivalries; but the ideological conflict has
now detonated the power conflict. There is no easy
answer to this double polarization. If we believe in free
society hard enough to keep on fighting for it, we are
pledged to a permanent crisis which will test the moral,
political and very possibly the military strength of each
side. A "permanent" crisis? Well, a generation or two
anyway, permanent in one's own lifetime, permanent in
the sense that no international miracle, no political

sleight-of-hand will do away overnight with the tensions
between ourselves and Russia.

Indeed, we have no assurance that any solution is possible. The twentieth century has at least relieved us of the
illusion that progress is inevitable. This age is straining
all the capacities of man. At best, it is an age of transition;
at worst, an age of catastrophe. And even an age of transition, as John C. Calhoun has reminded us, "must always
necessarily be one of uncertainty, confusion, error and
wild and fierce fanaticism." [5] There is no more exciting
time in which to live — no time more crucial or more
tragic. We must recognize that this is the nature of our
age: that the womb has irrevocably closed behind us, that
security is a foolish dream of old men, that crisis will
always be with us.

Our own objective is clear. We must defend and
strengthen free society. The means are somewhat more
difficult. Surrender to totalitarianism — whether the surrender of military strong points or the surrender of standards and values — is the most certain road to the destruction of free society. War is the next most certain road.
The first question is: how to protect free society short of
war? The answer will involve all dimensions of activity —
political, economic, moral and military.

We must first understand more clearly *why* free society
has failed. Then we must examine the nature of the
totalitarian challenge. Then we may acquire some notion
of the strategy and tactics of a democratic counteroffensive.

II

The Failure of the Right

Free society has its roots deep in our classical and religious past. In the modern sense, however, it began as the political expression of youthful and exuberant capitalism. The rise of commerce and industry burst the bonds of the medieval economy. The new middle class set limits on feudal and royal power, generalizing rights against authority in order to claim privileges for themselves. The American and French declarations of natural right were the ideological reflection of the bourgeois revolution. And the men of business, by their application and their thrift, by their readiness to take trading risks, by their organizing and productive genius, not only carved out the area of freedom but created the material abundance to keep freedom going.

Since businessmen laid the economic foundations for free society, one would look for them to have provided

11

the political leadership which kept it in operation. Both apologists and critics of capitalism have assumed the political genius of the businessman. The Marxist myth, indeed, glorifies the capitalist with particular assiduity, portraying a demonic figure of infinite calculation and ruthlessness, committed to the pitiless destruction of every obstacle to the maximization of profits. In Marxist works (such as Harold J. Laski's *The American Democracy,* for example) the Capitalist dwarfs and dominates the other characters much as Satan dwarfs the good angels in *Paradise Lost.*

The two social philosophies of our time — in Karl Mannheim's useful phrase, the ideology and the utopia — thus both revolve around the notion of the political mastery of the businessman. Yet Professor Laski, for instance, appears perfectly aware of the contradictory fact that the normal American businessman is insecure and confused — uncertain what he wants or where he is going. Tear away the veil of Rotarian self-congratulation or of Marxist demonology, and you are likely to find the irresolute and hesitating figure of George F. Babbitt.

How is one to define the political capacities of the businessman? Certainly the capitalist has been uniquely great as organizer of production. His managerial and commercial skills have transformed the face of the world. These economic gains were not achieved, moreover, without the boldness to risk the political consequences of human suffering. For many decades, businessmen fought almost every measure looking to the improvement of conditions of labor, pursuing their quest for economic power with callous disregard for their weaker competitors or for the workers. The prodigious accomplishments of capitalism have rested in great part, in other words, upon the

confidence, intelligence and ruthlessness of the businessman.

Yet these qualities have been exercised in a peculiarly
narrow field. They have dwindled as the businessman has
got farther away from the factory or the counting-house
and nearer to the parliament or the executive chamber.
The capitalists have not been, in the political sense, an
effective governing class. They have constituted typically
a plutocracy, not an aristocracy.

A plutocracy is a possessing class founded, not on the
complex values of status which arise in a stable and inter-
dependent society, but on the naked accumulation of
money. Aristocracy at its best has something of the character of a family relationship with the nation. The ruler
rules but still retains some responsibility for the ruled;
noblesse oblige compels him to consult other interests
than those of his own immediate cash profit. Plutocracy,
on the other hand, neither rules nor protects the ruled.
Men accustomed to the exclusive pursuit of their own
interests find it hard to assume the rôle of the politician,
who must balance and reconcile the conflicting interests
of many groups. * The plutocracy thinks in terms of class
and not of nation, in terms of private profit and not of
social obligation, in terms of business dealings and not of
war, in terms of security and not of honor. With its
power founded on finance and thus dependent on the
preservation of the delicate skeins of promissory con-

* "When a man of business enters into life and action, he is more apt
to consider the characters of men, as they have relation to his interest,
than as they stand in themselves; and has his judgment warped on every
occasion by the violence of his passion." Hume, "Essay on the Study of
History."

fidence, the plutocracy above all dreads violence and
change, whether internal or external. Incapable of physical combat itself, it develops a legal system which penal-
izes the use of force and an ethic which glorifies pacifism.

The businessman, in other words, rescued society from
the feudal warrior, only to hand it over to the accountant.
The result was to emasculate the political energies of the
ruling class. "Experience shows that the middle classes
allow themselves to be plundered quite easily, provided a
little pressure is brought to bear, and that they are intimidated by the fear of revolution," as Georges Sorel wrote a
few years before the First War; "that party will possess the
future which can most skillfully manipulate the spectre
of revolution." [1] On the historical record, the business
community appears to lack the instinct, will and capacity
to govern.

This fact was not much noticed during a century of
comparative placidity, like the nineteenth. Then the appearance of Hitler, after a century's erosion of the com-
bative virtues, called the plutocratic bluff. To deal with
Hitler, the governments of Britain and France developed
a classically plutocratic foreign policy — a policy founded
on middle-class cowardice, rationalized in terms of high
morality ("peace in our time"), and always yielding to
threats of violence. The government of the plutocracy,
indeed, doomed France. It enfeebled its resolution, destroyed its unity, crippled its will to resist and hamstrung
its means of resistance. In Britain the plutocracy was expelled in time; the shift from Chamberlain to Churchill
reveals clearly the advantages of an intelligent aristocracy.

Chamberlain expressed with fearful accuracy the sentiments of the British business classes — their longing for

quiet and for a sure return on investments, their incomprehension of violence, their terror of social upheaval. These sentiments foundered on the phenomenon of Hitler. When commercial negotiation failed and class and profit no longer mattered, Chamberlain and the Birmingham plutocracy were impotent. They turned to resistance as a last resort; but even this was in the dubious and halfhearted spirit which produced the inglorious "phony war."

Churchill was a tougher breed. He spoke for something older and deeper in Britain than the shopkeepers who had come to power after the Industrial Revolution. As Léon Blum remarked, "Il n'a pas du tout l'ame capitaliste." * The business community knew this and always mistrusted him. His instincts were those of an imperial aristocrat, with power founded, not on finance, but on land and tradition, bold, vigorous, somewhat contemptuous of "trade," soaked in the continuities of history, schooled to standards and values alien to the plutocracy. He was devoted to an island and an empire rather than to particular business interests, and he was not afraid to fight. In the end, he saved Britain.

The feudal residues in British Toryism, the sense of history, the capacity occasionally to place national above class considerations, have created a broadly responsible conservatism, which today is collaborating in its own liquidation. This ability of the propertied interests to accept change, when change appears inevitable, has been

* As reported by Vincent Sheean, *New York Herald Tribune,* June 20, 1948. Churchill was, of course, sufficiently radical in his youth for the American socialist William English Walling to describe him as one of the precursors of collectivism. See *Progressivism and After,* New York, 1914.

an important source of British stability.* "If you do not
give the people social reform," as Quintin Hogg once
warned his party, "the people will give you social revolution"; [2] and the Tories have always heeded the warning
just short of the barricades. Today, British Tories and
businessmen are taking socialism much less hard than the
bulk of Republicans took the relatively gentle improvisa-
tions of the New Deal.

American conservatism too began on a genuinely lofty
plane. The Federalist Party of Washington, Hamilton
and Adams had a high sense of national welfare and a
capacity to think in terms other than those of immediate
class interest. The Federalists were men of intellectual
candor and robustness. They knew history, and the War
for Independence had given them a strong sense of public
responsibility. Their ideas were founded on a realistic
picture of social conflict, and they did not shrink from
following out the implications of these ideas. They performed an extraordinary job in laying solidly and accurately the foundations for the American union. Posterity
should be grateful that men who believed in strong government created the precedents of the republic and not
men, like Jefferson, who feared strong government.†
Even the Jeffersonians, it should be remembered, eventually concurred in the leading measures of Hamilton.

But the quarter-century after Hamilton saw a change
in the character of American economic life. The new
generation of conservatives, coming in on the shoulders
of the Industrial Revolution, were not the patricians of

* "When rape is inevitable, relax and enjoy it." — OLD PROVERB.
† It is appropriate that Alvin Hansen and other Keynesians cite Alexander Hamilton in arguing for the social usefulness of a national debt.

the eighteenth century; they were *parvenu* traders whose interest lay in profits rather than in public policy. Federalist tough-mindedness — on such questions as class conflict, for example — confronted this new generation with a dilemma. If they were to follow Hamilton and Adams in a class theory of society, they had to accept the possibility that this theory might have radical as well as conservative implications. The insurgency of other classes during the age of Jackson thus terrified them into dropping the whole theory of class conflict. The revolution which had schooled the Federalists in public responsibility was now remote. Their successors lacked their sturdiness and their culture.

The Whigs were the first party of the American plutocracy. For all the splendor of the Websters and the Clays, the Whig Party was essentially an incarnation of opportunism and platitude. "Of all the parties that have existed in the United States," observed Henry Adams, "the famous Whig party was the most feeble in ideas." * A new, raw class in politics, innocent of tradition, ignorant of history, it construed its own present advantages as the end toward which society had been evolving since the creation. Having no framework within which to fit the inexorable impulses toward social change, it interpreted each mild attempt to limit its own power to harm others as the hot breath of revolution. It bitterly fought the ten-hour day, the regulation of wildcat banking, the secret ballot, the abolition of imprisonment for debt, the organization of trade unions. In its war against Andrew

* Henry Adams, *Life of Albert Gallatin*, Philadelphia, 1879, p. 635. It is to be noted that Adams was writing before the Republican party had reached the full flower of intellectual development.

Jackson, it whipped itself into a lather of hysterics over proposals which every one, including the fighters themselves, would regard as innocuous a few years later. This was only the first (and the New Deal only the most recent) of a number of occasions in American history when the business community, having overindulged in the heady liquors of its own propaganda, ends up in what can only be described as a fit of political *delirium tremens*.

After the Whigs came the Republicans. The Republican Party, born of the union between Free Soil Democrats and Conscience Whigs, came to power in a great cause and under a great leader. But it soon resumed the Whig tradition. The forces of business, in the main opposed to Lincoln and Republicanism in 1860, captured the party after Lincoln's death. They speedily converted it into a political auxiliary for the business community, drove out its ablest leaders and drained from it most of the energy to govern.

The last serious attempt to regenerate the Republican Party, to make it the vehicle of what Sorel has called a propertied class "of serious moral habits, imbued with the feelings of its own dignity, and having the energy necessary to govern the country," [3] throws light on the problem of conservatism in the United States. This attempt sprang from the frustrations of ambitious men in the last part of the nineteenth century, who wished to serve (i.e., to rule) their country and found the road to power blocked by the men of business. These new spirits themselves came largely from the remnants of our abortive aristocracy. They were Adamses and Lodges of Massachusetts, Roosevelts of New York; and their great fortune lay in having in Theodore Roosevelt a man with enough vitality and vulgarity to impose himself upon a timid and reluctant political scene.

Matthew Josephson has aptly described this impulse as "neo-Hamiltonian." [4] The great document of neo-Hamiltonian frustration was, of course, *The Education of Henry Adams.* Henry's younger brother, Brooks Adams, is an even more revealing ideologue of the aristocratic revolt against plutocracy. The testimony of the Adamses, of Theodore Roosevelt, of Henry Cabot Lodge represents the last experiment in organized self-criticism on the part of American conservatives.

The basic emotion on the part of the neo-Hamiltonians was contempt for business in politics. This contempt was not based on their own failure to make good. Charles Francis Adams, for example, brother to Henry and Brooks, met the challenge of the day at its own terms and ended up as president of the Union Pacific Railroad. But financial success did not reconcile him to the age of the "gold-bug." "I have known, and known tolerably well," Charles Francis Adams wrote, "a good many 'successful' men — 'big' financially — men famous during the last half-century; and a less interesting crowd I do not care to encounter. Not one that I have ever known would I care to meet again, either in this world or the next; nor is one of them associated in my mind with the idea of humor, thought or refinement. A set of mere money-getters and traders, they were essentially unattractive and uninteresting." [5]

The dislike for business came, not from sour grapes, but from a reasoned analysis of the political incapacity of businessmen. To Brooks Adams the great difference between the historical ruling classes and the business community consisted in "the elimination of courage as an essential quality in a ruling class." Earlier rulers were characterized above all by dedication to honor and by the associated martial values: daring, self-sacrifice, energy, strength, "the ferocity mixed with gentleness," the ineptitude for business. But the Industrial Revolution had raised "a timid social stratum to the position of a ruling caste. A social stratum which had never worn the sword, which had always been overridden by soldiers, and which regarded violence with the horror born of fear." [6] The result was the disappearance of the heroic virtues, the displacement of valor by craft and cunning, the enthronement of the attorney, the detective, the usurer and eventually of the international banker.

The Adamses had always had somewhat these ideas but, since the defeat of John Quincy in 1828, had not been able to do much about them politically. In the late nineties they suddenly acquired fellow travelers who were good at politics. Theodore Roosevelt and Henry Cabot Lodge had similar beginnings. Respectable families and respectable education apparently consigned them to frustration in an epoch dominated by *arrivistes*. Both dallied with law after finishing Harvard. Both turned with relief to history. * Both admired the Federalists excessively and yearned for the splendid public careers young men like themselves would have enjoyed a century earlier. Some instinct of political realism kept them out of the Mug-

---

* It is notable how often a knowledge of history separates the responsible conservative from the plutocrat. In our own day Churchill is a great writer of history; Roosevelt, Willkie and Stimson were avid students. It is not evident from his writing that Herbert Hoover, for example, has any vigorous understanding of or interest in history; and Henry Ford expressed the pure plutocratic view that history was bunk.

wump movement, and they stayed restlessly in the Republican Party, chafing at the unimaginative leadership of the businessmen and their political agents. "The businessman dealing with a large political question," Lodge would say with Bostonian and Hamiltonian disdain, "is really a painful sight. It does seem to me that businessmen, with a few exceptions, are worse when they come to deal with politics than men of any other class." [7]

Lodge was a man without juices. But Theodore Roosevelt, with his toothy grin, his squeaky voice, his thick glasses and his incurable delight in self-dramatization, was a great political educator. Brooks Adams and Admiral Mahan could write lengthily about the difference between the martial virtues and the greed and timidity of commercial life. But it took Roosevelt, sharing, as he said, "Brooks Adams' gloomiest anticipations of our gold-ridden, capitalist-bestridden, usurer-mastered future," to invent the "strenuous life" as the antidote and sell it to the American people. [8] "I preach to you, then, my countrymen, that our country calls not for the life of ease but for the life of strenuous endeavor. . . . If we seek merely swollen, slothful ease and ignoble peace, if we shrink from the hard contests where men must win at the hazard of their lives and at the risk of all they hold dear, then the bolder and stronger peoples will pass us by, and will win for themselves the domination of the world." [9]

Such a philosophy threatened to commit the nation to domestic and international adventures which would upset the tranquilities prized by business. Mark Hanna, the boss of the Republican Party, perceived the dangers in Roosevelt. But the irrepressible Teddy, living up to his creed, helped bring on the Spanish-American War, then captured San Juan Hill and the governor's mansion at Albany. The bosses next hoped to solve the Roosevelt problem by sentencing him to the vice-presidency. They reckoned without the anarchist who murdered McKinley in 1901. "That damned cowboy," as Hanna called him, became President.

For all his adolescent brag, Roosevelt's recoil from business rule was clear and consistent. "We stand equally against government by a plutocracy and government by a mob. There is something to be said for government by a great aristocracy which has furnished leaders to the nation in peace and war for generations; even a democrat like myself must admit this. But there is absolutely nothing to be said for government by a plutocracy, for government by men very powerful in certain lines and gifted with 'the money touch,' but with ideals which in their essence are merely those of so many glorified pawnbrokers." [10]

Roosevelt hated socialists, whom he associated with pacifism, dogoodism and other forms of mollycoddle flapdoodle, when he did not associate them with the Terror and the guillotine. But he felt that the Republican policy of serving the wishes of the business community was only strengthening the socialists. "I do not believe that it is wise or safe for us as a party to take refuge in mere negation and to say that there are no evils to be corrected. . . . We Republicans [must] hold the just balance and set ourselves as resolutely against improper corporate influence on the one hand as against demagogy and mob rule on the other." [11]

Herbert Croly's exposition of Hamiltonian ideas in *The Promise of American Life* gave Roosevelt's neo-Hamiltonianism a dynamic intellectual setting. By 1910 the ex-President was declaring that "every man holds his property subject to the general right of the community to regulate its use to whatever degree the public welfare may require it." [12] In 1912 he sought to bring this issue to sharp choice; he sought to make the Republican Party decide between property rights and "the general right of the community." The choice was complicated, of course, by personal and political rancors and by Roosevelt's own theatrical insincerities. Yet the Republican convention of 1912 was nevertheless a historical turning point. By rejecting Roosevelt, the Republicans turned their backs on responsible conservatism.

No contemporary perceived this more clearly than Brooks Adams. He thought that the capitalists would have been lucky to get fifty more years of protection on terms as favorable as those held out by Roosevelt. When the Republicans repudiated the only strategy by which the business community could ride out the inevitable surge of change, Adams could only conclude that "privileged classes seldom have the intelligence to protect themselves by adaptation when nature turns against them, and, up to the present moment, the old privileged class in the United States has shown little promise of being an exception to the rule." [13]

The Progressive revolt killed progressivism in the Republican Party, just as the Free Soil revolt of 1848 killed antislavery in the Democratic Party. By removing the radicals from the party hierarchy and stamping their views with the brand of heresy, revolt made it impossible for them to return to the circle of power. Progressivism did, however, have a powerful impact on individuals. It is

astonishing how many of the few Republicans who played
a creative rôle in the thirties were Bull Moosers or, at
least, were shaped politically by T.R.: Henry L. Stimson,
Frank Knox, Harold Ickes, John G. Winant, Charles
Evans Hughes, Gifford Pinchot, William Allen White.

But most of these men were on the fringes of their own
party, and some even deserted to the enemy. The Progressive bolt left the plutocracy in unchallenged control
of Republicanism. Never in American history have any
administrations served the business community so faith-
fully — one might well say, so obsequiously — as the Republican administrations of Harding, Coolidge and
Hoover. It was an era whose political sterility was equaled
only by its complacency. "Given a chance to go forward
with the policies of the last eight years," as Hoover
summed up in 1928 the smugness of that incredible
decade, "and we shall soon with the help of God be in
sight of the day when poverty will be banished from this
nation." [14] This was the euphoria of capitalism: one phase
of the manic-depressive cycle which has characterized the
businessman in politics. The next phase would come a
brief five years later when Lewis Douglas, one of Roosevelt's less happy experiments with the businessman, cried
in despair as the nation went off the gold standard, "This
is the end of Western civilization." [15]

In spite of the Lincolns and the Theodore Roosevelts,
the American business community has not had an inspiring record in politics. Business fought Jackson; it fought
Lincoln; it fought Theodore Roosevelt and Wilson and
Franklin D. Roosevelt; and, on virtually all the issues of
controversy, Americans now believe the business community to have been wrong. In quiet times power gravitates

to business as the strongest economic group in society; but it has never been able to use that power long for national purposes. Dominated by personal and class considerations, business rule tends to bring public affairs to a state of crisis and to drive the rest of the community into despair bordering on revolution. When the crisis comes, businessmen must always turn for protection to some non-business group. In Britain the business classes have had the aristocracy, and now the socialists, to protect them. In America when the chips were down the businessmen have always been bailed out by the radical democracy, often under aristocratic leadership.

Why has American conservatism been so rarely marked by stability or political responsibility? In great part because conservative politics here has been peculiarly the property of the plutocracy. The aristocracy — people whose position derives from land and status rather than from stock holdings — exists only in certain side-pockets and backwashes in American life: in Boston and in Philadelphia, in New York and in Virginia, in a few other places where conscience and permanence have invested a plutocracy with social responsibility. The aristocracy has made valuable contributions to our politics in every generation — from the Jeffersons, and the Edward Livingstons and James Fenimore Coopers who backed Jackson, to the Oliver Wendell Holmeses, Henry L. Stimsons and Franklin D. Roosevelts, the Averell Harrimans and Adlai Stevensons. But such men have never, since Federalist days, controlled conservative politics; and in most cases, thwarted by the stand-pat leadership of the business community, they have allied themselves with the left against business rule.

History thus gives little reason to expect organized political intelligence from the dominant forces in the business community. And today the problem has become more complicated, for the business community itself is evidently entering a new phase. Its past incapacity for politics is now being aggravated by what would appear to be a gradual disappearance of the capitalist energies themselves. Not only does the business community lack the skill to govern society in its own interests. It is increasingly lacking the will to do so. Capitalism has visibly begun to lose the qualities which made it great: the zest for competition, the delight in risk-taking, the bold, creative vigor. The dynamism of capitalism is trickling out in a world where the passion for security breeds merger and monopoly. At the same time that it achieves new economic success and a new and altogether desirable economic stability, the capitalist system has begun to destroy the psychological interest in its own survival.

This process of capitalist suicide is complex but apparently remorseless. * A fundamental part of the liberation of energy under capitalism, for example, was the idea of property. Yet the whole development of capitalism — the rise of big business, the development of mass production and mass organization — has slowly taken the guts out of the idea of property. The basis in day-to-day experience of private property and of the free contract has disappeared. Organization impersonalizes all it touches; and, with the loss of personality, ownership loses its ability to command vital loyalties. The capitalist process, as Schumpeter puts it, "loosens the grip that once was so strong —

* It is most brilliantly analyzed in Joseph A. Schumpeter, *Capitalism, Socialism and Democracy*, New York, 1947.

the grip in the sense of the legal right and the actual
ability to do as one pleases with one's own; the grip also
in the sense that the holder of the title loses the will to
fight, economically, physically, politically, for 'his' factory
and his control over it, to die if necessary on its steps." [16]
In the end there will be no one ready to go down swinging for institutions so abstract, impersonal and remote.

The intellectual repercussions of capitalism have
speeded up the process by which vital faith in capitalism
has decayed. Capitalism created an atmosphere of intellectual freedom, of belief in science and technology. The
spread of rationalism set in motion a skepticism which
ended by holding no social authority sacred. Capitalism,
furthermore, could not defend itself by suppressing
skeptics: it had to protect intellectuals in their right to
criticism if it were going to preserve businessmen in their
right to initiative. The business community can bribe,
corrupt or denounce the intellectuals; it cannot discipline
them without jeopardizing liberties it needs for itself.
Businessmen, moreover, come themselves to believe the
criticisms made against them. The result is a profound
instability which invites collectivism as a means of holding society together.

Capitalism, in brief, at once strengthens the economic
centralization and stretches the moral bonds of society.
The first process lays the foundation for a socialist
economy; the second creates the case for a socialist
discipline. In a mature capitalist system, the basic
capitalist impulses atrophy from disuse when they do
not dry up under the heat of hostile criticism. As
Schumpeter puts it, capitalism "socializes the bourgeois
mind." [17]

One result has been the rise in some business circles of what can be accurately called a capitalist death-wish — a tendency, working silently within the organism, causing it to make the decisions which will guarantee its own disintegration. "The millionaires in all countries," wrote Lenin, "are behaving on an international scale in a way that deserves our heartiest thanks." [18] No one should be surprised that the Communists continue to get their most effective co-operation from the frightened, ignorant and despairing rich, driven by dark impulses beyond their own control to conspire in their own destruction.

Even in America, the capitalist fatherland, the home of the world's most confident and energetic business community, the death-wish far exceeds the normal limits of political incompetence and geographical security. After the First War Trotsky predicted that American capitalism would now make its stunning début on the world stage. Instead, American capitalism crept back into bed and pulled the covers over its face. With the whole world to conquer, it chose instead the womblike comfort of the Smoot-Hawley tariff and the fantastic belief of Mr. Hoover that the federal government should not build a power project at Muscle Shoals or feed starving people. American capitalism responded to the depression by an attack of hysterics. It responded to the challenge of Nazism by founding the America First Committee. It responded to the opportunities opened up by the Second War by rushing to dismantle the instrumentalities of American military and economic influence in the name of tax reduction.

There are signs today, it is true, of a new spirit stirring in the business community. The stabilization of economic life has given some business circles, at least, a clearer sense of their responsibility to the general welfare. Indeed, the very withering away of capitalist motivation, while rousing intimations of death-wish in some businessmen, has served as a means of liberating others from the tyranny of the profit motive. The modern American capitalist as a result has come to share many values with the American liberal: beliefs in personal integrity, political freedom and equality of opportunity. This process is reflected in the general support for the Marshall Plan, in the establishment of liberal business organizations like the Committee on Economic Development, in the proposals of some of the more forward-looking Republican politicians. A man like Senator Robert A. Taft, whose myopia on foreign policy is somewhat redeemed by a sense of responsibility in the domestic field, understands very clearly that the capitalist system must meet human needs in areas like housing, health and education if it is to survive. "If the free-enterprise system does not do its best to prevent hardship and poverty, even for those who can't be shown to deserve it," Taft has said, "it will find itself superseded by a less progressive system which does." [19]

But can we look to the business community to save free society? One questions whether the new spirit has gone far enough. Taft's own not very enthusiastic attempts to mitigate hardship and poverty have won him a reputation for "socialism" in the neanderthal circles in the Republican Party. As for the really advanced social thinking in the business community, it generally turns out on closer examination to consist of little more than accepting the New Deal. There are powerful forces in the business community of 1949 who still see few flaws in those policies with which Herbert Hoover in 1928 proposed to banish poverty from the land. They remain bitterly opposed to measures which would make the working class feel itself part of the nation because they believe that public housing or health insurance or some other newfangled idea is going to destroy the American way of life.

In spite of the shame of an enlightened business minority, the National Association of Manufacturers remains the characteristic expression of the capitalist libido. Few housewives have forgotten the full-page advertisement which the NAM placed in leading newspapers during the fight against price control in 1946. "If OPA is permanently discontinued," promised the NAM, "the production of goods will mount rapidly and, through free competition, prices will quickly adjust themselves to levels that consumers are willing to pay." One scholar recently subjected himself to the heroic task of looking up the positions on public policy taken by the NAM in the past decade and a half. His conclusion, published in the presumably non-subversive organ of the Harvard Business School, was as follows, and the italics are his own: *"Without exception* the measures favored by the NAM provided some sort of aid to business and industry. *Without exception* rigid opposition was maintained against similar assistance to other groups and against all regulatory measures pertaining to industry." *

The attitude of the business community toward foreign policy is equally inconclusive. The new spirit has had even more striking results in this area. Senator Vandenberg has played a genuinely statesmanlike rôle in the past few years; and the conversion of such former isolationists as Vandenberg and John Foster Dulles has helped bring the Republican Party as a whole about up to where it was

* A. S. Cleveland, "N.A.M.: Spokesman for Industry?", *Harvard Business Review*, May, 1948.

in Theodore Roosevelt's time — a considerable advance over where it was in the Hoover-Coolidge era. Yet there is no sign that the Hoovers, Tabers and Wherrys have been expelled to the outer darkness. The Young Fogy movement in the Republican Party, led by Harold Stassen (who was briefly considered as a liberal by those who mistook youth for liberalism), is dedicating itself today to a crusade against democratic socialism; British socialism and Soviet Communism, says Stassen, "are two peas from the same confining pod." [20] An important segment of business opinion still hesitates to undertake a foreign policy of the magnitude necessary to prop up a free world against totalitarianism lest it add a few dollars to the tax rate.

Terrified of change, lacking confidence and resolution, subject to spasms of panic and hysteria, the extreme right-wing elements keep the American business community in far too irresponsible a condition to work steadily for the national interest, at home or abroad. A Republican who wishes to be a strong and progressive leader of his party in the manner of Theodore Roosevelt or Wendell Willkie must take on and defeat those neolithic forces who took on and defeated T. R. and Willkie. Governor Dewey approached this problem in altogether too unctuous and slick a mood. For the neanderthals are alive and hungry, not to be appeased by slogans; they are shambling around, supporting the Un-American Activities Committee, campaigning against Keynesian textbooks in the colleges, conspiring against the trade-union movement, inveighing against free milk for school children and smearing all nonconformists as Communists. Henry L. Stimson may talk about "the variety of forms which free societies may take," but there are always the Ayn Rands to say, "The basic

principle of inalienable rights . . . can be translated into
practical reality only in the form of the economic system
of free enterprise." * It is hard to dispute Senator Henry
Cabot Lodge, Jr., in his interpretation of the 1948 election: the American people were saying to the Republican
Party, surmised Lodge, "You have made some real progress
in liberalizing yourselves and in making yourselves a forward-looking instrument of the popular will — but you
have not progressed far enough. We are still afraid that
you may backslide." [21]

The business community remains everywhere dependent on those non-business groups capable of political
leadership — which may mean aristocrats or radical democrats in a stable society, such as Britain and the United
States, or political gangsters in a society which still has
reserves of violence. The susceptibility of a confused and
frightened business community to fascism is a source of
danger to free society. But, up to now, fascism has come
to power in countries like Germany and Italy, Spain and
Argentina, where the bourgeois triumph was never complete enough to eradicate other elements who believe in
what the business community fears more than anything
else — violence, and who then use violence to "protect"
the business community.

One source of hope for the United States today lies in

* The contrast between Mr. Stimson's remarkable article "The Challenge to Americans," *Foreign Affairs*, October, 1947, and Miss Rand's
equally remarkable attempt to formulate the principles of Americanism
for the Motion Picture Alliance for the Preservation of American Ideals,
"Screen Guide for Americans," *Plain Talk*, November 1947, shows strik-
ingly the difference between responsible conservatism and plutocratic
reaction. Miss Rand's novel *The Fountainhead*, surely one of the most
curious novels of the century, is an attempt to give her political ideas
symbolic form.

the fact that our social situation makes the rise of fascism unlikely. A thoroughly middle-class country, we have no organized resources of violence — whether Junker, militarist, caudillo, feudal or proletarian — which an ambitious demagogue can offer to a terrified business community.* Only the South has the tradition of violence to sustain even an appearance of fascism; and it is doubtful whether even Huey Long could have organized that appearance into a nationwide reality. Governor Dewey actually won the Republican nomination after he opposed outlawing the Communist Party in the debate which settled the crucial primary election. Cheered by the example of the voters of Oregon, we can consider ourselves to be still a little distance from fascism.

Yet this is a minimum hope. While our business community will probably not go fascist in the next few years, it will probably not produce the leadership to save free society either. Experience does not lead us to expect from businessmen a creative attack upon the basic anxieties which are unnerving our civilization. Certain conservative leaders in the aristocratic tradition can briefly and by

* Some writers discern in the growing importance of the Army the missing element in the pattern of American fascism. If we do move toward a fascist society, it will undoubtedly be as a result of an alliance between big business and the Army. My own belief, however, is that the appearance of generals in public life at this time is due as much as anything to the fact that they are men of ability, exempt from partisan criticism and used to working for the government at a low rate of pay — and hence are available as are few civilians of corresponding capacity. There is no evidence of the development of a unified military position on political questions. Some generals, indeed, notably Bradley, Eisenhower, Marshall, Bedell Smith, Stilwell, have shown clearly democratic political tendencies. We are still far from a militarist society. The theory that Universal Military Training is going to convert the youth of the country into willing agents of a military despotism can only have been concocted by people who have never had to undergo military service.

instinct resolve these anxieties, as Winston Churchill restored to Britain a sense of family solidarity under enemy
fire. But take away the enemy fire, and even aristocratic
conservatism seems to lack the boldness and the understanding to root out the social sources of anxiety. Businessmen have essential contributions to make as individuals and as producers of goods — but not, in the judgment
of the American people, as the ultimate makers of public
policy. The free society can lose by default as irrevocably
as by a positive error. It can perish by inanition as finally
as by the sword.

III

The Failure of the Left

SINCE progressives, on the whole, create our contemporary climate of opinion, the impression exists that the present perils to free society result exclusively from the failure of the conservatives. In a sense, this is true — in the sense that the conservatives have had the power, notably in the period between the wars, and have failed to use it intelligently. Yet one reason for their failure, as D. W. Brogan has reminded us, is the failure of their critics, whose hearts were in the right place, but whose heads were too often "muddled, full of sentiment, empty of knowledge, living on slogans and clichés, unwilling to realize how complicated is the modern world and that the price of liberty is eternal intellectual vigilance." [1] Compared with the conservatives, the progressives were indeed innocent; but is innocence enough?

During the years of plutocratic stagnation, why did not

progressivism have strong faith and lucid purposes? And, in the cases where progressives were sure of their diagnosis and of their remedy, why has that certitude now vanished? Let us concede at once the relative superiority in practice of left-wing governments — at least of the pragmatic left, though not of the doctrinaire left. The New Deal government of Franklin D. Roosevelt, for all its confusions and defects, kept its eye more steadily on the ball than any other government of our time, conservative, socialist, Communist or fascist. Yet history has discredited the hopes and predictions of doctrinaire progressivism about as thoroughly as it has those of conservatism. The progressive "analysis" is today a series of dry and broken platitudes, tossed out in ash-heaps (where they are collected and dusted off by the editors of the liberal weeklies).

What is the progressive? The defining characteristic of the progressive, as I shall use the word, is the sentimentality of his approach to politics and culture. He must be distinguished, on the one hand, from the Communist; for the progressive is soft, not hard; he believes himself genuinely concerned with the welfare of individuals. He must be distinguished, on the other, from the radical democrat; for the progressive, by refusing to make room in his philosophy for the discipline of responsibility or for the danger of power, has cut himself off from the usable traditions of American radical democracy. He has rejected the pragmatic tradition of the men who, from the Jacksonians to the New Dealers, learned the facts of life through the exercise of power under conditions of accountability. He has rejected the pessimistic tradition of those who, from Hawthorne to Reinhold Niebuhr, warned that power, unless checked by accountability, would corrupt its possessor.

The type of the progressive today is the fellow traveler or the fellow traveler of the fellow traveler: see the Wallace movement or (until fairly recently) the columns of the *New Republic* and the *Nation*.* His sentimentality has softened up the progressive for Communist permeation and conquest. For the most chivalrous reasons, he cannot believe that ugly facts underlie fair words. However he looks at it, for example, the USSR keeps coming through as a kind of enlarged Brook Farm community, complete with folk dancing in native costumes, joyous work in the fields and progressive kindergartens. Nothing in his system has prepared him for Stalin.

This is not a new breed in American history. A century ago, after Jacksonian democracy had split over the slavery question, one wing of northern Jacksonians under Martin Van Buren went into the Free Soil Party. The other wing refused to turn against the South. Many of this prosouthern group retained a Jacksonian desire for social reform; they certainly held no brief for slavery; yet as men implicated in the industrial evils of the north, who were they, they would cry, to pronounce judgment on the social system of the South? "The only difference between the negro slave of the South, and the white wages slave of the North," as one member of this group put it, "is, that the one has a master without asking for him, and the other

* Both journals began to show healthy schizoid tendencies in 1948. The *Nation* is now in good part liberated from the Soviet mystique, except for the devotional essays of Señor Del Vayo and pious genuflections by Miss Kirchwey herself. The *New Republic*, after waiving Mr. Wallace out of the league, has shown increasing evidence of waking up to realities. [In 1962, the *New Republic* is once again an excellent liberal magazine. The *Nation* still shows Doughface tendencies.]

has to beg for the privilege of becoming a slave. . . . The one is the slave of an individual; the other is the slave of an inexorable class." *

The members of this group were known as Doughfaces — that is, "northern men with southern principles." The infiltration of contemporary progressivism by Communism had led to the same self-flagellation, the same refusal to take precautions against tyranny. It has created a new Doughface movement — a movement of "democratic men with totalitarian principles."

The core of Doughface progressivism is its sentimental belief in progress. The belief in progress was the product of the Enlightenment, cross-fertilized with allied growths, such as science, bourgeois complacency, Unitarianism and a faith in the goodness of man. It dispensed with the Christian myths of sin and atonement. Man's shortcomings, such as they were, were to be redeemed, not by Jesus on the cross, but by the benevolent unfolding of history. Tolerance, free inquiry and technology, operating in the framework of human perfectibility, would in the end create a heaven on earth, a goal much more wholesome than a heaven in heaven.

---

* The speaker was Mike Walsh, editor of the fiery radical weekly *The Subterranean* and one of the first authentic proletarian characters in American political history. He went on to challenge the abolitionists to produce "one single solitary degradation" heaped on the slave which a northern worker was not liable to suffer through poverty. "It is all very well for gentlemen to get up here and clamor about the wrongs and outrages of the southern slaves; but, sir, even in New York, during the last year, there have been over thirteen hundred people deprived of their liberty without any show or color of offense, but because they were poor, and too honest to commit a crime." Walsh speaking in the House of Representatives, May 19, 1854, *Congressional Globe*, 33 Congress 1 Session, 1224. Clearly the false comparison, which Arthur Koestler has called the Fallacy of the Unequal Equation, is no invention of the modern Doughface.

The nineteenth century, with its peace and prosperity, supplied protective coloration for the enthronement of history and for the rejection of the dark and subterranean forces in human nature. Darwin furnished the scientific underpinnings, Spencer the philosophical superstructure, and even Marx accepted the psychological assumptions. At times one cannot but wonder at what psychic cost the Victorians purchased their optimism. How else to explain the fantasies of violence — the poorhouses and the mad-houses, the public cruelties and the secret insanities — which run through the Victorian novel like a deep stain of fear?

Yet the official optimism triumphed. Only a few dis-reputable aesthetes, a few obstinate Christians dared openly to compute this psychic cost. The nineteenth century had, indeed, its underground movements — its doubters and skeptics, shaken by nightmares which we have come to see as often only too exact probings into reality, but which their respectable contemporaries dis-missed as bad dreams. While the sun of optimism was still high in the sky, Dostoievsky, Kierkegaard, Nietzsche, Sorel, Freud were charting possibilities of depravity. Then, slowly the sun sank in the twentieth century, and practical men, like Hitler, Stalin, Mussolini, began to transform depravity into a way of life. Progress had betrayed the progressives. History was abandoning its votaries and un-leashing the terror.

Why was progressivism not prepared for Hitler? The eighteenth century had exaggerated man's capacity to live by logic alone; the nineteenth century sanctified what re-mained of his non-logical impulses; and the result was the pervading belief in human perfectibility which has disarmed progressivism in too many of its encounters with actuality. As the child of eighteenth-century rationalism and nineteenth-century romanticism, progressivism was committed to an unwarranted optimism about man.

Optimism gave the progressives a soft and shallow conception of human nature. With the aggressive and sinister impulses eliminated from the equation, the problem of social change assumed too simple a form. The corruptions of power — the desire to exercise it, the desire to increase it, the desire for prostration before it — had no place in the progressive calculations. As a result, progressivism became politically inadequate: it could neither persuade nor control the emotions of man. And it became intellectually inadequate: it could not anticipate nor explain the tragic movements of history in the twentieth century. Ideologies which exploited the darker passions captured men by appeals unknown to the armory of progressivism.

Doughface progressivism — the faith of the present-day fellow traveler — may be defined briefly as progressivism kept alive by main force in face of all the lessons of modern history. It is this final fatuity of progressivism which has turned it into, if not an accomplice of totalitarianism, at least an accessory before the fact. For its persistent and sentimental optimism has endowed Doughface progressivism with what in the middle of the twentieth century are fatal weaknesses: a weakness for impotence, because progressivism believes that history will make up for human error; a weakness for rhetoric, because it believes that man can be reformed by argument; a weakness for economic fetishism, because it believes that the good in man will be liberated by a change in economic institutions; a weakness for political myth, because Doughface optimism requires somewhere an act of faith in order to survive the contradictions of history.

The weakness of impotence is related to a fear of responsibility — a fear, that is, of making concrete decisions and being held to account for concrete consequences. Problems are much simpler when viewed from the office of a liberal weekly than when viewed in terms of what will actually happen when certain ideologically attractive steps are taken. Too often the Doughface really does not want power or responsibility. For him the more subtle sensations of the perfect syllogism, the lost cause, the permanent minority, where he can be safe from the exacting job of trying to work out wise policies in an imperfect world. Politics becomes, not a means of getting things done, but an outlet for private grievances and frustrations. The progressive once disciplined by the responsibilities of power is often the most useful of all public servants; but he, alas, ceases to be a progressive and is regarded by all true Doughfaces as a cynical New Dealer or a tired Social Democrat.

Having renounced power, the Doughface seeks compensation in emotion. The pretext for progressive rhetoric is, of course, the idea that man, the creature of reason and benevolence, has only to understand the truth in order to act upon it. But the function of progressive rhetoric is another matter; it is, in Dwight Macdonald's phrase, to accomplish "in fantasy what cannot be accomplished in reality." [2] Because politics is for the Doughface a means of accommodating himself to a world he does not like but does not really want to change, he can find ample gratification in words. They appease his twinges of guilt without

committing him to very drastic action. Thus the expiatory
rôle of resolutions in progressive meetings. A telegram of
protest to a foreign chancellery gives the satisfaction of a
job well done and a night's rest well earned. The Doughfaces differ from Mr. Churchill: dreams, they find, are
better than facts. Progressive dreams are tinged with a
brave purity, a rich sentiment and a noble defiance. But,
like most dreams, they are notable for the distortion of
facts by desire.

The progressive attitude toward history is sufficiently
revealing. The responsible conservative, we have seen,
finds in history a profound sense of national continuity
which overrides his contemporary fears and trepidations.
The Doughface, less humble in his approach, is like the
neanderthal conservative, looking at history long and wistfully until it reassembles itself in patterns which support
his current vagaries. Mr. Wallace and his followers, for
example, have proclaimed repeatedly that they are doing
no more on behalf of the Russian Revolution than
Thomas Jefferson did on behalf of the French: it is their
support of social change that exposes them to the same
reactionary persecutions as those which harried Jefferson
in the nineties. It is quite true that Jefferson was an enthusiast for the French Revolution. But he was too intelligent a man and too profound a believer in human freedom to let his enthusiasm survive the transformation of
the Revolution into an aggressive military despotism.
Napoleon, Jefferson observed, was "the Attila of the age
. . . the ruthless destroyer of ten millions of the human
race, whose thirst for blood appeared unquenchable, the
great oppressor of the rights and liberties of the world
. . . a cold-blooded, calculating, unprincipled usurper,

without a virtue." [3] Mr. Wallace, who restrained his passion for Soviet Russia in its revolutionary days and opposed its recognition as late as 1933, became a great enthusiast for the Soviet Union only after it was embarked on its Napoleonic phase. *

In life one must make a choice and accept the consequences; in Doughface fantasy, one can denounce a decision without accepting the consequences of the alternative. Ask a progressive what he thinks of the Mexican War, or of our national policy toward the Indians, and he will probably say that these outbursts of American imperialism are black marks on our history. Ask him whether he then regrets that California, Texas and the West are today part of the United States. And was there perhaps some way of taking lands from the Indians or from Mexico without violating rights in the process? Pushed to it, the progressive probably thinks that there is some solution hidden in the back of his fantasy; but ordinarily he never has to push the question that far back, because he never dreams of facing a question in terms of responsibility for the decision. For him it is sufficient to dissociate himself from the Mexican War so long as he is not required to dissociate himself from the fruits of victory.†

* The Morgenthau Diaries document Wallace's opposition to the recognition of Russia; see Henry Morgenthau, Jr., "How F. D. R. Fought The Axis," *Collier's,* October 11, 1947. Wallace's comment is characteristic: "That was in 1933 and if I opposed it at that time it was because I was not thoroughly familiar with it." *Boston Herald,* October 4, 1947.

† This discussion could be pushed further. Progressives, in pronouncing dogmatic judgments about the Mexican War, will undoubtedly refer to it as a slaveholders' conspiracy. Why then was John C. Calhoun opposed to it? . . . But ignorance is never any bar to certitude in the progressive dreamworld.

Or take the question of the "robber barons." The phrase itself suggests the attitude of disfavor with which the progressive regards the industrialists of the second half of the nineteenth century.* The robber baron, of course, used to sally forth from his castle and steal the goods of innocent travelers. His was a thoroughly non-productive form of economic enterprise. Does even the most unregenerate Doughface consider this to be analagous to the achievements of Andrew Carnegie or John D. Rockefeller? And, to save the nation from the "robber barons," would the Doughface reduce our industrial capacity to the point where it was when the "robber barons" came on the scene? Or has he some other formula for industrialization in a single generation? The fact is, of course, that this nation paid a heavy price for indus-trialization — a price in political and moral decadence, in the wasteful use of economic resources, in the centraliza-tion of economic power. But the price we paid, though perhaps exorbitant, was infinitely less in human terms than the price paid by the people of Russia; and it is not clear that the managers who charged more have done the better job.

Everyone has seen the ignorant dogmatism of Dough-face progressives at work on current issues. People who had barely heard of Spain in 1934 became world cham-pion Spanish experts by 1937, though if you asked them what a Carlist was they would have been hard pressed for an answer. They did not know anything about his-tory, but they knew what they liked. The system of falsi-fiction operated on contemporary lines, too, so that the

* Matthew Josephson, whose admirable book bears this unfortunate title, actually errs much less in this respect than the Doughface.

average American progressive got the impression that the Spanish Republicans were a united group undone by the wicked fascists. Dreams are better than facts. Books like Franz Borkenau's *Spanish Cockpit* and George Orwell's *Homage to Catalonia* were simply not published in America; it was left to Mr. Hemingway and Mr. Dos Passos a few years later to report the savage political differences in the Loyalist ranks and, in particular, the unsavory rôle of the Communists in delivering Spain to fascist tyranny.

The belief that man is perfectible commits the progressive to the endless task of explaining why, in spite of history and in spite of rhetoric, he does not always behave that way. One favorite Doughface answer, borrowed from the Communists, is that contemporary man has been corrupted by the system of private ownership; let us change all this, they say, and our problems will be solved. This form of economic fetishism can be seen nakedly in the Webbs' dreamlike *Soviet Russia: a New Civilization*, where the nationalization of the means of production is believed to have liquidated injustice in society and evil in man.

But is private ownership the root of all evil? Private property, Reinhold Niebuhr has reminded us, is "not the cause but the instrument of human egotism." [4] It is only one embodiment of the will to power. "By abolishing private property," as Freud puts it, "one deprives the human love of aggression of one of its instruments, a strong one undoubtedly, but assuredly not the strongest." [5] Some social arrangements pander more than others to the human love of aggression; but aggression underlies all social arrangements, whether capitalist or Communist, and it remains a question whether aggression is more checked and controlled by Russian totalitarianism than by American pluralism. In any case, the root remains man.

At the bottom of the set of Doughface illusions is a need for faith. As the gap has widened between the sentimental abstractions of Doughface fantasy and the cruel complexities of life, the need has increased for mythology to take up the slack. One myth, to which the Doughface has clung in the face of experience with the imperturbable ardor of an early Christian, is the mystique of the proletariat. This myth, given its classical form by Marx, himself so characteristically a bourgeois intellectual, states that the action of the working class will overthrow capitalist tyranny and establish by temporary dictatorship a classless society. Its appeal lies partly in the progressive intellectual's sense of guilt over living pleasantly by his skills instead of unpleasantly by his hands, partly in the intellectual's somewhat feminine fascination with the rude and muscular power of the proletariat, partly in the intellectual's desire to compensate for his own sense of alienation by immersing himself in the broad maternal expanse of the masses. Worship of the proletariat becomes a perfect fulfillment for the frustrations of the progressive.

At one time perhaps there was *prima facie* support for the myth. Before capitalism raised mass living standards, the working classes had a genuinely revolutionary potential. This was visible in Britain and America in the early days of the nineteenth century and in France as late as the Paris Commune. In countries like Spain and Yugoslavia, where industrialization and its benefits have been delayed, the revolutionary potential existed well into the twentieth century. But, contrary to Marx's prediction of increasing proletarian misery, capitalism, once it has had the chance, has vastly increased the wealth and freedom of the ordinary worker. It has reduced the size of the working class and deradicalized the worker. *

As a result, workers as a mass have decreasingly the impulses attributed to them by Marxism. They too often believe in patriotism or religion, or read comic strips, go to movies, play slot machines and patronize taxi dance halls. In one way or another, they try to cure their discontent by narcotics rather than by surgery. The general strike is in principle the most potent weapon in the world, but it always remains potent in principle. The last great moment for the general strike was perhaps 1914, when syndicalist agitation had at least kept alive mass revolutionary emotions. But, even had Jaurès survived and led the call, the working classes would probably have succumbed to the bugle, the flag and the military parade. Marx recognized that many workers were not Marxists and so invented a classification called the *Lumpenproletariat* in which were dumped those who did not live up to theory. Lenin recognized this too and so invented a disciplined party which announced itself as the only true representative of the proletariat, reducing non-Communist workers to political non-existence.

Progressives defending their belief in the proletariat sometimes cite the trade-union movement.† Yet the trade

---

* In the United States, between 1910 and 1940, the common laborer dropped from 38 per cent of the labor force to 25.9 per cent; white-collar workers increased from 10.2 per cent to 17.2 per cent.

† Communists do not have any such illusions except for propaganda purposes. "Trade unionism," wrote Lenin, "signifies the mental enslavement of the workers to the bourgeoisie." David Shub, *Lenin*, New York, 1948, p. 54.

union has, in fact, surely been the culminating agency in the deradicalization of the masses. As an institution, it is as clearly indigenous to the capitalist system as the corporation itself, and has no real meaning apart from that system. Thus trade unions, while giving the working masses a sense of having an organization of their own, insure that the goals of this organization are compatible with capitalism. And, as unions become more powerful, they increase their vested interests in the existing order. Labor leadership acquires satisfactions in terms of prestige and power. Only acute mass disaffection could radicalize the union leadership; and, up to this point, at least, the increase in capitalist productivity has enabled the labor movement to bring the rank-and-file steady benefits in the shape of higher wages, reduced hours and better working conditions.

What operational meaning, indeed, does the conception of the proletariat as an agency of change have? Can it mean anything more than the proletariat as a pool of discontent from which leaders can draw recruits for a variety of programs? The technical necessity for organization, as Robert Michels showed long ago, sets in motion an inevitable tendency toward oligarchy. The leadership after a time is bound to have separate interests from the rank-and-file. A working-class organization will soon stand, not for the working class, but for the working class plus the organization's own instincts for survival plus the special bureaucratic interests of the organization's top leadership. No loopholes have yet been discovered in the iron law of oligarchy.

For these various reasons, the mystique of the working class has faded somewhat since the First War. In its place has arisen a new mystique, more radiant and palpable, and exercising the same fascinations of power and guilt: the mystique of the USSR. Each success of the Soviet Union has conferred new delights on those possessed of the need for prostration and frightened of the responsibilities of decision. In a world which makes very little sense, these emotions are natural enough. But surrender to them destroys the capacity for clear intellectual leadership which ought to be the progressive's function in the world. In an exact sense, Soviet Russia has become the opiate of the progressives.

"The facts of life do not penetrate to the sphere in which our beliefs are cherished," writes Proust; "as it was not they that engendered those beliefs, so they are powerless to destroy them; they can aim at them continual blows of contradiction and disproof without weakening them; and an avalanche of miseries and maladies coming, one after another, without interruption into the bosom of a family, will not make it lose faith in either the clemency of its God or the capacity of its physician." [6] The Soviet Union can do very little any more to disenchant its believers; it has done about everything in the book already. I remember in the summer of 1939 asking a fellow traveler what the USSR could possibly do which would make him lose faith. He said, "Sign a pact with Hitler." But two months later he had absorbed the pact with Hitler; and so the hunger to believe, the anxiety and the guilt, continue to triumph over the evidence. *

* The pact with Hitler might have been justified at the time on the ground that Stalin did not know the West would fight. But the more determined fellow travelers now argue that Stalin was right in any case — even if he had known the West would resist. Cf. Henry Wallace: "If Stalin were doing it all over again, in the light of his present knowledge of Hitler, France and England, he could hardly act differently than [sic] he did." *New Republic,* February 9, 1948.

Conservatism in its crisis of despair turns to fascism: so progressivism in its crisis of despair turns to Communism. Each in a sober mood has a great contribution to make to free society: the conservative in his emphasis on law and liberty, the progressive in his emphasis on mass welfare. But neither is capable of saving free society. Both, faced by problems they cannot understand and fear to meet, tend to compound their own failure by delivering free society to its totalitarian foe. To avoid this fate, we must understand as clearly as possible the reasons for the appeal of totalitarianism.

IV

The Challenge of Totalitarianism

Modern technology created free society — but created it at the expense of the protective tissues which had bound together feudal society. The protective tissues of medievalism suffocated some individuals; in the end they had to be destroyed in the interests of the release of economic energy; but, while they lasted, they consoled and fortified the bulk of the people. They helped, on the whole, to constitute a society where many men could live whole lives.

Our modern industrial economy, based on impersonality, interchangeability and speed, has worn away the old protective securities without creating new ones. It has failed to develop an organizational framework of its own within which self-realization on a large scale is possible. Freedom in industrial society, as a result, has a negative rather than a positive connotation. It means a release

51

from external restraints rather than a deep and abiding sense of self-control and purpose. Man is not free: he is out on parole.

This freedom has brought with it frustration rather than fulfillment, isolation rather than integration. "Anxiety," writes Kierkegaard, "is the dizziness of freedom"; [1] and anxiety is the official emotion of our time. The vogue of existentialism is due in part to the fact that the existentialists have made perhaps the most radical attempt to grapple with the implications of this anxiety. "Man is condemned to be free," remarks Jean Paul Sartre [2] — and from this Sartre concludes that man is absolutely responsible for the use he makes of his freedom. By making choices, man makes himself: creates or destroys his own moral personality. This is a brave and bleak expression of our dilemma. But such a philosophy imposes an unendurable burden on most men. The eternal awareness of choice can drive the weak to the point where the simplest decision becomes a nightmare. Most men prefer to flee choice, to flee anxiety, to flee freedom.

The "escape from freedom," as Erich Fromm has called it, is a characteristic pattern of our age. Man is used to belonging but no longer belongs: the society of status has given way to the society of contract, and the ordeal of consummating or breaking contracts breeds anguish and exhaustion. "In society as it is now constituted," Albert Brisbane, the American Fourierite, cried a century ago, "monotony, uniformity, intellectual inaction and torpor reign: distrust, isolation, separation, conflict and antagonism are almost universal: very little expansion of the generous affections and feelings obtain. . . . Society is spiritually a desert." [3] People, in Thoreau's

stabbing phrase, live lives of quiet desperation. Eliot
notes today

> . . . the strained time-ridden faces
> Distracted from distraction by distraction
> Filled with fancies and empty of meaning
> Tumid apathy with no concentration
> Men and bits of paper, whirled by the cold wind.[4]

As organization towers higher and higher above him,
man grows in forlornness, impotence and fear. As monopoly or state capitalism enlarges its power, the outlets in
economic enterprise dwindle. Man longs to escape the
pressures beating down on his frail individuality; and,
more and more, the surest means of escape seems to be to
surrender that individuality to some massive, external
authority. Dostoievsky remarks, "Man is tormented by no
greater anxiety than to find some one quickly to whom he
can hand over that gift of freedom with which the ill-fated
creature is born." [5] The psychological stigmata of the
fugitives from freedom, Erich Fromm finds in his remarkable analysis, are the strivings for submission and for
domination, the losing of self in masochism or sadism.

The totalitarian state, which has risen in specific response to this fear of freedom, is an invention of the twentieth century. It differs essentially from old-style dictatorship, which may be bloody and tyrannical but yet leaves
intact most of the structure of society. Totalitarianism,
on the contrary, pulverizes the social structure, grinding
all independent groups and diverse loyalties into a single
amorphous mass. The sway of the totalitarian state is unlimited. This very fact is a source of its profound psychological appeal. On an economic level, it seeks to supply
the answer to the incoherence and apparent uncontrol-

lability of industrial society. On the political and psychological level, it holds out hope of allaying the gnawing anxieties; it offers institutional outlets for the impulses of sadism and masochism. As a system of social organization, it purports to invest life with meaning and purpose. Against the loneliness and rootlessness of man in free society, it promises the security and comradeship of a crusading unity, propelled by a deep and driving faith.

Man under freedom, in Marshal Zhukov's expressive phrase, is "an undisciplined, unoriented entity"; under totalitarianism, says Konstantin Simonov happily, each person becomes "a particle of the Soviet system." "To be a socialist," as Goebbels put it, "is to submit the I to the thou; socialism is sacrificing the individual to the whole." Or, in Simonov's candid statement, "I, personally, cannot bear loneliness. . . . If you ask me what the Soviet system has done for the writer I should answer that, first of all, it has erased from his inner self all sense of loneliness, and given him the feeling of complete and absolute 'belonging' to society and the people." [6]

These are the overriding reasons for the appeal of totalitarianism — not the politics of *Mein Kampf* or the economics of *Das Kapital*. Ideology and logic play a minimal part. "I did not join the Party for ideological reasons," writes a young Italian Communist. "I had not then read a line of Marx. I did not adhere to a philosophy when I joined the Party. I joined the struggle and I joined men." [7] Outsiders sometimes wonder how Communists can endure the strict party discipline. How foolish a speculation! Members of a totalitarian party *enjoy* the discipline, they revel in the release from individual responsibility, in the affirmation of comradeship in organized mass solidarity.

"Formerly, our people were disciplined because they were Communists," remarks the Malraux hero; "now plenty of people become Communists because the Party stands for discipline." [8] "The Party is a thong," cries a character in Kirshon's play *Bread*. " . . . It often cuts into my flesh, but I can't live without it. . . . I need someone to give me orders. I must feel another shoulder next to mine." [9]

Against the western sense of being out of joint with history, the totalitarians proclaim their oneness with history — "the thousand-year Reich" or "the proletarian revolution." While free society feels a sense of estrangement from its destiny, the Hitlers and Stalins are in the school of Ralph Waldo Trine; they are "in tune with the infinite." The honest defender of the free individual can only confess the uninspiring belief that most basic problems are insoluble. The totalitarian promises a new heaven and a new earth.

In a society which is uncertain and fragmented, its institutions undermined and its members paralyzed by doubts, this dynamic faith exerts the magnetic influence of a lodestone on iron filings. It affects not only the weak and sentimental but also the highly sophisticated — those most subtly aware of the shaky foundations of existing society. E. H. Carr, the British historian and one-time leader writer for the London *Times,* is the type of intellectual convinced almost in spite of himself by the absolute confidence of totalitarian power. The nature of the power matters little: when Hitler was in the ascendancy, Carr argued (in *The Twenty Years' Crisis*) for the necessity of coming to terms with Nazism; now he argues (*Conditions of Peace,* etc.) for the necessity of coming to terms with Soviet Communism. "Even those — or perhaps par-

ticularly those — who have rejected most vigorously the
content of the creed," as he wrote recently of Communism,
"have been conscious of its power of attraction." [10]

The "anxious man," we have seen, is the characteristic
inhabitant of free society in the twentieth century. The
final triumph of totalitarianism has been the creation of
man without anxiety — of "totalitarian man." Totalitarianism sets out to liquidate the tragic insights which gave
man a sense of his limitations. In their place it has
spawned a new man, ruthless, determined, extroverted,
free from doubts or humility, capable of infallibility, and,
on the higher echelons of the Party, infallible. The
"totalitarian man" is Koestler's Commissar — "the human
type which has completely severed relations with the sub-
conscious." [11] He is the Hero of André Malraux, the man
incarnating mass purpose and historical destiny, in contrast to an individualism based on the cultivation of personal differences. [12]

The "totalitarian man" is oriented against his own individuality. "True Bolshevik courage," observes Stalin,
"does not consist in placing one's individual will above
the will of the Comintern. True courage consists in being
strong enough to master and overcome one's self and subordinate one's will to the will of the collective, the will of
the higher Party body." [13] The totalitarian man denies
the testimony of his private nerves and conscience until
they wither away before the authority of the Party and
of history. He is the man persuaded of the absolute infallibility of the Party's will and judgment, the agent who
knows no misgivings and no scruples, the activist who has
no hesitation in sacrificing life to history. We know well
the visages of these new men in the Gestapo or the MVD,

in the Politburo or in the Assembly of the United Nations — the tight-lipped, cold-eyed, unfeeling, uncommunicative men, as if badly carved from wood, without humor, without tenderness, without spontaneity, without nerves.

Against totalitarian certitude, free society can only offer modern man devoured by alienation and fallibility. The great issue of this century is who is right. Is man a creature of doubt and ambiguity, undone by "the fire and treason crackling" in his blood? [14] Or has he mastered the secrets of history and nature sufficiently to become ruthless, monolithic and infallible, to know whom to spare and whom to kill? For the very insights into man which strike democrats and Christians as the marrow of experience convince the totalitarians of our decadence. *

By one means or another — by strength through joy and joy through strength, by incantation, hypnosis and conversion — the totalitarians have eliminated the conflict between man and the universe, healed the estrangement, brought man into full and living contact with his comrades and with history. The invalids throw away their

* For a vulgar statement of the Communist viewpoint, see a recent definition of existentialism by a party-line literary critic. "What, after all, is existentialism? The bourgeois intellectual transfers to humanity and the universe his sick soul, his enormous egocentrism, his inability to achieve genuine comradeship or love, his actual and potential treacheries, his nebulous hatred, frustration and insecurity, his illusions that the miseries of capitalism are eternal, and dignifies his projection by a name and by maxims from Pascal and Kierkegaard. . . . Let us turn from Auden's mummified existentialist man to Maxim Gorky's complete, unambiguous man, the man who has taken his side with the forces of life . . . 'the miracle-worker and the future master of all the forces of nature.' . . . The City of Man will be built by those who speak with the voice of Maxim Gorky, not with the whine of W. H. Auden." Samuel Greenberg, "Auden: Poet of Anxiety," *Masses and Mainstream,* June, 1948. The question is a very simple one. Is or is not man, in fact, a "miracle-worker and the future master of all the forces of nature"?

crutches as they leave the Soviet shrine. We may suspect a delusion, when we see them whimpering and crawling a little way down the road. But the power of faith is great, especially in a time of despair.

"The horror which No. 1 emanated," muses Rubashov on Stalin in Koestler's *Darkness at Noon,* "above all consisted in the possibility that he was in the right." [15] Pascal's wager appears in a new and terrible form. Why not gamble on his being right? — you have a world to win, and, if you lose, you are no worse off than before. "We came out against the joy of the new life," cried the desperate, despairing Bukharin before the icy judges of Moscow. What could sustain his frail, belated individual defiance against the certitudes of power, which might well mask the certitudes of history? "When you ask yourself: 'If you must die, what are you dying for?'" Bukharin went on, " — an absolute black vacuity suddenly rises before you with startling vividness. There was nothing to die for, if one wanted to die unrepented. And, on the contrary, everything positive that glistens in the Soviet Union acquires new dimensions in a man's mind. This in the end disarmed me completely and led me to bend my knees before the Party and the country. And when you ask yourself: 'Very well, suppose you do not die; suppose by some miracle you remain alive, again what for? Isolated from everybody, an enemy of the people, in an inhuman position, completely isolated from everything that constitutes the essence of life. . . .'" [16]

The fear of isolation, the flight from anxiety lie at the bottom of the totalitarian appeal — especially when the fear and anxiety are converted into frenzy, into "an absolute black vacuity," by conditions of economic and moral hopelessness few Americans can imagine. Against the background of demoralization and exhaustion, the sheer dynamism of the totalitarian promise acquires a glistening certainty which few men can stand up against — not only those like Bukharin, who went to the school of Communism too long to refuse the diploma, but people in general, who tend to confound immediate power with the ultimate verdicts of history.

Thus the twentieth century, which began as the century of democracy, has become the century of the totalitarian revolt against democracy. Thus fascism, Nazism and Communism have risen to challenge fundamentally the whole conception of a free economic or political choice. There are important differences between Communism and fascism, which one must understand if one is to cope with each effectively. But, from one viewpoint, the similarities are vastly more overpowering and significant than the differences.

The similarities result, of course, from the fact that both faiths arose in response to the same frustrations; they bear the imprint of the same defects and failures of free society. Both have displaced the "anxious man" by the "totalitarian man." Both exploit the mystique of revolution, basing themselves on the deep popular disgust with vested inequalities. In both, the suppression of political opposition and intellectual freedom has invested the ruling Party with an absolute power; and, in both, an all-pervasive and merciless secret police has made sure that the power remains absolute. In both the significant contests for power take place within the ruling group; in both the masses are plunged in a profound and trancelike political apathy.

The essential kinship among all totalitarians is illustrated by their historical record of collaboration against the moderates, whether in the Prussian diet or the Berlin transport strike before Hitler, or in the French Assembly against the Third Force. The interchangeability of personnel is notorious. Mussolini consorted with the friends of Lenin in Switzerland before the First War; and Jacques Doriot was a key figure in the Comintern before he began his career as a collaborator with Hitler. From Nils Flyg in Sweden to Pierre Laval in France to Borgida in Italy to Rola-Zmyierski in Poland to J. B. Matthews in the United States to Wang Ching-Wei in China the passage from the extreme left to the extreme right and back has been fast and easy.

"There is more that binds us to Bolshevism," Hitler once observed, "than separates us from it. There is, above all, genuine revolutionary feeling. . . . I have always made allowance for this circumstance, and given orders that former Communists are to be admitted to the Party at once. The *petit bourgeois* Social Democrat and the trade-union boss will never make a National Socialist, but the Communist always will." [17] The Communists signaled their agreement with the sentiment after the death of its author by making a special campaign to bring small-fry Nazis into the Communist-dominated Socialist Unity Party in the Soviet zone of Germany. One concentration-camp survivor concluded after fifteen months at Buchenwald, where the Communists ran the camp's "inner government" in alliance with SS guards, "The Communists were merely Nazis painted red, neither better nor worse, pawning their souls and their fellows' lives for a mock abstract power . . . power to undo all moral or material structure which kept others from joining their herd and rushing with them into anarchy." [18]

There are many elements in this kinship: the contempt
of the man of will for the man of talk, of the activist for
the bourgeois. Both Lenin and Hitler were stirred by the
novels of Knut Hamsun. Men like André Malraux have a
taste for Heroes; and, when the Communist hero became
unendurable, Malraux simply moved on to what he calls
curiously the "liberal hero" — T. E. Lawrence, General
Leclerc and General de Gaulle. [19] Others on a lower level
share a consuming envy, a hatred of the existing order, a
passion for violence, an appetite for gangsterism, which
can be gratified indiscriminately by fascism or by Communism.

In both forms of totalitarianism, moreover, the impulses
of idealism suffer similar fates. Both had their share of
"genuine revolutionary feeling," but, as in all revolutions,
each reached the point of Thermidor, when the tension
between the needs of the revolution and the needs of the
new régime became unbearable. Organization eventually
destroys the revolution, and in so doing is likely to destroy
some of the leading revolutionaries. People have forgotten the revolutionary wing of Nazism. Gregor Strasser
had an honestly radical vision of National Socialist Germany leading an international alliance of the oppressed —
Bolshevik Russia, Nationalist India, Nationalist China —
against the forces of world capitalism. Strasser, Ernst
Juenger and others exploited this "anti-capitalist nostalgia" among the German people — a feeling of which
anti-Semitism was in certain respects only a particularly
crude and repulsive manifestation. * In the inter-Party
conflicts the more conservative Hitler defeated Strasser

* For some it is only a short (if fatal) step from hatred of usurers and
international bankers to hatred of Jews. Early signs of this extrapolation
are to be found in the writings of William Cobbett and of Henry and
Brooks Adams.

and his program of socialist revolution and a Soviet alliance. Yet revolutionary appetites had been excited in the masses; and, after Hitler came to power, they found an outlet in the SA, the only Nazi organization with a strong proletarian following.

The leader of the SA, Captain Ernst Roehm, was a thoroughly vicious character. But he still sensed and expressed the discontent of working-class Nazis afraid of being cheated of social violence. By 1934 Roehm was calling for a "second revolution." It had taken several years of the French Revolution, he would say, before the guillotine really got started. Conservative forces perceived the danger and the Army compelled Hitler to choose between itself and the SA. Once he had chosen, Hitler acted swiftly. The putsch of June 1934 eliminated Roehm and Strasser and drove such revolutionary fellow travelers as Goebbels and Erich Koch into submission.

A few days later Hitler pronounced the proper elegy on the victims of all Thermidors — on the "revolutionaries who favored revolution for its own sake and desired to see revolution established as a permanent condition. . . . Incapable of any true co-operation, with a desire to attack all order, filled with hatred against any authority, their unrest and disquietude can find satisfaction only in some conspiratorial activity of the mind. . . . This group of pathological enemies of the state is dangerous; it represents a reservoir of those ready to co-operate in every attempt at revolt, at least just for so long as a new order does not begin to crystallize out of the state of chaotic confusion." [20]

In Russia the apostle of "permanent revolution" was, of course, Leon Trotsky. The Soviet purge, culminating in the famous Moscow trials, ranks with Hitler's purge of

1934 as a textbook case of the organization destroying the revolution, of the bureaucracy turning upon the radicals. Of the members of Lenin's Politburo, of the original revolutionaries, only Lenin died naturally and only Stalin survives; the rest — Tomsky, Trotsky, Kamenev, Zinoviev, Rykov, Bukharin, Sokolnikov — were all murdered by the Stalinists. Stalin, as he finished up the job in 1938, might well have echoed Hitler's denunciation of "revolutionaries who favored revolution for its own sake." Or perhaps Mussolini had the most apt comment of all. "Normally, a revolutionary movement can be channeled into legality," observed the old maestro in his *Autobiography*, "only by means of forceful measures, directed, if necessary, against the personnel of the movement. . . . At certain historical hours, the sacrifice of those who were the deserving lieutenants of yesterday might become indispensable for the supreme interest of tomorrow." [21]

Fascism and Communism thus rise from a genuinely revolutionary dissatisfaction with existing society; but the revolutionary impulses are doomed to frustration and die under the heels of the new ruling class they have installed in power. Yet there remain important differences. While fascism is a fairly candid expression of nihilism, Communism retains an appearance of existing within a framework of intelligible values. What argument survives in fascism is somnambulistic: it is argument in terms of myth, psychosis and blood. But Marxism has endowed Communism with a respectable intellectual lineage saturated in nineteenth-century values of optimism, rationalism and detailed historical inquiry.

It is important to understand the process which transformed Marxism into a totalitarian faith. Marx himself, for all his abstract and polemical pronouncements of an anti-liberal character, was a man whose general flavor remains western and whose thought can be assimilated into the democratic tradition. Socialists like Léon Blum and Aneurin Bevan, for example, have seized upon the humane and liberal aspects of Marxism. But the Russian adaptation of the Marxist inheritance gave it a more sharp and sinister form. Marx, with his complex sense of history, may well have had apprehensions over what Russia, with the weight of its collectivist past, might do to his doctrines. "I am not of the opinion," he once wrote, "that 'old Europe' can be re-juvenated by Russian blood." [22]

His apprehensions would certainly have been warranted. Lenin exposed Marxist socialism to the play of two influences which divested it of libertarian elements and thrust it toward totalitarianism. First was the broad influence of the Russian past — a past in which individualism played no part and in which the massive movements were movements of the group and of the folk. Second was the narrow influence of the Russian revolutionary experience — an experience dominated by the Okhrana, by Siberia, by clandestinity and exile, and resulting in the enthronement of a psychology of conspiracy.

Marx had repudiated Bakunin, and even Lenin paid little formal respect to Nechayev or Tkachev. Yet Lenin's ideas were plainly shaped by the theorists of the anti-tsarist underground. With his call in 1902 for the professional revolutionary, he set in motion the Communist process of taking the revolution away from the people. We need, he said, a "small compact core, consisting of reliable, experienced and hardened workers, with responsible agents in the principal districts, and connected by all the rules of strict secrecy with the organizations of revolutionists." [23] This tight, disciplined élite, plotting in secrecy and mistrusting the world, impregnated Bolshevism with conspiratorial obsessions which easily survived the conquest of power in 1917. This conspiratorial paranoia has become the conditioned reflex of Communism. It is in great part responsible today both for the Soviet ruling class's fear of internal opposition and for its aggressions toward the outside world.

Totalitarianism in Germany is the pure case of the escape from freedom. In Nazism the impulses toward sadism and masochism consequently found their most violent gratification. But totalitarianism in Russia is a more complex phenomenon. In so far as Stalinism is the contemporary expression of the collectivist instincts which have been continuous in Russian history, it has a certain legitimacy.* It lacks, to that degree, the psychotic and compulsive qualities of totalitarianism in a land that has

* A glance at a book like the Marquis de Custine's account of his travels through Russia in 1839 suggests the extent to which political and intellectual life in Russia has always been ruled by a police despotism. "In Russia, whatever be the appearance of things," de Custine wrote, "violence and arbitrary rule are at the bottom of all. Tyranny rendered calm by the influence of terror, is the only kind of happiness which this government is able to afford to its people." And again: "Despotism is never so much to be dreaded as when it pretends to do good, for then it thinks the most revolting acts may be excused by the intention; and the evil that is applied as a remedy has no longer any bounds." The very completeness of the popular submission, de Custine argued, was launching Russia inexorably on a career of world conquest. "To purify himself from the foul and impious sacrifice of all public and personal liberty, the slave, upon his knees, dreams of the conquest of the world." Astolphe de Custine, *Russia*, New York, 1854, pp. 484, 474, 488. But it is hardly correct to infer from expressions such as these of de Custine that a tradition of despotism explains and excuses the present-day USSR. At its worst, tsarist absolutism never approached the Soviet in the efficiency or comprehensiveness of its terror. A book like the memoirs of Herzen, in which the author describes the intolerable persecutions of the tsarist police, has an opera-bouffe quality compared with the reminiscences of those who have had to deal with the MVD.

known freedom. But it acquires those qualities in so far
as it goes on to repress and thwart burgeoning desires for
greater freedom. The mixture of legitimate and psychotic
elements in Soviet Communism — the question of deciding what is Russian and what is totalitarian — make enormously difficult the problem both of estimating its own
potentialities and of devising an effective democratic
policy toward Russia.

There are other important differences between the two
varieties of totalitarianism. Fascism preserved the structure of private economic ownership. The state, it is true,
took over the power of basic economic decision; and leading political figures, like Goering, sliced themselves huge
fiefdoms in the economic world. But there was no systematic dispossession of the owning class and, as a result,
no liquidation of the old ruling elements. As a lower
middle class movement, Nazism envied the great accumu-
lations of property more than it disapproved them; unlike
working-class Communism, it had no profound desire for
the abolition of private exploitation.

The consequence was to give Nazism a short-term
strength and a long-term vulnerability. By forming an
alliance with compliant persons among the large capitalists, the landed nobility, the civil service and the Army,
Hitler gained immediate access to an invaluable reservoir
of technical skills; where Lenin had too often to start
from scratch with generals who could not command, engineers who could not build and diplomats who had never
been out of Russia. But a generation of rolling their own
gave the Soviet Union generals, engineers and diplomats
whom it could more or less trust — whose treason, at worst,
was individual and not that of a class. Hitler, on the other
hand, as the tide turned against him, found himself sur-

rounded by potential traitors in the Army, the Foreign Office and the civil service — men who used the resources and facilities of their class in opposing him. In his last days Hitler would remark wistfully to intimates that Lenin and Stalin had been right in annihilating the upper classes in Russia, and that he had made a mistake in not doing likewise. [24] Perhaps, as he looked back, he felt he had made the wrong choice in 1934.

The price of his error was, of course, the attempted putsch of July 20, 1944. The anti-Hitler conspiracy had found room to breathe in the sections of the aristocracy and bureaucracy which Hitler had left intact after 1934. In an alliance as incongruous as that of the "bloc of rights and Trotskyites" in Russia, conservatives like Goerdeler made an uneasy coalition with a group of radical activists, led by Count von Stauffenberg, in which the old Gregor Strasser longing for a truly revolutionary National Socialism based on an alliance with the Soviet Union was curiously revived. The putsch failed; and in the purge of the summer of 1944 Hitler did what he could to make up for his miscalculation of ten years earlier.

The liquidation of the old ruling élites certainly complicated the problems of transition for the Russians. But it makes their present position much more secure. Nazi Germany was at best an imperfect totalitarianism. Too many elements of pre-Nazi Germany survived in relatively good shape for the state to become identical with society. But the Soviet Union appears to have achieved a virtually complete identity between state and society. Its seams are calked against the wind and waves. For the long haul, it will prove a considerably more seaworthy vessel than the patchwork structure of Nazi Germany.

V

The Case of Russia

Soviet totalitarianism lays greater initial claim on democratic sympathies than does fascism. Its hopes and ideals appear to be in an intelligible humanitarian tradition; and for a time the harshness of its methods seemed almost justified by the magnitude of its problems, the unpreparedness of the Russian people and the implacability of the reactionary opposition. In the figure of Lenin, the Soviet Revolution had a leader whose combination of will and selflessness made him appear the embodiment of the inevitabilities of history. His lack of vanity, his force and directness, and his absolute impersonal devotion diffused over the Russian Revolution itself a character of sacrificial dedication to the good of humanity. These very qualities of Lenin, indeed, have long preserved him from the opprobrium which disillusioned Communists have flung upon his successor.

Yet Lenin's revision of Marxism laid the foundations upon which Stalinist absolutism rests. Soviet apologists have made much of the great capitalist encirclement as the cause for the policies of totalitarianism. Certainly in the years immediately after the Revolution the need for self-defense required peremptory measures of consolidation; but by the middle twenties the threat had receded. The most determined apologist can hardly argue that it was necessary to press the totalitarian terror in order to defend the Socialist Fatherland from such pathetic adventurers as Sidney George Reilly. External dangers were always the pretext; the design for absolutism lay deep in the conceptions of Lenin.

Lenin's special innovation was the deification of the Communist Party. At the start, he tolerated the existence of other working-class parties, such as the Socialists, Social Revolutionaries and Anarchists. The Workers' Opposition groups were allowed to carry on their fight for trade-union autonomy. But after 1920 the bureaucracy began to tighten its controls. The band of professional revolutionaries, emerging from the conspiratorial darkness, began to become the anointed of the Lord; Sir John Maynard finds their historical analogue in the Russian medieval church. The climax came with the uprising in March, 1921, of the revolutionary sailors of Kronstadt in a desperate attempt to arrest the consolidation of party power. The Kronstadt program is worth examining. Its aims were limited. New freedoms were demanded only for workers and peasants, not for members of the bourgeoisie. But these freedoms included elections by secret ballot, freedom of speech and press for all the left-wing Socialist parties, freedom of assembly for trade unions and peasant organizations, release of Socialist and Anarchist prisoners, and the end of state favoritism to the Communist Party and of special Communist power in state institutions.

To grant these demands would have been to destroy the Communist monopoly on power. Looking hard, Lenin claimed to discern White Guardists behind the Kronstadt radicals and ordered the bloody suppression of the rebels. The next Party Congress ended internal democracy within the Party. The large-scale arrest of political prisoners began; and Socialists and Anarchists began to make the long exodus to the stretches of Siberia and the bleak coasts of the White Sea. The trade-union fight came gradually to a dismal end. The labor movement turned into a labor front for disciplining the workers, and Tomsky, the great champion of the unions, perished mysteriously in the early thirties.

It is true that for Lenin the use of terror was, on the whole, principled; that is to say, it was restricted to class enemies or to open rebels. He refrained from applying it to his own people, to his comrades in the Revolution. Yet by his own acts he laid down the framework within which his successors could complete the extermination of all independent thought. "The Communists," Marx and Engels had written in 1848, "do not form a separate party opposed to other working class parties." [1] But for Lenin the Communist Party "does not and must not share leadership with any other party"; within its own ranks it must maintain "iron discipline"; and the dictatorship of the proletariat can be realized *only* through it as the directing force. [2] Thus the workers themselves were denied ideas and instrumentalities not totally under Party control. In the name of Party infallibility, all the institutions which might challenge the Party were ruthlessly subordinated to it or broken by it.

Both Lenin and Trotsky, as Bertram D. Wolfe has pointed out, had moments of insight before the Revolution when they saw the monstrous conclusions to which the deification of the Party might lead. "Whoever attempts to achieve socialism by any other route than that of political democracy," Lenin wrote in 1905, "will inevitably arrive at the most absurd and reactionary results, both political and economic." Trotsky had already predicted that centralism would lead to a situation where "the organization of the Party takes the place of the Party itself; the Central Committee takes the place of the organization; and finally the dictator takes the place of the Central Committee." [3] But neither Lenin nor Trotsky had the essential will to stand by these insights; they were corrupted by a passion for powers which each believed he could be trusted to use for good ends.

Lenin's policy of concentrating all authority and wisdom in the Party leadership and smashing all opposition thus made "Stalinism" inevitable. Nor would Trotsky's triumph over Stalin have made much difference. Trotsky was certainly the more attractive and appealing figure of the two, especially to other literary men and intellectuals. His dash and intransigence, his disdain for the petty detail of political maneuvering, the brilliance of his logic and the nobility of his rhetoric — all combine to romanticize a figure already invested with a devotion to democracy by his opposition to the ruling clique and with a special pathos by the circumstances of his exile and his shocking death.

Yet it was this same Trotsky who boasted in 1920: "As for us, we were never concerned with the Kantian-priestly and vegetarian-Quaker prattle about the 'sacredness of human life!' "[4] It was this same Trotsky who crushed the rebels of Kronstadt. His devotion to democracy, his fight against bureaucracy, were the product of the period when the bureaucracy was organized against him and "democracy" provided his only hope. Even then he made no appeals to the people. He represented, in short, merely the left wing of the bureaucracy. "Trotsky as well as Stalin wished to pass off the State as being the proletariat, the bureaucratic dictatorship over the proletariat as the proletarian dictatorship, the victory of State capitalism over both private capitalism and socialism as a victory of the latter." *

To the end Trotsky remained prisoner of one controlling delusion — the notion that nationalization of industry made the Soviet Union a "workers' state" which, however much it might degenerate under the Stalinist bureaucracy, still remained sound at bottom. Thinking always in terms of bureaucratic supremacy, he failed to see that totally centralized nationalization of the Soviet type made it inevitable that the bureaucracy be "Stalinist." Too many still share his delusion that the state ownership of industry somehow makes up for the excesses of a one-party system. "Whatever you say about Russia," the modern Doughface will cry, "at least you must admit that the workers are not exploited; they are the owners of the factories themselves. The USA may have political democracy; but the USSR has economic democracy."

* A. Ciliga, *The Russian Enigma*, London, 1940, p. 104. This book, written by a former Yugoslav Communist, presents a remarkable account of developments in the USSR.

This claim demands close examination. In the sense of legal forms, it is doubtless true that the workers "own" the factories. Yet no people are more ardent than the Communists themselves in exposing this identical legal fiction when a corporation boasts that it is "owned" by large quantities of widows and orphans. The fact is, as Professor Michael Polanyi has put it, the Soviet workers "are not owners of their factories any more than the British citizen is the owner of the British navy." [5]

The crucial point, of course, is not the legal fiction of ownership but the operating reality of control. The experiments in workers' control in Russia are long since extinct; independent labor organization and strikes are dreams of a forgotten past; free movement from job to job has disappeared; the speed-up, long hours and low wages have reduced even the nominally free worker to conditions of servitude which would not be tolerated in a capitalist state; and a part of the economy rests indispensably on millions of slave laborers. What kind of "economic democracy," what kind of workers' state is this? At least, Western workers have indirect supervision over the post offices and battleships they technically own. But the Soviet worker has no recourse — by ballot, by trade union, or by share in management — which will concede him any power in the economy supposedly his by birthright. Power resides in the officialdom which controls the economy.

"Soviet Russia," as Dennis Brogan more accurately puts it, "is one vast company town." In the old Republican days, steel companies used to own towns in the minefields of western Pennsylvania. The company towns had their own police, their own schools, their own churches, their own stores, their own unions. If any of the workers had been stockholders in the company — i.e., "owners" of it — they would have been in the same position as the workers in Russia. Of course, the American company town had its vulnerable points. Frances Perkins could come in and speak from the steps of the post office, which the company did not own; or workers could go to Pittsburgh for a rendezvous with members of the Steel Workers Organizing Committee; or they could cast their votes for Roosevelt. "Soviet Russia is a Pennsylvania or West Virginia from which there is no escape," and in which the steel companies and the Government are united in indissoluble bonds. [6]

The Russian Revolution, in short, has not liberated the workers. In the economic as in the political sphere, it has brought into existence a new ruling class. As absolute masters, not only of government, but of the means of production as well, the Communist bureaucracy has more power than any capitalist ruling class has ever had; and its interests are at least as much opposed to those of the working class. Soviet society, in other words, has taken no recognizable socialist shape, if socialism implies anything about the active participation of the workers in political and economic decisions. As sensible a designation as any for this new society is the phrase "bureaucratic collectivism." [7]

The process of bureaucratization has thus divided Soviet society into the amorphous masses and their active and purposeful masters. It is not yet a rigid caste society. An efficient system of recruitment, for example, pulls young men of ability into the Party machine before a sense of exclusion might drive them to organize opposition against it. But the children of officials and Party leaders are already enjoying privileges which certainly tend toward class stratification. At twenty-eight young Vasily Stalin was a major general, an eminence possibly not due entirely to merit.

The common people are once again an inert majority, sunk back into the state of political apathy from which the Communists helped rouse them a generation before. Denied political or intellectual initiative, deprived of organizations of their own, pursued everywhere by the argus eye of the secret police, worn out by the unrelenting tension of totalitarianism, the Russian masses have apparently become as blank and shapeless politically as the masses of the Third Reich.

> Comrade Stalin is our Party,
> Comrade Stalin is our people,
> Comrade Stalin is our banner,
> Comrade Stalin is our victory.*

Reassuring sentiments perhaps, but hardly an entire

* From an article by Yaroslavsky in *Propagandist*, Summer, 1942, quoted by Avrahm Yarmolinsky, "Inside Russia," *New Republic*, March 29, 1943. This kind of thing is carried to a nauseating length and is drenched in religious imagery. *Pravda*, for example, on August 28, 1936, produced the following:

> "Oh, great Stalin, oh, leader of the people,
> You who created man,
> You who populated the earth,
> You who made the centuries young,
> You who made the springtime flower. . . . "

Suzanne Labin quotes this, along with other examples, in *Staline le terrible*, Paris, 1948, pp. 74 ff. *Zemlia Russkaya*, a book published by the Young Communist League, Moscow, 1946, contributes the following gem: "Stalin! . . . Here in the Kremlin his presence touches us at every step. We walk on stones which he may have trod only quite recently. Let us fall on our knees and kiss those holy footprints." Victor Serge provides more examples of Stalin-worship in *From Lenin to Stalin*, New York, 1937, pp. 98 ff.

political vocabulary. Yet people under totalitarian rule are hypnotized by such incantatory slogans into a condition of political exhaustion from which they can be stirred only by the most ferocious rhetoric. Hence the mad-dog fascist-beast language which characterizes totalitarian oratory.

The lavatory-wall imagery of a typical Goebbels or Zhdanov speech serves the further purpose of giving popular frustrations and discontents something to work themselves out upon. No one should count too much on these discontents. The Russian people fought for Stalin during the war — and would fight again — with fully as much devotion as they fought for tsarist Russia against previous invaders. Still, many thousand Russians joined General Vlasov's Russian Army of Liberation in alliance with Hitler against Stalin; and many thousands more today — ex-soldiers, workers, peasants, officials — are in the displaced persons camps of Europe, ready to do anything except return to the Soviet Union. Within Russia the dull bitterness of the people is seeping over and, according to recent reports, is expressing itself increasingly in anti-Semitism.[8] Bad morale presents no serious threat to a totalitarian régime, of course, because modern science has given the ruling class power which renders mass revolutions obsolete. Yet its existence casts a strange light on the beauties of life in the Soviet paradise.

Many people who will concede this account of development in the USSR still wonder whether these developments are not perhaps the result of crisis. Will not age, prosperity and international peace mellow the totalitarians and lead them to relinquish their absolute power?

It is certainly true that pressures toward relaxation — the restlessness and discontent — may accumulate to the point where they will affect totalitarian policy. But experience suggests that they will affect totalitarian policy in the direction, not of moderating, but of intensifying the ruling psychosis. Totalitarianism, as we have seen, means that all social energy — all loyalty, emotion and faith — is focused upon a single object; and this concentration requires the maintenance of a high pitch of tension throughout society. Totalitarian states have generally maintained this tension by playing up external or internal threats: an aggressive foreign state, or a diabolical domestic conspiracy. But the very disappearance of real threats, far from enabling the régime to relax its controls, only compels it to rely increasingly on internal terror as a means of maintaining the necessary pitch of tension.

Lenin's terror, being attached to objective conditions, like a still-existing capitalism, had some limits. But Stalin's terror, operating after the liquidation of capitalism, is directed at thoughts — the "vestiges of capitalism," as Molotov calls them, adding that they "are extremely persistent in people's consciousness." [9] It is consequently unlimited in its application. "The tasks of the ideological front," observes Zhdanov, " . . . are not removed, but, on the contrary, grow more important under conditions of peaceful development." [10] Concentration camps, as Hannah Arendt points out, multiplied in both Russia and Germany, not at the height of effective opposition to the régime, but after its disappearance. The longer the totalitarian régime is established and the more secure it is from internal and external enemies, it would seem, the more essential the terror, the more fierce the heresy hunts, the more violent the requirements for total conformity.*

One cannot be dogmatic about the general point that totalitarianism waxes rather than wanes with time. Both Germany and Russia in their later phases were doubtless influenced by real or imagined fears of foreign aggression. And a marked increase in living standards might well reduce the terror by reducing the need for coercion and tension. Yet a totalitarian ruling class is in some sense the victim of the dynamism of its own system. Once the Politburo reaches a decision, it cannot admit its own fallibility. If the totalitarian man too begins to feel fire and treason crackling in his blood, if humility or doubt lead him to grant other views equality with his own, then his claim to infallibility disappears. Anxiety is the enemy and must not be permitted within the gates. So he is driven eternally to confirm his conviction of absolute rightness, to destroy not only those who would challenge him directly, but those whose activity sets up currents in society away from the all-devouring center. Everything in a totalitarian state is eventually sucked into the vortex where totalitarian man interminably revindicates himself.

The recent Soviet campaign against cultural freedom and diversity becomes all too comprehensible in this light. The totalitarian man requires apathy and unquestioning

---

* In 1930 Freud raised a significant question. "It is quite intelligible," he wrote, "that the attempt to establish a new communistic type of culture in Russia should find psychological support in the persecution of the bourgeois. One only wonders, with some concern, however, how the Soviets will manage when they have exterminated their bourgeois entirely." (*Civilization and its Discontents,* p. 91.) The answer is now clear: the Soviet régime turns upon the intellectuals and the working class.

obedience. He fears creative independence and spontaneity. He mistrusts complexity as a device for slipping something over on the régime; he mistrusts incomprehensibility as a shield which might protect activities the bureaucracy cannot control. After all, the mission of art is clear and definite. In the words of Konstantin Simonov, "We must show the Soviet person — the builder of the future — in such a light that the audience and the whole world will see the moral and spiritual superiority of people who have been reared in a socialist society." [11] "We have in real life, living," adds Alexander Fadeyev, the secretary of the Soviet Writers Union, "those heroes who created the new social order, who are the personification of the new moral values." [12]

The paintings of Picasso, the music of Stravinsky are strangely disturbing. They reflect and incite anxieties which are incompatible with the monolithic character of "the Soviet person." Their intricacy and ambiguity, moreover, make them hard for officialdom to control; they thus tend to create intellectual enclaves within the totalitarian whole. Nicolas Nabokov quotes a character in a famous anti-tsarist satire: "What I don't understand is undoubtedly dangerous to the security of the state." * Complexity in art further suggests the whole wicked view of "cosmopolitanism" summed up for the Communists in

---

* N. Nabokov in his brilliant article, "The Music Purge," *Politics*, Spring, 1948. Where are the famous anti-Communist satires? Zoshchenko, a brilliant satirist, has long since fallen into disgrace for making fun of aspects of Soviet life. As David Zaslavsky, the Westbrook Pegler of *Pravda*, defines the somewhat restricted rôle of satire, "Humour serves Soviet society by ridiculing the survivals of the old capitalist system." *Soviet Writers Reply*, p. 53. Like most other things, humor goes underground in a totalitarian society.

the conception of Europe. "It is not by chance that the Russian Communists attack Picasso," Malraux has written. "His painting is the presence of Europe in its most acute form. In the order of the spirit, all that which Russia calls formalism and which she has been deporting or tirelessly destroying for ten years, is Europe." [13]

The conclusion is clear. Let artists turn their back on Europe. Let them eschew mystery, deny anxiety and avoid complexity. Let them create only compositions which officials can hum, paintings which their wives can decipher, poems which the Party leaders can understand. This is the *Diktat* of the state. And the consequent attacks on "formalism" and "decadence" are fully as vulgar and as determined as those which used so to amuse the Doughface progressives when they were conducted by the Nazis. The delicate phrases of Alexander Fadeyev at the World Congress of Intellectuals are characteristic: "If hyenas could type and jackals could use a fountain pen," they would write like T. S. Eliot, Dos Passos, Sartre and Malraux.*

In an article for dissemination by the USSR Society for Cultural Relations with Foreign Countries, Vladimir Kemenov exhausts the arsenal of philistinism in his denunciations of Picasso, Henry Moore, Georgia O'Keeffe, even of individualists so comparatively restrained as Cézanne and the impressionists. Modern art, says Kemenov, is "a mixture of pathology and chicanery, which

---

* London *Times,* August 26, 1948. Professor F. O. Matthiessen, who once wrote an excellent book about Eliot, apparently now can take Fadeyev in his stride without succumbing to any fascist doubts about cultural freedom in the Soviet Union. Matthiessen's *From the Heart of Europe,* New York, 1948, is an astonishing revelation of the modern Doughface justifying totalitarianism to himself.

trace their origin to the daubs painted by the donkey's tail. . . . In order to analyze this work, the healthy normal people of the future will seek the services not of the art expert, but the psychiatrist." * The healthy normal art of the future, one would gather, will be modeled on Alma-Tadema, if not on James Montgomery Flagg. Official Soviet painting today certainly bears out the inference.

The campaign against the free creation of music is even more notorious. Stravinsky, Prokofieff, Shostakovich and the others have sinned against the desired banalities of form and sound. "This music," observes the president of the Association of Soviet Composers, "openly harks back to the primitive barbaric cultures of prehistoric society, and extols the eroticism, psychopathic mentality, sexual perversion, amorality, and shamelessness of the bourgeois hero of the twentieth century." [14] *Pravda* even lashes out periodically against the jazz bands: "Instead of the popular Soviet songs . . . they reproduce melodies filled with tavern melancholy and alien to the Soviet people." [15] No form of esotericism is too small to be dangerous to totalitarianism.

The Communist slide rule has similarly produced absolute equations for literature, for the films, for philosophy, even for drama critics and for clowns. Zhdanov, in his day the lord-high executioner, laid down the specifications. Alexandrov, the leading Soviet historian of phi-

* Vladimir Kemenov, "Aspects of Two Cultures," *Voks Bulletin No. 52.* People who still have illusions about the fate of art in the USSR should read this weird article. Oddly enough, modern art is obviously one field where the Politburo and President Truman could have got together. The saving grace of free society is that Truman's views about "ham and eggs art" remain his private prejudices and do not become the rules according to which all future paintings are to be painted.

losophy, fell under the interdict because, in Zhdanov's words, his exposition was "abstract, objectivist, neutral." *
Varga, the economist, argued that regulated capitalism, in the New Deal or British Labour Government model, might delay the expected post-war crash; he was fired as director of the Institute of World Economics, and subsequently the Institute itself was shut down.

Nor is science itself immune. The fantastic attempt to settle controversies in genetics by official edict is a scandal in the scientific world. The fruitful work of Vavilov and his associates was stopped, because traditional genetics did not emphasize the environment enough for political leaders who proposed to remake the world in a generation. Vavilov eventually died, apparently in a concentration camp; his main colleagues in genetics and cytology were castigated, and some have disappeared; and a home-grown Luther Burbank named T. D. Lysenko, whose theories are without serious experimental verification or scientific standing, now sits upon the ruins of what once was a promising scientific enterprise. Science has no recourse against totalitarianism. As one of Russia's last Mendelians put it in his avowal of penance, "I, as a party member, do not consider it possible for me to retain the views which have been recognized as erroneous by the Central Committee of our party." †

* A. A. Zhdanov, "On the History of Philosophy," *Political Affairs,* April, 1948. Zhdanov, in the characteristic manner of totalitarian debate, goes on to urge Soviet philosophers to note that "gangsters, pimps, spies, and criminal elements" are being recruited by western philosophers in the ideological struggle against Marxism.

† The literature on the Lysenko affair by fully qualified geneticists is now extensive; see C. D. Darlington, "The Retreat from Science in Soviet Russia," *Nineteenth Century and After,* October, 1947; H. J. Muller (who has worked in the Moscow Institute of Genetics), "The Destruc-

The fact that other sciences have not yet been so seriously deformed as genetics is not especially relevant. More
important and ominous is the demonstration that the
deformation is possible and that scientists have no effective means of protecting the integrity of their inquiries.*

"What previous despotism has ever interfered so brutally
with the liberty of writers, painters and musicians?" asks
Raymond Mortimer in the *New Statesman and Nation*
(where it was about time that that question was asked) .[16]
Yet the true horror from the western viewpoint lies in the
fact that the artist practically always gives in. For every
Mayakovsky, who kills himself, a thousand exhibit maso-
chistic delight in accepting correction and promising
never, never to do it again. "I know the Party is right,"
cries Shostakovich, "that the Party wishes me well and

tion of Science in the USSR" and "Back to Barbarism — Scientifically,"
Saturday Review of Literature, December 4, 11, 1948; C. H. Waddington,
"Lysenko and the Scientists," *New Statesman and Nation,* December 25,
1948, January 1, 1949; Eric Ashby (who has worked in the Moscow Institute of Cytology) , "Science without Freedom," *New Leader,* January 1,
1949. Needless to say, Professor Muller was promptly denounced by the
Soviet Academy of Science as being in the category of "racialists and reactionaries in science." For the quotation of the repentant Soviet
geneticist, see Professor Anton R. Zhebrak's letter to *Pravda,* quoted in
Time, September 6, 1948. The distinguished British scientist and Communist J. B. S. Haldane, in commenting on this situation, has made a
classical party-line response to criticisms of Russia: "In London the
research grant to my department has been so far reduced during the
present year that I have had to dispense with the paid services of three
research workers. . . . I confess that I would prefer to have been ad-
monished by *The Times,* or even the *Daily Herald,* for my incorrect
genetical theories." *New Statesman and Nation,* September 11, 1948.

* Since I wrote this sentence, the attack has been extended to physics.
V. Lvov, writing in the *Literary Gazette,* has called for war against the
reactionary, idealistic and formalistic theories of bourgeois physics. The
principle of indeterminacy, of course, and the western emphasis on the
observer as a factor in the experiment, are unacceptable to the Soviet
version of Marxist materialism. For the Lvov article, see the New York
Herald Tribune, November 25, 1948.

that I must search and find concrete creative roads which will lead me toward a realistic Soviet people's art. It would be impossible for me not to look for such roads, because I am a Soviet artist. . . . I must and I want to find a way into the heart of the Soviet people." [17] "A stern and timely warning of the Central Committee," said the repentant Eisenstein, the ex-great film director, "stopped us Soviet artists from further movement along the dangerous and fatal way which leads toward empty and non-ideological art for art's sake." * "I highly value the critical articles about my novel," writes the novelist Kostylev after an official rebuke. ". . . The only thing I might regret is that such articles have been, perhaps, too favorable to my works." [18]

No one should be surprised at the eagerness for personal humiliation. The whole thrust of totalitarian indoctrination, as we have seen, is to destroy the boundaries of individual personality. The moral balance of power is always with the Party as against the person. Those who cave in, as Dwight Macdonald accurately notes, do so not so much because they lack moral courage as because they lack good conscience.† They can never be confident in

* "The sense of historical truth," Eisenstein goes on to say in a revealing inadvertency, "betrayed me in the second part of *Ivan The Terrible*." Significantly enough, his specific sin had been to portray Ivan as a man prey to anxiety, a character with his Hamlet moments. "It is difficult to think," says Eisenstein, "that a man who did such unheard-of and unprecedented things in his time never thought over the choice of means or never had doubts about how to act at one time or another." Yet such a conception was clearly incompatible with the official demand for the portrayal of the "totalitarian man." For Eisenstein's letter to *Culture and Life*, see *New Leader*, December 7, 1946.

† The artists and writers, Macdonald observes, are the ones who feel guilty; the bureaucrats "feel that reason (historical materialism), justice and the people are on their side." "Bureaucratic Culture," *Politics*, Spring, 1948.

asserting their own individuality against the Party; after all, Number One may always be right. The totalitarian psychosis thus sickens the whole society. Stalinism on closer examination turns out to be what Dostoievsky called Shigalovism.

"Cicero will have his tongue cut out," [cries Verhovensky in *The Possessed*] "Copernicus will have his eye put out, Shakespeare will be stoned — that's Shigalovism. . . . Every member of the society spies on the others, and it's his duty to inform against them. Everyone belongs to all and all to every one. All are slaves and equal in their slavery. . . . The one thing wanting in the world is discipline. The thirst for culture is an aristocratic thirst. The moment you have family ties or love you get the desire for property. We will destroy that desire; we'll make use of drunkenness, slander, spying; we'll make use of incredible corruption; we'll stifle every genius in its infancy. We'll reduce all to a common denominator! . . . That's for us, the masters, to look after. Slaves must have masters. . . . Desire and suffering are our lot, but Shigalovism is for the slaves." [19]

So Marx's dream of a classless society, of a benevolent proletarian socialism, dissolves into the harsh realities of Shigalovism. A contemporary of Marx's was wiser in these matters. George Fitzhugh, writing in the United States in the eighteen-fifties, shared Marx's views of capitalism. The false philosophy of economic individualism, said Fitzhugh, had brought about social conflict, class cruelty and mass unemployment: "free society has failed." Man must now understand that "he has no rights whatever, as opposed to the interests of society . . . whatever rights he has are subordinate to the good of the whole." Only this faith can make "society a band of brothers, working for the common good, instead of a bag of cats biting and

worrying each other." The answer in other words was
socialism — a system which would guarantee to all what
Fitzhugh called "THE RIGHT TO EMPLOYMENT".

But Fitzhugh approached the problem of socialism (I
use here Fitzhugh's own terminology; he was referring to
a society based on the suppression of civil freedoms or
what we would call today, not socialism, but Communism) with a candid recognition of what it involved in
terms of power. The efficient combination of labor could
not be brought about, he argued, "till men give up their
liberty of action and subject themselves to a common
despotic head or ruler. This is slavery, and towards this
socialism is moving."

"All human experience," wrote Fitzhugh, "proves that
society must be ruled not by mere abstractions, but by men
of flesh and blood. To attain large industrial results, it
must be vigorously and severely ruled. Socialism is already slavery in all save the master. It had as well adopt
that feature at once, as come to that it must to make its
schemes at once humane and efficient. . . . Our only
quarrel with Socialism is that it will not honestly admit
that it owes its recent revival to the failure of universal
liberty, and is seeking to bring about slavery again in
some form."

Fitzhugh, a Virginian, frankly defined slavery as "a
form, and the very best form, of socialism." Trade unionism, social insurance, full employment — all were feeble
attempts to graft on free society the securities of slavery.
"Socialism proposes to do away with free competition; to
afford protection and support at all times to the laboring
class; to bring about, at least, a qualified community of
property, and to associate labor. All these purposes,

slavery fully and perfectly attains. . . . A Southern farm is the beau ideal of Communism." [20]

Fitzhugh's slave plantation was a relatively amiable, mid-Victorian beau ideal of Communism. The image of twentieth-century totalitarianism is infinitely more bleak and hopeless; it is, as Hannah Arendt has brilliantly argued, the concentration camp. For the essential dynamism of totalitarianism is toward the unlimited domination and degradation and eventual obliteration of the individual; and only in the concentration camp does this process achieve its evil perfection.

The camps play no rational rôle in a system of justice nor even in a system of labor. Many of the prisoners do not know why they are there; nor do their jailers; nor can the central officialdom always tell who is alive and who is dead; and the forced labor is more a part of the process of control than it is a contribution to productivity. The very essence of the system lies in the arbitrariness and meaninglessness of the arrests, and in the utter and calculated viciousness of the life — a life which robs man of nobility, his spirit of the capacity for loyalty or for resistance, and his death of martyrdom. The individual disappears into what Malraux called "that pitiful fraternity, without a face, almost without a real voice (all whispers resemble one another) ." [21] The ghastly, shambling anonymity, who shuffles obediently into the gas chamber, is the end-product of the totalitarian state. "Such a citizen," Hannah Arendt writes, "can be produced only imperfectly outside of the camps." [22]

The concentration camp represents the bureaucratization of unlimited terror, the final education of the élite in power and of the masses in submission. Without the camp, normality might reassert itself, and the totalitarian mystique would fall to pieces. The camp is the culmination of dominance and surrender, of sadism and of masochism; it is the climax of the system of tension which keeps totalitarianism taut and triumphant.

The camp takes care of the masses. As for the élite, theirs is a vision of power, magnificent if sinister. Let us not delude ourselves into thinking that the primary motive of the Soviet rulers is personal or national aggrandizement. Their goal is to save mankind — to drive anxiety from the world; and in this effort they are prepared to assume the awful burden of freedom themselves. The Politburo, after all, is probably the one place in the Soviet Union where free speech exists. It has a monopoly of decision. It consequently bears to the highest degree the terrible anxiety over choice. The Soviet leaders seek to deny the existence of anxiety; but it is, above all, anxiety which commits them to their savage, compulsive, unending campaign against freedom. "Desire and suffering are our lot. . . . Shigalovism is for the slaves."

It is Dostoievsky again, in his parable of the Grand Inquisitor, who best explains the corruption of the Soviet vision: the nobility of the dream and the cruelty of the results. One can imagine a contemporary adaptation of Dostoievsky's fable in which an Abraham Lincoln might appear in Moscow at a time of trials and terror. He would come, like Dostoievsky's Christ to Seville, softly, unobserved. Yet the people somehow would be drawn to him, would recognize him, would surround him. The humility, the compassion, the grandeur would suggest the grandeur of freedom itself, would stir in the people memories of old promises of liberty. There would be cries, sobs, con-

fusion, until the Leader would appear, the Grand Inquisitor, with his armed guards, who would break up the
crowd and arrest the gaunt, merciful man.

In the night, the Leader, if he were some one like
Lenin, might visit the stranger in the depths of the
Lubianka. "Why have you come to hinder us?" he would
say. "For you have come to hinder us, and you know
that. Do you know what will happen tomorrow? Tomorrow I shall destroy you. I shall send you to the firing
squad as the worst of deviationists. And the very people
who flocked after you today will confess their guilt tomorrow at the faintest sign from me."

And Lincoln would remain brooding, silent, impene-
trable.

"In your time you spoke to men of freedom," Lenin
would continue, "but now you have seen these 'free' men.
Yes, we've paid dearly for your words. But at last we have
completed that work in your name, in the name of freedom and democracy. Let me tell you that now, today,
people are more persuaded than ever that they have perfect freedom; yet they have brought their freedom to us
and laid it humbly at our feet. Was this what you intended? Was this your freedom?

"You went into the world," Lenin would continue,
"with a promise of freedom which men in their simplicity
and their natural unruliness could not even understand,
which they fear and dread — for nothing has ever been
more insupportable for a man and a human society than
freedom. Thousands and tens of thousands may be strong
enough to live by your freedom. But what of the millions
and hundreds of millions who do not have the strength to
turn their backs on security? Or do you only care for the

strong? We care for the weak, too. They are sinful and rebellious, but in the end they will become obedient. They will marvel at us, because we are ready to endure the freedom which they have found so dreadful. We tell them that we are your servants and rule in the name of your liberty. We shall deceive them, for we will permit them no liberty. But that deception will be our suffering.

"Instead of destroying human freedom, you made it greater than ever. Did you forget that man prefers peace and even death to freedom of choice in the knowledge of good and evil? And, instead of simplifying that choice for him, you made it enigmatic and difficult. Men will cry aloud at last that the truth is not in freedom, for the fearful burden of free choice imposes too many cares, too many unanswerable anxieties.

"There are three powers, and three powers alone, able to conquer the conscience of these impotent rebels — miracle, mystery and authority. You have rejected them all. But are all men as strong as you? Is the nature of men such that at the moments of their deepest spiritual difficulties they can reject miracle, mystery and authority and cling only to their individual impulses? You ask too much from man. For men are slaves, of course, if rebellious by nature. We have corrected your work; we have founded it upon miracle, mystery and authority. And men rejoice that they are again led like sheep, and that the terrible gift that had brought them such suffering is, at last, lifted from their hearts. Why have you come now to hinder us? Why do you look silently and searchingly at me with your mild eyes?

"Our work has only begun. It has long to await completion and the earth has yet much to suffer, but we shall triumph and shall be Caesars, and then we shall plan the universal happiness of man. With us all men will be happy; they will no longer rebel nor destroy one another as under your freedom. Oh, we shall persuade them that they will only become free when they renounce their freedom to us and submit to us. And shall we be right or shall we be lying? They will be convinced that we are right, for they will remember the horrors of slavery and confusion to which your freedom brought them. Freedom led them into such straits that the fierce and rebellious destroyed themselves, others, rebellious but weak, destroyed one another, while the rest, weak and unhappy, crawled whining to our feet. . . . Too, too well they know the value of complete submission! And until men know that, they will be unhappy.

"Yes, we shall set them to work, but in their leisure hours we shall make their life like a child's game, with song and dance. We shall allow them even sin, and tell them that every sin will be expiated if it is done with our permission. We shall have an answer to the the most painful secrets of their conscience. And they will be glad to believe our answer, for it will save them from the terrible agony of making a free decision for themselves. And all will be happy, all the millions of creatures — all except those who rule over them. For we, the Party, shall be unhappy. We alone shall be free. But we alone are strong enough for the burdens of freedom. We have corrected your work."

VI

The Communist Challenge to America

Toward the end of the Second War, Russia had gained the admiration and confidence of all elements in the West as never before. Bankers and industrialists vied with each other in contributing to Russian war relief and in discerning evidences of growing Soviet nationalism and conservatism. Liberals and socialists felt a new hope for collaboration with Communism on terms of trust and equality. Yet, before war's end, the Soviet Union abandoned the wartime coalition and embarked on a policy of expansion. Why did Soviet policy take this fatal turn?

Some have argued that the death of Roosevelt was followed by a basic change in American policy; that Truman's subservience to bankers and generals revived in Russia an ancient and justified fear of capitalist encirclement; and that the American policy of imperialist aggression, particularly the Truman Doctrine of 1947, forced the Communists in self-defense to consolidate their own position.

It is clearly of basic importance in understanding the dynamism of Soviet Communism to determine whether post-war Soviet policies were in their essence a response to hostile Western policies. But a quick glance at the relevant dates shows conclusively that Moscow decided to leave the wartime coalition *before Roosevelt's death* — in other words, that if any American policies were responsible for "alienating" the Russians, they were those of Franklin Roosevelt himself.

Co-operation with the West, it must never be forgotten, was for the Russians a wartime program, to be continued so long as Nazism was a threat. As late as January, 1945, in the shadow of the Rundstedt counteroffensive of December, Maurice Thorez at Ivry could call on French Communists to submit themselves to the leadership of General de Gaulle. British Communists were urging that the Labour Party enter a post-war coalition with Churchill. Spanish Communists were flirting with Gil Robles. American Communists were talking about an indefinite extension of the no-strike pledge. The wartime mood of co-operation found its last notable expression in the Yalta Conference in early February, when the memory of the Nazi comeback in the Ardennes was still vivid in the minds of the Allied leaders.

But the Yalta Conference coincided with the beginning of the last phase of the war. The military picture was altering in February with great rapidity. The Crimean discussions had barely started before the Third Army breached the Siegfried Line. A fortnight after Roosevelt left Yalta, the Ninth Army had reached the Rhine at

Duesseldorf. With the end of the war in sight, the need for wartime co-operation was disappearing: it was now time to begin the post-war political battle for Europe. In the weeks after Yalta, the Soviet Union, so far as one can tell from the overwhelming external evidence, swiftly re-organized its strategy in terms of the new political battle.

Jacques Duclos, the French Communist, signaled the change of line in an article in the April 1945 issue of *Cahiers du Communisme*. The Duclos article was plainly an announcement by the Comintern official formerly re-sponsible for the western Communist parties that the period of anti-fascist collaboration was over. In making this announcement, Duclos harped on the sins of the American Earl Browder, no doubt to spare embarrass-ment to European Communist leaders like Thorez who had taken the same position as Browder but whom Moscow did not wish to stigmatize. The Duclos piece appeared before Roosevelt's death; it obviously had been planned and scheduled six or eight weeks earlier — prob-ably right after Yalta. Indeed, the National Committee of the American Communist Party, noting in its discussion of Duclos that the publication had preceded the death of Roosevelt, severely criticized the previous policy of sup-porting the Roosevelt régime. William Z. Foster, who re-placed Browder as the American Communist leader, could boast of having said as early as January, 1944, "A postwar Roosevelt administration would continue to be, as it is now, an imperialist government." [1]

The Russian performance in eastern Europe supplies even more conclusive evidence of a Moscow decision in favor of nonco-operation. Within a few weeks after Yalta, the Soviet Union took swift action in Rumania and

Poland in brutal violation of Yalta pledges of political freedom. Such action may have been necessary to protect the USSR from the resurgent strength of these powerful nations; but the vital point here is that the action was taken while Roosevelt was still alive. At the same time, the USSR opened up a savage political offensive against the United States. In a cable which enraged Roosevelt, Stalin charged that the United States and Britain were engaged in separate peace negotiations with Germany. The evidence for the charge was as flimsy and perfunctory as the evidence which would later sustain charges of "war-mongering" against the US and Britain in the United Nations. In accordance with an agreement between Germany and the West, Stalin said, the Germans had been allowed to move three divisions from the Italian to the Russian front. Roosevelt replied that he deeply resented these "vile misrepresentations." The movement of the divisions, he pointed out, had begun weeks before there could have been any possibility of negotiations. Stalin's informants, he said, were apparently trying to destroy the friendly relations between the two countries.

By the end of March Roosevelt cabled Churchill that he was "watching with anxiety and concern the development of the Soviet attitude" and that he was "acutely aware of the dangers inherent in the present course of events, not only for the immediate issue involved but also for the San Francisco Conference and future world co-operation." On April 1, Roosevelt told Stalin that he could not conceal "the concern with which I view the development of events" since Yalta. By this time, Stalin had decided not to send Molotov to San Francisco — another act expressing the Soviet retreat from collaboration. An hour before his death Roosevelt wrote a last cable to Churchill: "We must be firm . . . our course thus far is correct." [2]

The statement that Russia changed its policy after the death of Roosevelt and because of the policies of Truman is thus a pure specimen of propaganda fabrication. The actions of Stalin after Yalta, and the switch in policy announced through Duclos show conclusively that the Politburo decision long preceded Roosevelt's death and was to be carried out whoever the American president might be. The real reasons for Soviet aggression go much deeper than the change from one person to another as head of the American government.

Why, then, did the USSR abandon co-operation? The true reason, I suspect, lies partly in the history of Russia, mainly in the nature of Soviet society. Russia is an immense and sprawling land entering the stage of its historic development when national consolidation is leading to outbursts of international energy — a stage long since passed through by Britain, France, Spain, Germany and the United States. Russia, indeed, has been poised on the verge of manifest destiny for well over a century. Tocqueville, Brooks Adams and many others have long predicted the day when Russia and America would dominate the world. "The arrest of the Russian scheme of annexation," Karl Marx himself could write in 1853, "is a matter of the highest moment." [3]

Had the Romanovs followed the policies of someone like Count Witte, had they pushed through industrialization and ridden out the political consequences, Russia would be confronting the world today with much the same immediate problems of expansion — with the same thrusts into western Europe, the Mediterranean, the Middle East and China. But Imperial Russia necessarily had limited objectives. It could mobilize only the resources and energies of Russia itself — at most, those of Pan-Slavism. Its attempts to master other lands roused deep national opposition, just as did the similar attempts of Imperial Germany. Dynastic imperialism stood for wars of conquest, not for social revolution. It generated its own antidote because few other peoples were likely to regard annexation by an Imperial Russia or Germany as a form of national or social self-fulfillment.

But, as National Socialism gave Germany briefly a new ideological weapon, capable of splitting other nations asunder, so the infinitely more exportable creed of Communism adds a fearful warhead to the traditional energies of Russian expansionism. As a social faith, lacking obvious national implications, Communism can rally its fifth columns in any corner of the world where injustice and poverty give it a foothold. At the same time, Communism creates a society where imperialism becomes an almost inevitable weapon of state. A totalitarian system, as we have seen, is a system of tension; and a convenient way to maintain the tension is to invoke the threat of external war. The presence of foreign foes, moreover, is an essential part of the psychological economy of a totalitarian régime; for it is only by turning hates outward that totalitarianism can work off the inner aggressions which a free society ventilates in politics, in private group activity, and in a thousand other ways. When internal discontents and internal contradictions press too hard upon the Hitlers and Stalins, foreign adventurism provides the irresistible solution.

Thus Russia today has aggressive possibilities because it is in the historic phase of expansion. But the psychoses of totalitarianism, loose in a world which almost falls apart at touch, transform the possibilities into facts. An industrialized Imperial Russia would have been a source of trouble; at some point, however, dynastic imperialism would have run down. But nothing less than the entire world can in the end satisfy totalitarian imperialism; for totalitarianism charges imperialism with the fear and frenzy of an ideological crusade. The Communist crusaders, indeed, apply ruthlessly the ancient and honored principle of religious wars: *cuius regio, eius religio* — who runs the government runs the mind. In a time of breaking-up of empires, such a crusade threatens a profound and terrible convulsion.

Thus the aftermath of the Second War. With Germany and Japan knocked out of the world-power equation, with Britain enfeebled and an already enfeebled France exhausted, great gaping holes appeared in the international fabric. Power abhors a vacuum; so Soviet expansion has flowed fast into the empty spaces, bringing a fanatic *religio* in the wake of an implacable *regio*.* Since 1939, the Soviet Union has added 280,000 square miles of new land. Today the satellite states of eastern Europe are being readied for incorporation into the Soviet Union itself. Tomorrow Soviet power will surely spread everywhere that it meets no firm resistance.

* There come too in many cases, of course, social changes which greatly benefit the mass of the population in a material sense. One cannot sneer at these changes; on the other hand, it is folly to think that they sanctify totalitarian methods. Progressives were not moved to admire Huey Long, though he greatly improved roads, hospitals and schools in Louisiana; why then should they admire Communist dictators who accomplish substantially the same results as Huey Long employing methods which are indescribably worse?

At the start, the expansion seemed justified in terms of Soviet security. No one would wish to deny a nation which had suffered so horribly from foreign invasion the reasonable requirements of security. But Soviet foreign policy is like the boxing style of the Soviet heavyweight champion: "such a defense," as Radio Moscow put it, "looks more like an attack." * One soon wondered what the limits were of Soviet security requirements. And it has gradually become clear that the totalitarian conception of security implies the elimination of all opposition or even indifference anywhere: it means the absorption of all in the central maelstrom of tension. "The state will wither away," writes P. F. Iudin, the Soviet academician, "[only] when the capitalist environment is replaced by a socialist environment. . . . Comrade Stalin has made certain that the state will not wither away as long as social-ism and communism are not victorious on an inter-national scale." [4]

As long as even vestiges of free society linger in people's consciousness, the fatherland is in danger; and Marxism has identified capitalism as the specific source of aggres-sion and evil. It is this fact which exposes most sharply the shallowness of the argument that a different US policy might have won the confidence of the Kremlin. For, so long as America remains a capitalist democracy, no American policy can win basic Soviet confidence;

* "The most popular Russian boxer is the heavyweight Korolev, typical exponent of the Soviet boxing style. Korolev is a non-stop fighter. He almost never does any blocking, relying almost exclusively on ducking, side-stepping and almost imperceptible back-stepping. Such a defence looks more like an attack. This is confirmed by the champions of Poland, Czechoslovakia, Yugoslavia and other European countries whom Korolev met and defeated last year, taking on an average two minutes a bout." Radio Moscow, February 20, 1948.

every American initiative is poisoned from the source.
Nothing short of the establishment of Communism in
America might suffice to relieve America of the curse of
capitalism; and the example of Tito has shown that even
this, alas, is not enough; that even Communism must be
entirely subservient to Moscow before it ceases to be a
threat to Soviet security. The Soviet fear is perfectly genuine; history, experience, the Hearst press and the anti-
Soviet forces in the West have given it a partial basis; but
the fear exists independently of history and experience
and will probably not be affected by them. It arises out of
Leninist doctrine, and it is intensified by the psychological
necessities of a system of tension. The Moscow *Literary
Gazette* draws the obvious conclusion: "We must write
about war in such a way that the generation of young
Soviet people which comes after us will love arms and be
ready for battles and victories." [5]

The Russian challenge consequently forces the western
world to pay close attention to the techniques of Soviet
expansion. The USSR uses, of course, the traditional
apparatus of international pressure — diplomats, armies,
political warfare, and so on. But the special Soviet advantage — the warhead — lies in the fifth column; and the
fifth column is based on the local Communist parties. Let
no one be deceived about the relations of these parties to
Moscow. Many of them from time to time affect a shrill
pseudo-nationalism — "Communism is Twentieth Century
Americanism" or "We must defend our national sover-
eignty against the Marshall Plan"; few of them insist upon
the instant reproduction in their own countries of the collective farm or the MVD; but all are faithful in their

essential mission, which is to run interference for Soviet foreign policy.

Soviet Deputy Premier Nikolai A. Voznesensky has defined the duty of the national Communist with precision: it is "to protect and defend the USSR, which represents the first socialist state in the world. Only he who unconditionally protects the USSR is an internationalist." [6] Edgar Snow has reported that the Cominform nations in their Warsaw meeting adopted a secret protocol agreeing that "the defense of the Soviet Union must be considered paramount" to all national interests. [7] If there are Communists who refuse to sacrifice local interests to the needs of the USSR, they are soon enough denounced and condemned. The Jay Lovestones and Heinz Neumanns did not last long in the Party, or, when Moscow could take care of it (as in the case of Neumann), in the world. In the early months of 1949, Communist leaders in nation after nation across the world rose in obedient sequence to pledge their allegiance to the Soviet Union in case of war between the USSR and their homelands. [8] In the meantime, the ever more implacable Soviet campaign against Tito showed how Moscow, its power dependent on its apostolic infallibility, was compelled to demand abject servility from its network of national parties.

The Soviet campaign against the United States, as against any nation, thus has two aspects: the pressures exerted in the traditional manner of power politics; and the pressures exerted through the network of Communist parties. The first is easy to handle. The United States can tell if Soviet planes or tanks cut loose across Europe or the Pacific. But the second is harder. The United

States cannot always determine the intentions and capabilities of the Communist Party of the United States.
Even if it could, the very traditions of free society tend to
inhibit our instinct of self-preservation. We are restrained
from outlawing the Communist Party; and some people
feel that it is somehow below the belt even to report on
Communist Party activities or to identify its influence.
Yet, given the nature of the Soviet drive against free
society, given the frightful tyranny implicit in the principle *cuius regio, eius religio,* there is surely no alternative
to paying exact and unfaltering attention to the Communists in our midst.

The American Communist Party, like all other Communist parties, originated in the split of left-wing groups
from the Socialist Party following the Russian Revolution. The American schism took place in the lurid atmosphere created by Attorney General A. Mitchell Palmer,
the Fighting Quaker (or Quaking Fighter), and his
notorious red hunts. Two main factions competed for
Moscow endorsement as the official Communist Party,
meanwhile squabbling with each other, issuing incendiary
proclamations to the American people and eking out a
precarious existence underground. Eventually the Comintern got the rival groups together; and, after a mass arrest
of delegates to a convention held in the woods near
Bridgman, Michigan, in 1921, the Party decided to abandon melodrama and come out into the open.

According to their own figures, the Communists had
only about 7500 members in 1929. Then came the depression, which the Party hopefully regarded as the long-
awaited final agony of capitalism. As Joseph Stalin observed encouragingly to the American section of the Com-

intern that year, "I consider that the Communist Party of the USA is one of the few Communist parties to which history has confided decisive tasks from the viewpoint of the world revolutionary movement. The revolutionary crisis has not yet arrived in the United States, but there are already numerous indications which lead us to believe that it is near. The American Communist Party must be ready to meet the crisis fully armed to take over the direction of the class war. You must prepare yourselves for this, comrades, with all your strength and by every means." [9]

The Communists accepted the directive and exploited the depression with energy and zeal, recruiting among the unemployed, the hungry, the homeless; among members of the middle class who felt a sense of guilt or confusion over the economic mess; and among intellectuals who feared the worldwide rise of fascism. In 1934 the Party claimed 25,000 cardholders; in 1936, 40,000; in 1938, 75,000 plus 20,000 in the Young Communist League. But the Moscow trials and the Molotov-Ribbentrop pact were body blows to the Party which even the pro-Russian enthusiasm of the war failed to make up. Earl Browder's wartime policy of subordinating everything to national unity brought membership to 80,000, however, by 1944. Then the radical phase under William Z. Foster lost many of the Browder adherents. Present membership (1949) is probably slightly under 70,000.

These statistics are always uncertain, quite apart from the Party's tendency to exaggerate the results of its campaigns in the best capitalist manner. The Communist Party of the United States (CPUSA) has always had a tremendous turnover. Thus there have been a hard core of perhaps ten per cent who have been in the Party for fifteen years or more, a fairly solid ring of fifty or sixty per cent who have been in from two to ten years, and a vaporous penumbra of people who join the Party because of some local strike or lynching, lose interest and are dropped when they fail to pay their dues.

The organization would fill Boss Hague with envy. Each candidate must be eighteen years old and duly certified by a member before he can be admitted to a local club. Cryptic communications bid the five to thirty cell members to regular meetings for instructions and assignments. As a matter of course, members work as part of the Communist bloc in outside organizations and thereby help increase Party influence far beyond the actual number of cardholders. The local clubs are the bottom of the chain of command, which stretches through county and state, or section and district, committees, to the National Committee and the National Secretariat, both housed in the Centre, the smoky brick Party headquarters on 12th Street in New York City, and finally to Moscow.

Why do people join the Party in the United States? One can understand Communist strength in countries like China or South Africa, where cruel oppression affords little choice. But America has been through the longest period of liberal government in its history. The labor movement has never been so strong. Why should Americans submit themselves to the intolerable discipline of party membership? Yet even America has its quota of lonely and frustrated people, craving social, intellectual and even sexual fulfillment they cannot obtain in existing society. For these people, party discipline is no obstacle; it is an attraction. The great majority of members in America, as in Europe, *want* to be disciplined.

It is hard work being a Communist in America, which is one reason the turnover is so great. But, once fully committed, the party member finds that his world has become totally the world of the Party. Communism fills empty lives. Surrender to the Party gives a sense of comradeship in a cause guaranteed by history to succor the helpless and to triumph over the wealthy and satisfied. Ben Gitlow, for many years a Communist leader and twice Communist candidate for Vice-President, describes concisely the impact of the organization on the individual member: "The Party winds him up and keeps him going." [10] One member explained why he had made the Party the beneficiary of his insurance policy: "The reason I did that was, in the first place, I am not married and have nobody to leave anything like that to, and in the second place the Communist Party is more in the world to me than anything else is." [11] A pro-Communist novel, such as Isidor Schneider's *The Judas Time,* shows more clearly than any hostile tract ever could the implacability of Communist social life.

The total assimilation of the individual to the Party creates for some a genuine selflessness and consecration. Like a platoon isolated behind enemy lines, the American Communists perform marvels of daring at their leaders' word, each acting as if he embodied the impersonal force of history. Their courage has impressed thousands of people with the invincible determination of their Party. But the price of such intimate relations with history is the intensive personal supervision, only to be duplicated in a religious order or a police state. There is even a clause in the Party constitution forbidding "personal or political relations with enemies of the working class." [12]

But this does not have to be invoked often. Most Communists voluntarily renounce non-Party friendships and activities.

In the end, they become so involved socially and psychologically that the threat of expulsion strikes them as excommunication would a devout Catholic. It is enough to keep many in line long after they begin to develop intellectual doubts about the infallibility of Russia. When Granville Hicks left the Party, a young woman wrote him, "So it all comes to this: that your whole life previous to this time . . . has gone up in a puff of smoke and lost its meaning. . . . What a pity to find one's life suddenly without meaning. What is left for you now?" * And many, once they make the break, have become so dependent emotionally on discipline that, like Louis Budenz and Elizabeth Bentley, they rush to another form of discipline in the Roman Catholic Church, moving from one bastion to another in their frenzied flight from doubt.†

* This Communist correspondent went on to remind Hicks of the words of A. P. Rosengoltz a few days before he was shot by the USSR for high treason: "Woe and misfortune will betide him who strays even to the smallest extent from the general line of the Bolshevik party. I want you to believe me, to believe in the sincerity of the words which I now utter." Granville Hicks, "Communism and the American Intellectuals," *Whose Revolution?* I. D. Talmadge, ed., New York, 1941, pp. 107–08.

† As Miss Bentley puts it, "People who are genuine Communists, as I was, aren't the lukewarm type. They can't go into a vacuum if they give up Communism. They must have something to tie to." *Time*, November 29, 1948. Mr. Budenz's memoirs are filled with similarly revealing remarks. When the Communists used to insist on all or nothing, it seemed to him insupportable intellectual tyranny; now he remarks with evident pleasure, "There is no compromise in the Church's stand. Catholic faith and the Catholic view must be accepted whole." One feels in him still a hankering after party discipline: "A Catholic has an obligation to live and act in a special manner. . . . We had to be sure that our whims and wishes did not supersede our duties to the Catholic cause." Louis Budenz, *This Is My Story*, New York, 1947, pp. 352, 351.

In its own eyes the CPUSA has two main commitments: to support and advance the USSR, and to promote the establishment of Communism in the USA. The second, of course, has much the lower priority, since the preservation of the workers' homeland in Russia is indispensable to the triumph of Communism anywhere else in the world. The consequent conflict between the requirements of Soviet foreign policy and the requirements of the American domestic scene has stunted the growth of the CPUSA. As the most impressive part of the Communist record in this country has been its courageous activity against local injustice and exploitation, so its least impressive has been its subservience to Soviet foreign policy. Yet the Party leadership has had no choice but to stifle its grass-roots initiative and squander its grass-roots assets in order to whip up American backing for Soviet adventures abroad.

The policy of the CPUSA, of course, is a carbon copy of Soviet policy. For a long time, indeed, the Party was billed as the American section of the Communist International. It has always received directives and in the past has received funds from Moscow. In the nineteen-twenties instructions flowed over the Moscow wire in such volume as to produce a wry joke among Party members: "Why is the Communist Party of the United States like the Brooklyn Bridge? Because it is suspended on cables." But Moscow's most effective control has probably been through Comintern representatives — the so-called "C.I. reps." In 1929, for example, when the Party convention elected Jay Lovestone leader by a large majority, Moscow cables to the C.I. reps in attendance caused a reversal of the decision in favor of Earl Browder and William Z.

Foster. From the famous John Pepper or Pogany in the twenties to Gerhart Eisler (Hans Berger) in the forties, inconspicuous foreigners in the background have made basic decisions for the American Communist Party.

From the Moscow viewpoint, the American is clearly one of the expendable parties, so far as its political activity is concerned. Stalin and Molotov amuse themselves by making jokes about the CPUSA with non-Communist Americans; and the Comintern at no time has exerted itself to give the American Party aid or to spare it embarrassment. No one in Moscow, for example, apparently ever dreams of giving the CPUSA a preview of an impending change in the party line; and every zigzag has caught the American leaders unprepared and red-faced.

The problem whether CPUSA operations are determined today by specific directives from Moscow or by New York attempts, through earnest reading of *Pravda* and *New Times*, to guess what such a directive would say is not important. The relation of Moscow to the CPUSA may be compared to that of a football coach to his team. The team has its quarterback to run it on the field, its set of plays and its general instructions. The coach will occasionally send in a substitute with new instructions or a new quarterback or an entire new team, but he is not likely to be giving play-by-play orders. (At times, though, it looks as if the Soviet Union had adopted the unlimited-substitution rule.) Since the team has complete confidence in the coach, it resents cracks from bystanders about taking orders from outside; after all, the players say, aren't the interests of the coach and team identical? As *Political Affairs*, the American Party organ, recently put it, "The policies of the Soviet Union, before, during, and since the anti-Axis war, have corresponded to the best interests of the American people." [13]

Jay Lovestone and Ben Gitlow were excommunicated for espousing various forms of the heresy of "American exceptionalism" — the heresy, that is, of arguing that special circumstances in the United States might justify occasional deviations from the Moscow line. Their disappearance signaled the Stalinization of the American Party; it meant the extermination of the last flicker of independence. Thereafter, when Russia was militant, the CPUSA was militant. No more extreme document survives from the period of bellicosity than William Z. Foster's *Toward Soviet America* (1932). When Russia became the great advocate of the united front, the CPUSA precipitately stopped kicking liberals in the teeth and started to embrace them. When Russia opposed Nazism, America had no stouter defenders of collective security than Earl Browder; when Molotov signed up with Ribbentrop, no one took more delight in writing off the war in Europe as a "family quarrel of rival imperialisms." [14]

Because the CPUSA has no mass following to take into account, local political realities do not restrain its passion to please Moscow. As a consequence, it has apparently won itself a low-comedy reputation in Comintern circles for always overdoing things — always jumping ten feet when the Comintern expects two. Thus in 1939 all Communist parties supported the Russo-German pact and denounced the British; but only the American Party dropped its boycott of Nazi goods. * Nor is it likely that

* It now appears that the Communist line was wrong everywhere when it denounced the war of 1939–41 as imperialistic. According to the ultimate authority, Comrade Stalin, in his speech of February 9, 1946, "The

Stalin, who was perhaps not deceived about Hitler's intentions, looked with great enthusiasm upon the activity of the CPUSA in inspiring strikes in such plants as North American Aircraft and Allis-Chalmers.

When the invasion of Russia brought on the national unity program, the Americans, as usual, carried Moscow hints to the extreme. Browder offered to shake hands with J. P. Morgan, who, having been dead for some months, was in no position to accept the invitation. * Harry Bridges talked about the extension of the no-strike

Second World War against the Axis states *from the very outset* assumed the character of an anti-Fascist war, a war of liberation." The italics are my own. The entry of Russia into the war, far from transforming its character, "could only enhance . . . the anti-fascist and liberation character of the Second World War." *The Strategy and Tactics of World Communism,* p. 169.

There were practical advantages to overreacting in the American manner, however. Harry Pollitt, the leader of the British Communist Party, was slow in drawing the anti-war conclusion from the Russo-German pact; as a native of a country in the line of Nazi fire, he could not abandon the fight against fascism as readily as did Earl Browder. "To stand aside from this conflict, to contribute only revolutionary-sounding phrases while the fascist beasts ride roughshod over Europe," Pollitt wrote in *How to Win the War,* published September, 1939, "would be betrayal of everything our forebears have fought to achieve in the course of the long years of struggle against capitalism." Toward the end of September, Pollitt and one other member of the Central Committee of the British Communist Party voted in favor of the war. Shortly afterward both dissenters wrote letters to the *London Daily Worker* not only accepting the new line but apologizing for votes which infringed party discipline. The decision which their votes violated was clearly not a decision of the British Communist Party, which was just then in the process of being reached, but a decision of Moscow. Pollitt was punished for his deviation by being removed for a time from his position as leader of the Party. See Victor Gollancz, ed., *The Betrayal of the Left,* London, 1941, pp. 174, 286.

* "If J. P. Morgan supports this coalition and goes down the line for it, I as a Communist am prepared to clasp his hand on that and join with him to realize it." Browder in *The Communist,* January, 1944.

pledge far into the post-war world. The CPUSA hailed with delight the prosecution of the Minneapolis Trotsky-ites under the Smith Act — an act which they subsequently denounced as unconstitutional when it was applied to themselves some years later. Then, when the end of the war revived Communist militancy, the Americans franti-cally leaped on Browder with hobnailed boots, rubbed his face in the dirt and kicked him out of the Party. ("They have failed Karl Marx," a wit has observed, "but remain faithful to Harpo.")

Browder had been leader of the Party for fifteen years. He had steered it from anti-Roosevelt militancy to pro-Roosevelt popular frontism to anti-Roosevelt isolationism to pro-Roosevelt war unity, all without a quiver of dis-taste. But the experience of the wartime coalition seems to have given him the vision of an Americanized Com-munist Party, working with its fellow American parties to solve the urgent questions facing the nation. He trans-formed the wartime tactic of national unity into a post-war strategy and argued the possibility that progressive capitalism, to save itself, would embark on policies favor-able to the workers at home and to the Soviet Union abroad.

In April, 1945, however, Jacques Duclos of the French Communist Party published the celebrated repudiation of Browderism in *Cahiers du Communisme*. The article lam-basted Browder and commended William Z. Foster, quot-ing at length from Foster's criticisms of Browder within the Communist Central Committee — criticism which Browder had suppressed and which Foster not long before had sternly denied making.

112   THE VITAL CENTER

The material in the article had clearly been handed over to Duclos by Moscow in order to announce the fundamental shift from the wartime policy of collaboration. As we have seen, it is likely that Moscow was simply using the CPUSA as a scapegoat in order to chart the new line for the somewhat more important Communist parties of western Europe. Browder, receiving his copy of the *Cahiers du Communisme* late in April, began to edge his way toward the new position. But the unexpected publication of Duclos's attack by the *New York World Telegram* forced the Communists' hand. Overdoing things as usual, spurred on, in addition, by the personal hatred which many party functionaries, led by Foster, had developed toward Browder, his erstwhile followers ganged up on him and expelled him from the American leadership. Subsequent developments suggest that Moscow neither expected nor, probably, desired this result; at most, it doubtless intended a suspension of the kind that Harry Pollitt, the British Communist leader, received for his anti-Nazi deviation of 1939.

The events of the next few weeks show Communist methods in full swing — comic perhaps on the scale employed, but appalling in their implications if applied to an entire nation. In June, 1945, the National Committee met to consider the case of Browder. With a vengeful Foster leading the attack, the members indulged in a three-day orgy of denunciation, while the unfortunate Browder, accused of such heinous offenses as "chronic tailism," slumped deeper and deeper in his chair, his head in his hands. The attacks were interlarded with confessions and avowals of penance on the part of the erring brethren attempting to explain how they had gone astray. Browder's speech in his own defense was subsequently suppressed by Foster lest it contaminate the membership — just as Foster's own criticism of Browder had been suppressed a year before. *

There followed recriminations of intense bitterness. Browder retired into inactivity; but attacks continued upon him unabated; and soon the Westchester County (*sic*) section of the Party was entertaining a motion for his expulsion from the Party itself. In February, 1946, the notice of expulsion appeared in the *Daily Worker*. Browder promptly accused the Secretariat of circulating charges against him which "ranged the whole gamut of social and political crimes excepting perhaps that of murder." One member of the National Board even proposed, according to Browder, that he be given the job of scrubbing floors in the National Office. "If there had been any evidence that there existed a real need for my services in this capacity, I would gladly have given them. However . . . I did not see fit to take the suggestion seriously." His refusal to give the National Board the names of all Party members to whom he had spoken since the convention the summer before evidently precipitated his expulsion. Browder's *Appeal . . . to the Members of the C.P.U.S.A.!* concluded starkly: "All effective interparty democracy has been destroyed." † Two months later he was on his way to Moscow.

---

* For the whole episode, see the vivid eyewitness account by Louis Budenz, *This Is My Story,* chap. 9.

† The strange document entitled *"Appeal of Earl Browder to the Membership of the C.P.U.S.A.!"* contains letters from Browder, one to the National Committee dated February 8, 1946, the other to the Yonkers Communist Club dated February 1, 1946.

The trip to Moscow was not unlike the pilgrimage made by Lovestone and Gitlow in 1929 after their repudiation by the Comintern. Both Lovestone and Gitlow were offered jobs if they promised to cease their opposition; both turned the propositions down. Browder accepted his offer and returned to America with a five-year contract as representative of Soviet publishing houses in the United States. He thus remains on the payroll in anticipation of a new shift in policy.

How did he happen to stay in favor? For one thing, he is an old Moscow favorite who served the Party loyally for a quarter of a century. For another, he might well have explained to Soviet officials that the question between himself and Foster was not a question of objectives; it was a question of timing. Were conditions in the United States in fact ripe for a militant policy on the part of the CPUSA? Browder's answer might well have been that 1946 was too soon. Let's wait five years — let's wait for the depression. By then we will have a strong party; we will have potent issues; and our self-restraint will meanwhile lull capitalist suspicions of the USSR. . . . This is always a line to which the USSR may return, and which appears to have support somewhere in the Politburo. It would not be the first time that Moscow has seen fit to adopt a policy of reinsurance.

What was the specific question on which Browder and Foster differed? That question, it is important to note, was the question of the third party. Browder wished, as he put it in his *Appeal,* "to do everything to maintain the Roosevelt-labor-democratic coalition and to support the Truman Administration in all its efforts to that end." But

Eugene Dennis, coming to the fore as the actual Party leader, promptly deduced from the new line, as he told the National Committee in July, 1945, that it would be "necessary from now on to create the conditions and base for organizing a major third party nationally." [15]

The third party quickly became the CPUSA's central post-war project. By February 12, 1946, Dennis was ready to place the detailed time-table before the National Committee. We must proceed, he said, "to lay the foundation now to establish in time for the 1948 elections a national third party — a broad people's anti-monopoly, anti-imperialist party. . . . If possible — and it is preferable — steps toward forming a third party should be taken early in 1947." [16] The mass base, Dennis added, would be found in the National Citizens' Political Action Committee and the Independent Citizens' Committee for the Arts, Sciences and Professions.

All went according to plan. In December, 1946, the NCPAC and ICCASP merged to form a new group called Progressive Citizens of America (PCA) ; and through the year PCA was steadily transformed into the recruiting apparatus for the third party. In the meantime, the departure from the Truman cabinet of Henry Wallace, formerly an enemy of all third parties, was a windfall for the Communists. This well-intentioned, woolly-minded, increasingly embittered man was made to order for Communist exploitation; his own sense of martyrdom was swiftly generalized to embrace all friends of Soviet totalitarianism.

During 1947 the Communist machine moved steadily toward its proclaimed objective. After the CIO convention in October, Eugene Dennis and Robert Thompson, the New York state chairman of the CPUSA, called a meeting of pro-Communist labor leaders, including Michael Quill, the head of the Transport Workers. "They told me they had decided to form a party and Wallace would head it up," Quill later reported after breaking with the Communists. [17] By December the Wallace candidacy was in the bag.

Wallace's decision evidently shocked some PCA members who had been unaware of the extent to which their own organization was Communist-controlled. Even Frank Kingdon, a co-chairman of PCA, woke up with a start. "Who asked Henry Wallace to run?" Kingdon wrote a few weeks later. "The answer is in the record. The Communist Party, through William Z. Foster and Eugene Dennis, were the first. I am no red-baiter. I believe it possible for American liberals to cooperate with Communists for social ends immediately desirable. The saddest lesson I learned in 1947 was that this is impossible. . . . All citizens, including Communists, have a right to put forward a candidate. All I am saying is that their candidate is theirs. They are his sponsors. He is named by them to serve their ends." [18]

The Wallace movement represented the most considerable political undertaking ever attempted by the Communists in the United States. [19] An effort was made, of course, to give the new party the protective coloration of American radicalism. Wallace was plainly not a Communist; Glen Taylor of Idaho, the Singing Cowboy, who had shown himself in the Senate as a kind of left-wing Pappy O'Daniel, was prevailed upon to run for the vice-presidency; and the party was named Progressive in a stab at capturing the prestige and possibly some of the adherents of the LaFollette party of 1924.

Some even affected to see in the Wallace movement a rebirth of the Populist tradition, in Wallace himself a renewal of the spirit of Bryan and LaFollette. Dwight Macdonald has exposed the Bryan analogy elsewhere. [20] The comparison with LaFollette is even more unscrupulous; for LaFollette had faced in 1924 the identical problems of Communist infiltration, and his blunt, principled reaction put to shame Wallace's evasions of 1948. "To pretend that the Communists can work with the Progressives who believe in democracy," LaFollette had written, "is deliberately to deceive the public. The Communists are antagonistic to the Progressive cause and their only purpose in joining such a movement is to disrupt it." The Communists, he charged flatly, are mortal enemies of democracy. "I believe, therefore, that all Progressives should refuse to participate in any movement which makes common cause with any Communist organization." [21] There might have been some excuse if Bob LaFollette had not seen the true nature of Communism a few years after the Russian Revolution. There seems little excuse for Henry Wallace a generation later appropriating the name of LaFollette's party while abandoning LaFollette's unconditional opposition to totalitarianism. The blood of Bryan and LaFollette was evidently running thin.

From the start, the key jobs in the Wallace Progressive Party were filled by Communists or fellow travelers. Stalin himself, who had never lifted a finger to help the

CPUSA, sent a letter to Wallace, as if to a head of state, laying down a basis for international negotiations. By the time of the Philadelphia convention in July, 1948, Communist control was arrogant and shameless. The Party platform was largely a paraphrase of the platform adopted a few weeks earlier by the Communist Party; and any deviations remaining were quickly brought into line. The first draft, for example, had carelessly called for a "unified homeland" for the Macedonian people. Someone noticed that this plank would have put the Progressive Party on the side of the recently discredited Tito in one facet of his dispute with the Soviet Union. The platform committee hastily purged the document of the offending reference. When a Vermont delegate sought to amend the foreign-policy plank by adding the statement "It is not our intention to give blanket endorsement to the foreign policy of any nation," he was shouted down. Delegates attacked the amendment as "an insinuation against a friendly ally of the United States" and as a concession to "the smear campaign of red-baiting." [22]

The Philadelphia convention completed the exposure of the Wallace movement. The New Dealers, the non-Communist leaders of American labor, the Negro leaders, and, in general, the men who had been on the firing line in the fight for democracy in America repudiated Wallace with startling unanimity. The CPUSA, the fellow travelers and that moonstruck fringe of the generous-hearted and muddleheaded were left in possession of the third party.

There is no need to note in detail the collapse of the campaign. Wallace's personal deterioration added a pathetic note: his claim, for example, that he was not familiar with the record of Senator Brooks of Illinois, who had carried on his reactionary and isolationist activity while Wallace presided over the Senate as Vice-President; or his veiled attack on Mrs. Roosevelt. * His series of evasions on the Communist issue provided a particularly weird chapter. He first said he would follow Roosevelt's policy on the question of collaboration with the Communists. When he learned that Roosevelt had repeatedly repudiated Communist support, he took refuge in the claim that he knew nothing about Communism and had met very few Communists; all the ones he knew, he said, seemed to him very good Americans. When it was pointed out that ignorance of Communism was hardly a qualification for the presidency in 1948, he adopted a new tack. "If they want to help us out on some of these problems, why God bless them, let them come along." He would tell aimless anecdotes about a woman Communist who had said that she was not an atheist. "Guffawing loudly,"

* Mrs. Roosevelt had written in "My Day" on January 2, 1948, "When Mr. Wallace assumes that by changing certain of our policies until we resemble Mr. Chamberlain, hat in hand, approaching Hitler, we will have the results which he calls 'peace and abundance,' I am afraid he is doing more wishful thinking than realistic facing of the facts." Wallace replied in the *New Republic,* February 2, 1948, "Those who liken me to Chamberlain are in the same category as those who initiated the anti-Comintern movement back in the late thirties. The anti-Comintern bloc of those days produced war and misery. Its spiritual descendants of today will produce a greater war and a greater misery." In a few months the Soviet *Literary Gazette* would be referring to Mrs. Roosevelt as "garrulous, feeble old Eleanor Roosevelt." *New York Times,* October 25, 1948. By December Katz-Suchy, the Polish delegate to the United Nations assembly, was calling Mrs. Roosevelt a tool of fascism. It seems possible that her husband, had he lived, might have ascended the ladder of fascist-bestiality even more rapidly.

as the *New York Times* soberly reported one incident, he added, " 'Probably there are just as many kinds of Communists as there are kinds of Republicans and Democrats.' " [23] By the end of the campaign Wallace had become, as Mr. Koestler observed in a frivolous moment, a Yogi in the hands of the Commissars.

The 1948 election gave the Communists a decided setback in politics. Today the great field of semi-overt Communist activity is the trade unions. The Communists have suffered stunning defeats here too in recent years — in Walter Reuther's rise to power in the United Automobile Workers and in the revolts after years of co-operation by Joe Curran of the National Maritime Union and by Mike Quill of the Transport Workers. Still the national leadership of the United Electrical Workers, the International Longshoremen's and Warehousemen's, the American Communications Association, the United Office and Professional Workers, the Fur and Leather Workers, the United Public Workers, the Farm Equipment Workers, the United Furniture Workers, the Food and Tobacco Workers, the Mine, Mill and Smelter Workers, and the Marine, Cooks, and Stewards, can be relied upon (1949) to follow the party line with fidelity. Communist influence, however, is now clearly labeled as a result of the third-party movement, and the responsible leadership of American labor is fully mobilized against it.

Also high in CPUSA priorities is the drive to organize the Negroes. As the most appalling social injustice in this country, the Negro problem attracted Party interest from the start. With the brilliant party exploitation of the Scottsboro case, Communist prestige among the Negroes rose tremendously. In countless small ways across the country Communists performed commendable individual acts against discrimination. The top leadership, however, continued to view the race problem mainly as a valuable source of propaganda. Angelo Herndon, a Georgia Negro, was sentenced to twenty years in prison for passing out Communist literature on a street corner in Georgia. When he was finally freed, after nation-wide agitation, he was rushed to New York. A group of Communist big shots met Herndon, an intelligent, light-skinned Negro, at Penn Station. In the cab on the way to Harlem, Herndon heard Anna Damon of the International Labor Defense, a top Communist leader, remark that it was a pity he was not blacker. [24]

Another objective is what the Communists call "mass organizations" — that is, groups of liberals organized for some benevolent purpose, and because of the innocence, laziness and stupidity of most of the membership, perfectly designed for control by an alert minority. Sometimes the Communists start the organization themselves; sometimes — as in the case of the Independent Citizens Committee of the Arts, Sciences and Professions in 1945 and 1946 — they take over an existing organization. The Attorney General's list of subversive groups (whatever the merit of this type of list as a form of official procedure) provides a convenient way of checking the more obvious Communist-controlled groups; the list includes such outfits as the Civil Rights Congress, the Joint Anti-Fascist Refugee Committee, the Congress of American Women, and the National Council of American-Soviet Friendship. * The Attorney General's list, however, leaves out organizations like PCA, which have a large proportion of non-Communist members, but rarely, if ever, oppose Communist objectives.

The infiltration into mass organizations is accompanied by a larger attempt to organize culture itself. During the thirties the Party engaged in ambitious projects — the cult of "proletarian literature" and the American Writers' Congress — by which they sought to establish firm control over the literary scene. These projects had a temporary success. But there seemed to be some basic incompatibility in the relationship between the CPUSA and the creation of literature. The promising writers either broke with the Party or abandoned serious writing in favor of Hollywood or disappeared entirely. Who can name today three "proletarian writers" of the early thirties?

Yet the Party has not given up. Where it still has power, it has sought systematically to enforce the doctrine that writing must conform, not to the facts, not to the personal vision of the author, but to a political line.† A *New Masses* controversy not so long ago displayed the

* The inclusion of such anti-Communist revolutionary groups as the Socialist Workers Party in the Attorney General's list seems to me foolish and unwarranted.

† Samuel Putnam, a disenchanted party-line author, describes an instance which took place in 1946. "I had a book in press in which I set forth certain opinions that the Party looked upon as unorthodox. No one, I take it, was supposed to know what the book contained except the author and his publisher; but somehow, doubtless through a loyal member somewhere along the line, the *Daily Worker* found out. . . . I was accordingly visited by a Party functionary, who insisted that I discuss my book with him. This I declined to do; and just to see what his reaction would be, I quoted to him the words of Emerson that had stuck in my mind ever since high-school days: 'Speak what you think today in words

exercise of Party discipline in the literary field in reward-
ing detail. Albert Maltz, a former novelist who had become a Hollywood writer, submitted an article to the *New
Masses*. Communist critics, the author suggested in mild
and tentative language, had perhaps employed political
standards a trifle too mechanically in judging literary
works. The *New Masses* itself, for example, had castigated
Watch on the Rhine as a play but praised it as a film, the
Nazi attack on Russia having intervened to transform the
party line toward Germany. Writers like James T.
Farrell and Richard Wright, Maltz went on, even though
anti-Stalinist, might still be able to write good novels.
The political criterion, Maltz suggested, was fatal to artistic creation. "I know of at least a dozen plays and novels
discarded in the process of writing because the political
scene altered," he confessed, in a significant revelation of
artistic methods in the Stalinist world. " . . . I even know
of a historian who read Duclos and announced that he
would have to revise completely the book he was engaged
upon. . . . Obviously the authors in question were not
primarily bent upon portraying abiding truths, either of
character or of the social scene, but were mainly concerned with advancing a political tactic." [25]

Isidor Schneider, literary editor of the *New Masses*, sent
Maltz a note of approval and printed the article. Then
all hell broke loose. Week after week in the *New Masses*
and the *Daily Worker* the bush-league Zhdanovs —

as hard as cannon balls, and tomorrow, speak what you think in words
just as hard though you contradict everything you said today.' 'That,'
he replied, 'is a luxury you can't afford in times like these.' And I think
it was then I finally realized what an unbridgeable gulf there was between us." *New Leader*, December 4, 1948.

Howard Fast, Mike Gold, Eugene Dennis, even Foster himself — attacked Maltz in the most unrestrained manner. Maltz's subsequent performance was a pathetic demonstration of the power of Shigalovism. Capitulating completely, he even turned on sympathizers who had written to the *New Masses* objecting to the abusive tone in which correction had been administered. "What should be clear is that my article made fundamental errors," wrote the purified Maltz, as repentant as any Russian geneticist. " . . . A serious and sharp discussion was required." [26]

As James T. Farrell has pointed out, writers who accept easy social formulas may gain a superficial and temporary clarity about the world they live in; but they pay a price for allowing others to tell them what they ought to think and write. "They lose their own insights, and harden their talents. Many writers who take this path become cynical, and even abandon writing. They finally reach the point where they don't know their own problems, and are completely disoriented." * The writer, it is clear, must have social perspectives — but they must be his own. The susceptibility to programs corrupts the artist by distorting and eventually superseding the personal truths by which he is nourished. Hence Balzac and Stendhal, whatever their politics, were more truly revolutionary than Victor Hugo or Eugène Sue; Henry James than a party line G. A. Henty like Howard Fast.

* James T. Farrell, "The Needs of American Literature," *Modern Review*, June, 1948. Existing in splendid isolation, writing generally in obscure magazines, Farrell, in my judgment, has written more ruthlessly honest and illuminating essays about the place of the writer in society than any other living American critic.

So direct political control either throttles the serious artist or makes him slick and false. Like Maltz, John Howard Lawson, Alvah Bessie and Dalton Trumbo, the fellow-traveling, ex-proletarian writers go to Hollywood and become film hacks.* Hollywood, indeed, has turned out to have a particularly favorable climate for the spread of Communism. The Hollywood writer, like the radio writer and the pulp fiction writer, tends to have a pervading sense of guilt. He feels he has sold himself out; he has abandoned his serious work in exchange for large weekly pay-checks; and he resents a society which corrupts him (it always seems to be society's fault in these cases). He has qualms of conscience, moreover, for making so much while others make so little. So he believes that he can buy indulgences by participating in the Communist movement, just as men in the Middle Ages bought remission for sins from wandering monks.

The result of the double corruption — first by the pay-checks, then by the Communists — is a corrupt criticism and a corrupt art. The larger result has been to create a dangerous inroad upon the moral fabric of American culture. Where direct political control cannot reach, the Communists and their friends have exerted their influence toward lowering and softening artistic standards in

---

* Until, that is, they refused to own up to their political beliefs before a committee of Congress — in response to which the film industry, rearing itself in an unwonted spasm of moral nobility, turned them out into the storm. I do not wish to imply approval of the question asked by the Un-American Activities Committee. I suspect, however, that if the Committee had been asking witnesses whether they were members of the Ku Klux Klan, the Silver Shirts or the Trotskyites, Mr. Lawson and his friends would be overflowing with indignation at the refusal to answer.

a pseudo-democratic direction. The wildly enthusiastic Communist claque for certain types of fake folk art is symptomatic. The vogue of *Ballad for Americans,* for example, or for the incredible radio plays of Norman Corwin only results in betrayal of taste. Words like "the little people," "the common man," "the folks," are used with cynicism as a sure way to provoke desired responses; and the consequence has been to discredit the words. The phony populism, the adaptation of slick advertising methods to politics, reached its climax in the cultural trimmings of the Wallace campaign. *

But these half-concealed exercises in penetration and manipulation represent only a part of the Communist mission in the United States. From the beginning, the Party has had in addition an underground arm, operating apart from the formal organization of the CPUSA and working as the American section of the Soviet secret intelligence corps. Because clandestine operations of this kind are utterly foreign to American political life, many Americans dismiss them as wild fabrication. They are naïve to do so. Doctrine and experience have equipped the CPUSA for underground activity. Leninism sanctioned the use by the Party of all methods in their war for survival against the American business classes; and the early history of the Party — A. Mitchell Palmer and the meeting at Bridgman, Michigan — confirmed in the minds of the Party leadership (both Foster and Browder were at

---

* One returns with gratitude to Joseph Mitchell's observation on the phrase "the little people" in his introduction to *McSorley's Wonderful Saloon* (New York, 1943) : "I regard this phrase as patronizing and repulsive. There are no little people in this book. They are as big as you are, whoever you are!"

Bridgman) an enduring psychology of clandestinity. Police raids, FBI penetration and civil persecution have fortified the Communist belief that they are a small and ill-armed band, acting in a ruthlessly hostile environment, and justified in using any methods to advance their cause.

The underground arm of the Party works through secret members and through fellow travelers. Secret members report directly to a representative of the National Committee; they have no local affiliations, are exempt from the usual Party discipline and are unknown to most of their Party brethren. Their Party cards usually are held in aliases, so that in the files they appear as "John Smith" with P.N. (party name) noted beside it. Fellow travelers are those who for one reason or another wish to keep some elbow room but maintain relations practically as close as actual membership. A curious freemasonry exists among underground workers and sympathizers. They can identify each other (and be identified by their enemies) on casual meeting by the use of certain phrases, the names of certain friends, by certain enthusiasms and certain silences. It is reminiscent of nothing so much as the famous scene in Proust where the Baron de Charlus and the tailor Jupien suddenly recognize their common corruption; "one does not arrive spontaneously at that pitch of perfection except when one meets in a foreign country a compatriot with whom an understanding then grows up of itself, both parties speaking the same language, even though they have never seen one another before." *

* Marcel Proust, *Remembrance of Things Past, Cities of the Plain,* Part I. Lionel Trilling's distinguished novel, *The Middle of the Journey,* New York, 1947, is the most subtle American study of the phenomena of

There can be no serious question that an underground
Communist apparatus attempted during the late thirties
and during the war to penetrate the United States Government, to influence the formation of policy and even to
collect intelligence for the Soviet Union. Though certain
of the individual accusations, especially those of Elizabeth
Bentley, are undoubtedly exaggerated, yet a hard substratum of truth survives in the stories told before the
federal grand jury.

The testimony of Harold Laski on this point is of interest, since he can hardly be written off as a red-baiter or
reactionary. "The Communist Parties outside Russia,"
Laski wrote in this pamphlet on Communism, which he
accurately entitled *The Secret Battalion*, "act without
moral scruples, intrigue without any sense of shame, are
utterly careless of truth, sacrifice, without any hesitation,
the means they use to the end they serve. . . . The only rule
to which the Communist gives unswerving loyalty is the
rule that a success gained is a method justified. The result
is a corruption, both of the mind and of the heart, which
is alike contemptuous of reason and careless of truth."
Professor Laski was writing about the British Party, but,
as he added prudently, its history was "relatively simple
compared with that of the Communist Parties in Germany
and France and, most of all, the United States." [27] We

fellow traveling and of Communist underground activity. For a British
view, see Humphrey Slater, *The Conspirator*, New York, 1948. Mr. Slater
was Chief of Operations on the International Brigade Staff in Spain in
1938. He was expelled from the Communist Party in 1940 for his activity
in organizing the British Home Guard against the possible Nazi invasion
and, in particular, for writing a book entitled *Home Guard For Victory!* Mr.
Slater's testimony can hardly be dismissed on grounds of incompetence.

would be well advised to take the necessary precautions.

These, then, are the proportions of the Communist movement in the United States: an organized party of 70,000 members, extending its influence by means of an underground apparatus and through the collaboration of fellow travelers; controlling a political party, several trade unions and a great many front organizations, and exerting a lingering power in cultural circles.

What kind of challenge does all this present to the United States? The espionage dangers, of course, are obvious and acute. No loyal citizen can underestimate these dangers, although there is probably little that he can do individually to grapple with them. All Americans must bear in mind J. Edgar Hoover's warning that counter-espionage is no field for amateurs.* We need the best professional counterespionage agency we can get to protect our national security.

Beyond this field, however, it is hard to argue that the CPUSA in peacetime presents much of a threat to American security. In every area where Communist influence can be identified and exposed, the Communists have lost ground in the last two years. Does anyone seriously believe that even the Communist Party is absurd enough to contemplate a violent revolution in the United States?

Far from being a threat to the status quo in America,

* As Mr. Hoover wrote in the January, 1949, issue of the *F.B.I. Law Enforcement Bulletin,* the overzealous amateur, "untrained in the use of proper investigative techniques, may constitute a serious menace to civil rights. . . . Patriotism and zeal cannot compensate for a lack of detailed, technical knowledge. . . . The work of the vigilante too often deserves the label 'witch hunt'; the work of the fifth columnist needs no label. Let us beware of both."

the CPUSA has been a great ally of the American conservatives because of its success, for a season, at least, in dividing and neutralizing the left. It is to the American left that the CPUSA has presented an immediate political danger. And it is in the revival of the free left, in America and through the world, that the answer to Communism lies.

VII

The Restoration of Radical Nerve

THE INDEPENDENT LEFT everywhere in the world has been in a state of moral paralysis at least since 1917. The commanding personality of Lenin and the unanswerable fact of the Russian Revolution gave Western radicalism a fatal complex of inferiority. Under the spell of that complex, the left committed itself to the long and corrupting enterprise of accepting in the Soviet Union crimes much worse than those it attacked in its own countries. Just as the left gained moral strength when it protested against Amritsar or the judicial murder of Sacco and Vanzetti, so it lost moral strength when it kept its silence before the anonymous victims of the Soviet despotism.

It is to the credit of certain individual radicals that they named the evil at the start and opposed themselves to it. The German Socialist Karl Kautsky, for example, early defined the totalitarian implications of the Leninist policy. Kautsky, a middle-of-the-road Social Democrat, may have only been flinching from the violent necessities of revolution. But no Socialist was a more true or faithful revolutionary than Rosa Luxemburg, the flaming leader of the German left Social Democrats; and Rosa Luxemburg saw that Lenin's bureaucratic collectivism was as much a threat to democracy in her sense — "the active, untrammeled and vital political life of the masses of the people" — as it was to the gradualist paradise of Kautsky's.

Rosa Luxemburg's indictment has a prophetic ring. "Freedom for supporters of the government only, for the members of one party only — no matter how big its membership may be — is no freedom at all. Freedom is always freedom for the man who thinks differently. This contention does not spring from a fanatical love of abstract 'justice,' but from the fact that everything which is enlightening, healthy and purifying in political freedom derives from its independent character, and from the fact that freedom loses all its virtue when it becomes a privilege. . . . The suppression of political life throughout the country must gradually cause the vitality of the Soviets themselves to decline. Without general elections, freedom of the Press, freedom of assembly, and freedom of speech, life in every public institution slows down, becomes a caricature of itself, and bureaucracy rises as the only deciding factor. No one can escape the workings of this law. Public life gradually dies, and a few dozen leaders with inexhaustible energy and limitless idealism direct and rule." [1]

But too few listened. If the Communist parties were becoming bureaucratic, at least they were bureaucratic in a hard way; they were effective. The Social Democratic parties, the only organized alternatives, were bureaucratic in a soft way; they were sedate, cautious and feeble — in Stalin's phrase "gross and stodgy." [2] So the Communists were able to manipulate their campaign against the independent left with brilliant success. They were tough and tender in bewildering alternation; they shifted from the united front from above to the united front from below; and they always invoked the indisputable fact that the USSR was the only "socialist" country in the world.

Beneath the tactical razzle-dazzle, however, the Communists proceeded to a single objective with unflagging determination. That objective was the extermination of the independent left — an objective which long antedated the Russian Revolution. Lenin used to boast in later years of the cold determination with which he had given moderate parties the embrace that killed. In 1901, as he wrote twenty years later, the Bolshevik Party concluded "a formal political alliance with Struve, the political leader of bourgeois liberalism." Yet "it was able at the same time to carry on an unceasing and merciless ideological and political struggle against bourgeois liberalism. . . . Between 1903 and 1912, there were periods in which we were formally united with the Mensheviks . . . but we *never* ceased our ideological and political struggle against them. . . . During the war we compromised to a certain extent with the 'Kautskians' . . . but we never ceased and never relaxed our ideological-political struggle against the 'Kautskians.' " And so on, far, far into the twentieth century. It was in this same amiable spirit that Lenin urged the British Communists to support the Socialist Arthur Henderson: "I wanted to support Henderson with my vote in the same way as a rope supports the hanged." [3]

Stalin drew very clearly from Lenin the lesson that the independent left was the great enemy. In his *Foundations of Leninism,* he reduced the three stages of the Russian Revolution, in his characteristic manner, to a set of diagrammatic outlines. The climax of each stage he labeled in his careful way as "direction of the main blow." In each case, one notes, the "main blow" was aimed, not at the forces of reaction, but at the democratic left.

Lenin's policy came in part from his rooted mistrust of gradualism — his belief that it was an elaborate decoy by which the capitalists would dissipate the revolutionary energy of the masses. Stalin, no doubt, added the perception that, if gradualism were to work, it would destroy the pretensions of the Soviet ruling class — and consequently, at all costs, it must not be permitted to work. The most deadly foe from the Communist viewpoint is no longer the reactionary whose blind folly will only speed the disintegration of his own society. For two generations it has been the radical democrat, who proposes to solve the problems of unemployment and want without enslaving the masses and setting up a police state. Whether you read Lenin in 1901 or William Z. Foster in 1932 — "The policy of the Social Democracy is basically that of Fascism" — or Kuusinen, the Finnish Communist, in 1948 — "The Right-wing Social-Democrats and the fascists serve one master; they are the two arms of the parasitic, reactionary bourgeoisie" — you find the same, inflexible Communist purpose of smashing the democratic left.[4]

The "direction of the main blow" policy is one reason why every experiment in democratic collaboration with the Communists has ended in failure. The Communists do not want to collaborate with democrats in any meaningful sense of the word; they want to absorb or destroy them. No co-operation on a common objective is possible because there is no common objective. The record on this point is unanswerable.

The only president in the Western Hemisphere (beside Batista of Cuba) to appoint Communists to his cabinet was Gabriel Gonzalez Videla of Chile. What was the sequel? "I have learned from bitter experience," testifies Gonzalez Videla. ". . . I found that the Communists are not really interested in the solution of the economic and social problems of the country. . . . They are only interested in creating economic anarchy which they expect to use to achieve their own ends." [5]

No American trade union leaders made a more wholehearted attempt over many years to co-operate with the Communists than Joe Curran of the National Maritime Union and Mike Quill the Transport Workers. Each suddenly realized the extent to which he had surrendered his independence to the Party machine. Each turned to fight for personal survival; and, after campaigns of amazing filth and vindictiveness on the part of the Communists, each won. Morris Muster, former president of the United Furniture Workers, was less fortunate. "These people are dangerously vicious," he said in denouncing Communist control of his union. "Anyone who goes along with them on the theory that this is the liberal thing to do is a fool. I know because I have been one." [6]

No American Negro leader tried harder to work with the Communists than Dr. Max Yergan. When he finally got tired of being pushed around and decided to break with the Communists, they smeared his character, beat him up physically and looted his office. "As a result of my

cooperation with the Communists in the past," said Dr.
Yergan, "I am convinced that they are unscrupulous and
irresponsible. They will resort to the foulest methods to
achieve their ends." [7]

Harold Ickes, who should have known better, went
through the experiment as director of the Independent
Citizens Committee for the Arts, Sciences and Professions
under the illusion that he could control the Communists.
If anyone could control them, it would probably have
been Harold Ickes. But Mr. Ickes' conclusion, on the
basis of bitter experience, was sufficiently definite: "Communism is a nonassimilable political ideology. . . . A true
progressive movement has no chance of success unless it
rigidly excludes Communists." [8]

The testimony could be prolonged indefinitely. It adds
up to a single fact; the personal word of the Communist
is worthless and cooperation with him impossible. The
phenomenon is worldwide. Dr. Sjarifoeddin, a former
Indonesian Prime Minister, announcing the fusion of his
Republican-Socialist Party with the Communists, blandly
disclosed that he had been a secret member of the Communist Party since 1935. [9] A group of American Communists and sympathizers, headed by Ella Winter, circu-
lated a statement attacking American efforts to influence
the Italian election — a statement which they claimed to
have been written by the revered anti-Fascist Professor
Gaetano Salvemini; Salvemini the next day exposed this
claim as a lie and denounced the "Communist deceit." [10]
Eleanor Roosevelt has pronounced the final word on the
Communists. "For years, in this country, they taught the
philosophy of the lie. They taught that allegiance to the
party and acceptance of orders from party heads, whose

interests were not just those of the United States, were paramount. . . . Because I have experienced the deception of the American Communists, I will not trust them." [11]

There always remain a group of the indefatigably bedizened who admit the major sins of the Communists but say nonetheless: Aren't they sincere in being for labor or for minorities, and can we not unite with them for immediate and limited objectives of a local character? Liberals will no doubt be active on the same issues as Communists; but experience should by now have warned them against personal or organizational collaboration. Quite apart from the practical consideration that Communist participation is enough to discredit any domestic reform movement, the Communist attitude toward immediate and limited reforms is entirely different from that of the liberal. Stalin was perfectly explicit on this point. "To a reformist," Stalin wrote, "reforms are everything." The reformer's object is to strengthen the existing system. But, to a Communist, reforms are of use only "as instruments that disintegrate the system, instruments that strengthen the revolution. . . . The revolutionary will accept a reform in order to use it as a screen behind which his illegal activities for the revolutionary preparation of the masses for the overthrow of the bourgeoisie may be intensified." [12]

This precept motivates much of Communist "co-operation" in reform movements. The other important motive, of course, is the hope of using domestic reform as the bait with which to lure innocent people to the support of Soviet foreign policy. Both motives figured in the Communist hit-and-run tactics on such questions as, for example, the Mundt-Nixon Bill, a drastic anti-Communist

bill with serious implications for civil liberties, introduced into the 80th Congress. The Republican leadership in the Senate announced in the press over the week-
end of May 29, 1948 that it would give three other bills
priority for Senate action in the few days remaining before
adjournment. This meant that the Mundt-Nixon Bill was
dead, so far as the 80th Congress was concerned. The
Communists promptly swung into action. On May 31 they
organized the Committee to Defeat the Mundt Bill. On
June 2 they staged a march on Washington. The object
of these tactics was unmistakable. The Communists hoped
by organized intimidation to antagonize indifferent sena-
tors and annoy those on the fence into reviving the bill.
"It is plain as any hidden intent can be," reported Alan
Barth of the *Washington Post,* "that the Communists want
to get the Mundt-Nixon bill enacted into law." [13] Enact-
ment would have given Henry Wallace a new and appealing issue; it would have provided the USSR with a potent
weapon in the psychological war. Fortunately, in spite of
the extreme irritation of some members of the Judiciary
Committee, the Senate was not to be stampeded into the
Communist trap.

Communists, as Stalin admits, like reforms which they
can exploit as instruments of disintegration. They dislike
reforms which will strengthen a democratic system.
Eugene Dennis put it simply in his post-election analysis:
The "main dangers" at present, he said, "are that Mr.
Truman will make concessions on domestic social
issues." [14] The choice of words illuminates vividly the
Communist attitude toward the welfare of the common
man in the United States.

The "main blow" tactic recommended by Stalin goes

much deeper, however, than the cynical manipulation of reform movements or the sudden reversal of a parliamentary line. It has plumbed the sickening depths of literal, physical betrayal of their supposed comrades of the left. The Communists collaborated, for example, with the Nazis in the revival of German nationalism and the campaign against the Social Democrats. Let us smash the bourgeoisie, the Communists cried, Hitler cannot last, and then we will take over. But Hitler turned out to be a little stronger than they expected; and the impartiality of his terror did much to change the Communist attitude toward the Social Democrats. All anti-Nazis became comrades within the grim palings of the concentration camp. Such comradeship, one would think, would be beyond violation. Yet that would be to underestimate the moral cynicism of the Communists.

In 1939 the Ribbentrop-Molotov pact transformed anew the Communist attitude toward the Nazis. Molotov decided that fascism was only "a matter of political views"; that the direction of the main blow should be toward Britain and France. * Appropriate orders went out to the

* *New York Times,* November 1, 1939. "One may accept or reject the ideology of Hitlerism as well as any other ideological system — that is a matter of political views. But everybody would understand that an ideology cannot be destroyed by force, that it cannot be eliminated by war. It is, therefore, not only senseless, but criminal to wage such a war as a war for the 'destruction of Hitlerism' camouflaged as a fight for 'democracy.' " Other portions of Molotov's speech are worth pondering today. "Today, as far as the European great powers are concerned, Germany is in the position of a state that is striving for the earliest termination of war and for peace, while Great Britain and France, which but yesterday were declaiming against aggression, are in favor of continuing the war and are opposed to the conclusion of peace. We have always held that a strong Germany is an indispensable condition for durable peace in Europe."

German Communists. Take, for example, the article published from Moscow in the official German Communist paper *Die Welt* on February 2, 1940. The article was signed by the Communist leader Walter Ulbricht, today a leader of the Communist-controlled Socialist Unity Party in the Soviet zone of Germany. Ulbricht's main contention was that the British Government was "the most reactionary force in the world." "The German workers have the proof before their eyes that the ruling class in Britain is carrying on the war against the working class, and that, if Germany were conquered, the German working class would be treated in the same way. The German workers know the big business men of England and the two hundred families of France, and are aware what an English victory would mean to them." Here was a clear appeal to the German workers to help Hitler in resisting the "worse" tyranny of Britain.

But Ulbricht went farther and struck lower. *"The British plan has the less chance of success,"* Ulbricht wrote (and the italics are throughout his own), *"the more deeply the friendship between the German and Soviet people is rooted in the working masses.* Therefore not only the Communists but also many Social Democratic and National-Socialist [*sic*] workers regard it as their task *not in any circumstances to permit a breach of the Pact.* [Double emphasis in original.] Those who intrigue against the friendship of the German and Soviet people are enemies of the German people, and are branded as accomplices of British Imperialism. Among the German working class greater and greater efforts are being made to *expose* the followers of the Thyssen clique, who are the enemies of the German-

Soviet pact." By the "Thyssen clique," Ulbricht made clear, he meant "the agents of British imperialism . . . and their friends among the Social-Democratic and Catholic leaders in Germany."

If this frightful passage meant anything, it was an invitation to the German working class, including the Nazi workers, to deliver Socialist and Catholic oppositional elements to the Hitler régime and to the Gestapo. This was only an extreme example of the pro-Nazi rôle which the Communist parties played in the early days of the war. * In Oslo, for example, the Norwegian Communist newspaper continued publication. The French Communists twice succeeded in winning official permissions from the Nazis to publish *L'Humanité* on the argument that it would help the Nazi war effort, only to be thwarted in this attempt by non-Communist French collaborationists, competing for Nazi favor. Even the heroism with which the Communists behaved in the Resistance — after the attack on Russia — can hardly erase the memory of the squalid diligence with which they sought a few months before to ingratiate themselves with Hitler.

For a time at the end of the war the mystique of the Resistance — the experience and memory of the common underground war against Nazism — renewed faith in the possibility of a united left. But Moscow was reading the European portents with special care. So long as Winston

* The memory of American liberals is too short. In general, people have forgotten the Communist performance in 1940–41 — a performance which, at the very least, destroys all subsequent Communist pretensions to moral leadership. The best analysis of Communist policy during these years is *The Betrayal of the Left,* edited by Victor Gollancz, with contributions by John Strachey, George Orwell and Harold Laski, published in London, 1941. The Ulbricht article is reprinted in its entirety in an appendix.

Churchill lived in Downing Street, the USSR knew that Britain could offer no competition in the struggle for the mind and faith of the people of Europe. So the British Communists favored a Labour coalition with Churchill. But the victory of the Labour Party on its own in the summer of 1945 changed the situation. It brought new hope to the people of Europe by signalizing an alternative to Moscow which promised the same economic advantages — but with political liberty in place of the MVD. It was at this point that the USSR stepped up its attack on the Socialist parties and began its concerted policy of hammering at the weak points, strategic and ideological, of the already crumbling British Empire.

This policy, and particularly the Soviet refusal to cooperate with the democratic Socialists in the reconstruction of the shattered continent, seems finally to have snapped the cord which bound the left to the Soviet Union.

In the end, after much heartbreak, the democrats have finally returned to the basic principles of democracy. For in the end they have remembered the greatest of all Lenin's questions — the magistral formula into which he had compressed the fundamental issue of politics: Who whom? "At bottom," Lenin had written, "the question of control is really the question: Who is it that exercises control? That is to say, what class controls and what class is controlled?"

Who whom? This is the question which the democratic left, through the years, has had to put with increasing insistence to the Soviet Union. For a generation, it had allowed itself to be turned away with evasions. Who whom? The Soviet Union has nationalized the means of

production, the answer would come; or capitalist encirclement has postponed the withering away of the state; or
Comrade Stalin has taken the drastic steps only to
save socialism from the Trotskyite-Bukharinite-mad-dog-
wreckers. But still the question would sound, louder and
louder: Who whom? And still the answers came back:
the Minister for Internal Affairs has restored folk dancing
in Azerbaijan; or the Soviet Union has entered the Nazi
alliance in order to save peace from capitalist betrayal; or
it is combatting the reconstruction of Europe in order to
protect Europe from the domination of Wall Street; or
"it knows what it wants, and brutalized as much of its
practice may have been [sic] it still points toward a goal
that gives the dispossessed their only hope." [15] But still
the question echoed implacably: Who whom?

Today the answer is clear. Who? — the Communist
bureaucracy. Whom? — the workers, peasants, intellectuals, all the human beings outside the ruling clique.
Rosa Luxemburg, Karl Kautsky and others knew this
answer from the start. They should be honored today
after the decades of Communist abuse and calumny. But
the highest honor would be to act upon their insight.
With the full comprehension of Lenin's conundrum —
Who whom? — comes the rebirth of the democratic left —
the rise, in the popular phrase, of the non-Communist
left.

The terminology of politics obscures more than it clari-
fies about the nature of the dilemma of our time. Left and
right were adequate to the political simplicities of the
nineteenth century, when the right meant those who
wished to preserve the existing order and the left meant
those who wished to change it. But the twentieth century,

here as elsewhere, introduced new ambiguities. The fascists, for example, were not conservative in any very meaningful sense. They did not wish to preserve the existing order, or even to turn back the clock to some more stable century. They purposefully planned to transform the existing order into a new and all-absorbing authoritarianism, based on the energies and frustrations of modern industrialism. The fascists, in a meaningful sense, were revolutionaries. Yet their totalitarian ideal hardly fitted into the pattern of the left, which had been the traditional home of greater freedoms and more generous aspirations. So, after boggling and uncertainty, they were assigned positions on the far right.

At the same time, the new complexities overtook the left. The Declaration of the Rights of Man, the spirit of the American and French Revolutions, the legacy of 1848 — all pointed in the direction of the enlargement of individual freedom. Yet the Communists, while clinging to the formal hope of the withering away of the state and the liberation of the individual, had committed themselves in practice to methods of terror, violence and dictatorship; and the methods seemed not only to defer but to corrupt and destroy the presumed objectives. But the Communists clearly did not belong to the right or center; so they have been allowed to retain positions on the far left.

The rise of fascism and Communism illustrated vividly the fallacies of the linear conception of right and left. In certain basic respects — the totalitarian state structure, the single party, the leader, the secret police, the consuming fear of political and intellectual freedom — fascism and Communism are clearly more like each other than they are like anything in between. This dilemma drove Professor

De Witt C. Poole to an inspired suggestion. Right and left, he said, should be conceived, not in terms of a line, but in terms of a circle, with the extremes of right and left — fascism and Communism — meeting at the bottom. You can then look at the circle in two ways: with respect to property, fascism and the moderate right are side by side against Communism and the moderate left; with respect to liberty, the moderate right and the moderate left are side by side against fascism and Communism.

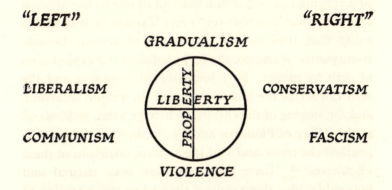

"LEFT"   **"RIGHT"**

                              GRADUALISM

LIBERALISM   LIB**E**RTY   *CONSERVATISM*

COMMUNISM   PROPERTY   *FASCISM*

                              VIOLENCE

This ingenious solution does reformulate the right-left classification in terms which correspond to the complexities of this ghastly century. But the Poole formula does not lend itself to the shorthand of mass communications — to the simplifications of the headline writer, for example, who hardly has time or space to plot his characterizations with a compass along the circumference of a circle. Thus the phrase "non-Communist left" seems to be the best way to designate the new political actuality. Subsequently Léon Blum, denouncing the twin dangers of Communism and Gaullism, used the phrase Third Force as the standard to rally the groups fighting to carve out an area for freedom.

The first principle of the democratic left was the affirmation of a belief in free society and an absolute repudiation of totalitarianism. For an older generation, nourished in the bright dreams of 1917, the rejection of the USSR was difficult. For some a gleam of hope, a fragment of some splendid vision still lurked underneath the machinery of terror. Victor Gollancz tells how he tried to resist the involuntary disgust which surged through his mind after first reading the verbatim transcript of one of the Moscow trials. He was shocked; yet "every Tycoon in Britain was using that trial to stir up hatred of Russia, because twenty-three years ago, she had abolished the exploitation of man by money. So I remembered Bolshevo, and the Red Corner in the Soviet ship, and the Prophylacterium, and the singing of the children when we went, in Moscow, to the Palace of Pioneers; and I published only books that justified the trials, and sent the socialist criticisms of them elsewhere." [16] These emotions were once natural and honorable. But there came a time when the extension of these emotions in the teeth of fact and human suffering became a source of irrevocable corruption.

My own generation escaped the lure of nostalgia. We were too young to feel the exultation of 1917 or to recall the lies from Riga. We do not know about Bolshevo; Hitler, we recall, also had his prophylacteria; and we could not hear the singing of children in the Palace of Pioneers because we could never get a Soviet visa. Our memories of Russia are shaped, not by the glory of Revolution, but by the horror of Thermidor. Mention the Soviet Union: the images which spring to mind are not those of the collective youth joyfully building the subway or doing mass calisthenics in the public square (images which in any case have been spoiled by Hitler), but those of the millions doomed to forced labor, of the intellectual Canossa of the scientists and historians, of mass starvation among the peasants, of the Old Bolsheviks babbling in the dock. It is not a question of disillusionment: we were too young to have that particular hope; we had no dream to lose. It is a question of distinguishing between nostalgia and actuality — or rather of holding fast to what one believes to be sane and true.

Thus for the Luxemburgs and Kautskys, insight acted as the spur; for the Gollanczs, disillusionment; for my own generation, a look at the corpse. Out of these mingled emotions, out of the agony of Europe, tormented by war and by tyrannies worse than war, out of the Soviet offensive against democratic socialism came a renewed sense of the meaning of freedom.

Its prophets were the writers who refused to swallow the fantastic hypocrisies involved in the defense of totalitarianism: Silone, with his profound moral sensibility; Gide, with his quivering sense of freedom; Koestler, with his probing, insatiable intellectual curiosity; Hemingway, who disliked people who pushed other people around; Reinhold Niebuhr, with his tragic sense of the predicament of man; George Orwell, with his vigorous good sense, his hatred of cant; Edmund Wilson, with his belief in moral and aesthetic taste. And its political leaders brought a new virility into public life, a virility compact of humanity and not of ruthlessness: Franklin D. Roosevelt, with his superb gaiety and his superb political insight; Aneurin Bevan, in whom is distilled the whole

tradition of British dissent; Walter Reuther, labor's man
of vision and will.

The non-Communist left has brought what measure of
hope there is in our political life today. Take a look at
Europe. What countries have achieved a fair degree of
political and economic stability? Britain, Denmark,
Norway, Sweden, Belgium, Netherlands, Austria. What
is the Communist strength in these countries? In every
case, negligible. What is the Socialist strength? In every
case, the Socialist Party participates in the government
and controls the national labor federation. What countries in western Europe are conspicuously lacking in political and economic stability? France and Italy. Here alone
in western Europe the Communist parties have a mass
following; here they dominate the labor federations; here
the Socialist parties are divided and weak.

Why has Socialism been able to contain Communism in
most of these countries and not in France and Italy? One
factor is certainly the fact that in the stable countries the
Socialist parties have always retained their faith in free
society; they have remained consistently anti-Communist;
as a result, Communism was permitted no foothold in the
labor movement or in the political world. But in France
and Italy, where the Socialist parties were more doctrinaire, they were weakened gravely by the disease of
united-frontism. The French Socialists ran through the
disease during the thirties; and have emerged today, clear-
headed if pale and faltering. But almost too late: the
working class does not trust their determination to carry
out reforms, and the middle class does not trust their
determination to resist Communism. The Italian Socialist
Party went through its united-front phase after the war;
today it is broken and helpless.

The health of the democratic left requires the unconditional rejection of totalitarianism. This line must be held fast for all time. And there is always danger of a relapse. The period of 1939–41, one would have thought, would be sufficient education in the meaning of the Soviet system. Yet some people returned to the Soviet mirage with new ardor on June 23, 1941; being attacked by the Germans somehow remitted for the Communists the sin of having collaborated with them. Like a youth regaining his beloved after a period of rebuff and separation, the Doughface found his infatuation more intense than ever; after all, he had always known she would never be happy in the embrace of the Nazi roughneck.

The same possibility of relapse exists today. Many pro-Soviet liberals, for example, refused to enter the cul-de-sac of the Wallace movement. A distinct quasi-Browderite faction remains in the American left, dissenting from current Soviet tactics but still clinging to the USSR as the only hope for the future. These people would blame the international impasse primarily upon the aggressive program of American monopoly, summed up in the Truman Doctrine; this US policy, they feel, has unfortunately if understandably provoked the USSR into politics almost as unwise. Such people were unhappy over the Communist opposition to the Marshall Plan; and they objected above all to the third party because it might help the Republicans. But, given any encouragement, they could return to the old flame. The great need, they continue to say, is to reunite Communists and liberals. Soviet totalitarianism and collaboration with it, this group feels, presents no serious moral or political problem for liberals.

The USSR may in time have to accept the fact of democratic revival in western Europe. Being unable to lick the democrats, it may then decide to try and join them. We must then expect a dusting-off of "Browderism" in the United States. Foster, the veteran militant, will once again vent his anarcho-syndicalist rages on deaf ears; Eugene Dennis will once again reverse himself in midair; and the pro-Communist liberals, the Doughfaces, so unhappy during the third-party adventure, will anticipate a joyful reunion. It will be up to the non-Communist liberals not to permit the left to forget the painful lessons of 1946 to 1949, as it once forgot the painful lessons of the Molotov-Ribbentrop liaison. My own conviction is that the failure of radical nerve is over. This time there will be no lamp in the window for the Communists.

If the distinguishing moral commitment of the new radicalism is its faith in freedom and the unconditional rejection of totalitarianism, the distinguishing political commitment is its belief in the limited state. The Soviet experience has caused a revaluation of the politics of Marxism — a revaluation which questions in particular the total concentration of all political and economic power in the apparatus of the single-party state. For the Soviet experience has proved, if it has proved anything, that concentration of power creates classes whatever the system of ownership — classes under Communism as well as under capitalism. Who whom? remains the crucial question; and in every system, as history has finally taught us, the tendency of the ruling class toward oppression can be checked only by the capacity of the other classes for resistance.

And resistance requires essentially an independent base from which to operate. It requires privacy, funds, time, newsprint, gasoline, freedom of speech, freedom of assembly, freedom from fear; it requires resources to which its own access is secure and which remain relatively inaccessible to the ruling class. Resistance is possible, in short, only when the base is clearly separate from the state. Under a system of total state ownership, the sinews of resistance are doled out to the opposition only by the charity of the ruling class.

Constitutions are no guarantee for political freedom; they acquire strength only with age, use, and support. A sheet of paper like the Soviet Constitution of 1936 has no function except to bemuse the Webbs and the Wallaces. "You may cover whole skins of parchment with limitations," John Randolph of Roanoke once wrote, "but power alone can limit power." [17] When all power is centered in the top hierarchy of a single party, there is none left over to serve as a check against the ruling class. The only check, in other words, is the state's own sense of self-restraint. History has shown how feeble a bulwark self-restraint is — especially when those who exercise the power believe they have a monopoly of the truth.

Totalitarianism does not abolish politics altogether, of course. Active and searching arguments go on within the ruling clique before a decision is reached. But, on the whole, totalitarianism reduces the appeal against a decision to the intrigues of a court or to the uprising of a praetorian guard. Or it perverts politics into something secret, sweaty and furtive like nothing so much, in the phrase of one wise observer of modern Russia, as homosexuality in a boys' school: many practicing it, but all those caught to be caned by the headmaster. Totalitarianism succeeds magnificently in abolishing politics in the high sense — politics as a source of and guarantee for freedom.

When a single group gets hold of the state and destroys all opposition, what hope is there for the withering away of the state? Will such a group of its own accord surrender power and establish freedom? Marxist theory itself is conclusive on the point. A ruling class does not abandon power voluntarily; it must be clutched by the throat until it chokes the power up. But you cannot bring pressure on a ruling class without leverage; and totalitarianism provides for the automatic liquidation of the leverage. The critic of a totalitarian régime shares the predicament and the wail of Archimedes: If I only had a place to stand, I could move the world!

The consequences of the unlimited state are so fatal to individual freedom and dignity that the new radicalism has no choice but to work with the limited state. But, in addition, experience suggests that the limited state can resolve the basic social questions which were supposed to compel a resort to the unlimited state.

A century ago, Marx dismissed the limited state in a somewhat cavalier manner. "The executive of the modern state," he wrote in *The Communist Manifesto*, "is but a committee for managing the common affairs of the bourgeoisie." [18] As a passive instrument of capitalistic power, the state in Marx's judgment was incapable of acting independently of the business community. But history in this case, as in so many others, betrayed Marx. Even Engels, before he died, was groping toward a more complex theory of the capitalist government. The state, as he saw it in 1890, was a "new independent power, [which] while having in the main to follow the movement of production, also . . . reacts in its turn upon the conditions and course of production." Legislation in the capitalist state, he added, "reacts in its turn upon the economic basis and may, within certain limits, modify it." [19]

It is surely Marx's mistaken analysis of the state which, more than any single factor, was responsible for the failure of his prophecies. The capitalist state has clearly not been just the executive committee of the business community. It has become an object of genuine competition among classes; it is the means by which the non-business classes may protect themselves from the business community, if not actually launch a counterattack against long-established bastions of business power. As a result, through using the state power, the other classes have been able to promote the systematic redistribution of wealth which has helped confound Marx's prediction of increasing proletarian misery. Through using the state power, the other classes are even now within measurable distance of the means of avoiding economic crises. Even the Soviet economist Varga has recognized this fact (to the acute displeasure of his masters).

The democratic left today has committed itself to the limited state — European Socialists, retreating precipitately from the abyss of totalitarianism, as well as American New Dealers advancing cautiously out of the jungle of private enterprise. In one direction lies the tyranny of the irresponsible bureaucracy; in the other, the tyranny of the irresponsible plutocracy. Somewhere between the abyss and the jungle the new radicalism will work out a sensible economic policy. There will certainly be changes in the structure of the economy. But these changes will be brought about in a way which will not disrupt the fabric of custom, law and mutual confidence upon which personal rights depend, nor will they liquidate the basis of future resistance. The transition must be piecemeal. It must be parliamentary. It must respect civil liberties and due process of law. Only in this way can it preserve free society.

The classical argument against gradualism was that the capitalist ruling class would resort to violence rather than surrender its prerogatives. Here, as elsewhere, the Marxists enormously overestimated the political courage and will of the capitalists. In fact, in the countries where the full triumph of the middle class wiped out those groups willing to exercise violence, capitalism has surrendered with far better grace than the Marxist scheme predicted. The British experience is illuminating in this respect, and the American experience not uninstructive.

There is no sign in either nation that the capitalists are putting up a really determined fight against those who would use the state to restrict their profits and reduce their power — even perhaps to take their property away from them. Alarmists who feel that the clamor of a political campaign or the noise of hired lobbyists constitutes a determined fight should read the history of Germany. In the United States an industrialist who turned a machine gun on a picket line would be disowned by the rest of the business community; in Britain he would be sent to an insane asylum.

Britain has already submitted itself to social democracy; the United States will very likely advance in that direction through a series of New Deals, and the advance will be accelerated if the country fails to keep out of a depression. In the depths of the last depression, as Frances Perkins has reported, the coal operators actually pleaded with the Government to nationalize the mines. They offered to sell "to the Government at any price fixed by the Government. Anything so we can get out of it." [20] But the Government was not ready to take over the coal mines in 1933 any more than it was ready to take over the banks, or any more than it had been ready to keep the railroads in 1919. The New Deal, however, has greatly enlarged the reserves of trained personnel; the mobilization of industry through the War Production Board during the war provided more experience; and another depression would probably mean a vast expansion in government ownership and control. The private owners will not just submit to this. In panic, they will demand it.

It is plain today that Marx's method was often better than his own application of it. "From a method to an ideology," writes Silone, " . . . the decay of Marxism is comprised within these two terms." [21] Experience is a better master than any sacred myth. The experience of a century has shown that neither the capitalists nor the workers are so tough and purposeful as Marx anticipated; that their mutual bewilderment and inertia leave the way open for some other group to serve as the instrument of change; that when the politician-manager-intellectual type is intelligent and decisive, he can usually get society to move fast enough to escape breaking up under the weight of its own contradictions; but that, when no one provides intellectual leadership within the frame of gradualism, then the professional revolutionist will fill the vacuum and establish a harder and more ruthless régime than the decadent one he displaces; and that the Communist revolutionist is winning out over the fascist and today operates in alliance with an expanding world power committed to the destruction of democratic radicalism.

The failure of nerve is over. The new radicalism need not invoke Marx at every turn in the road, or point its prayer-rug every morning to Moscow. It has new confidence in its own insights and its own values. It has returned in great part to the historic philosophy of liberalism — to a belief in the integrity of the individual, in the limited state, in due process of law, in empiricism and gradualism. Man in its estimate is precious but not perfect. He is intoxicated by power and hence most humane in a society which distributes power widely; he is intimidated by industrialism and thus most secure in a society which will protect him from want and starvation. We conclude with Pascal: "Man is neither angel nor brute, and the unfortunate thing is that he who would act the angel acts the brute." [22]

As the old order crumbles through the world, we know that any path which can preserve peace and freedom is narrow and hazardous. Our instruments must be as precise as possible, our analysis as dispassionate, our conclusions as honest and objective as we can make them. One false step may plunge the world into atomic war or deliver it into totalitarian darkness. The new radicalism seeks to fight for honesty and clarity in a turbulent and stricken society, to restore a serious sense of the value of facts, of the integrity of reason, of devotion to truth. Its final success will depend upon its immediate success in shaping the policy of the only one of the two great powers accessible to it: the United States.

VIII

The Revival of American Radicalism

The equalitarianism of the Declaration of Independence was a spontaneous expression of the American experience. Life on the frontier was making the national character intolerant of classes in the social sense; and the rise of the city would gradually release the forces which would carry on the struggle against class domination in the economic and political spheres. Born in revolution, "conceived in liberty and dedicated to the proposition that all men are created equal," America from its beginning has charted its history and its politics by the morning star of equality.

The faith that all men were created equal brought with it two political premises: that all men were endowed with certain unalienable rights; and that, if government became destructive of those rights, it was "the right of the people to alter or to abolish it." Embodied in the more sober language of the Constitution, these premises assured, on the one hand, the freedom of the individual, and, on the other, the right of the people to control the political and economic life of the nation. These guarantees have become the basic premises of American democracy.

Critics of democracy have claimed to detect an inherent incompatibility in this marriage of majority rule and minority rights. Nor can it be said that our democratic philosophers have been at their most lucid on the point. Thomas Jefferson's formulation is typical. "Absolute acquiescence in the decisions of the majority," he said, was the "vital principle of republics" — but he then went on in the same address to add in apparent contradiction that the will of the majority, though "in all cases" to prevail, yet "to be rightful must be reasonable." A few lines later he even placed a whole category of rights out of reach of the majority for fear that the majority might destroy them. "The minority possess their equal rights . . . and to violate [them] would be oppression." [1]

The problem of reconciling majority rule with minority rights is, in terms of strict logic, insoluble. But the incompatibility exists much more in these terms than it does in the practice of society. For any logical decision in favor of majorities or of minorities would be fatal to free government. Jefferson's language, however distressing to logicians, expresses the deep and healthy instincts of a free people who require a margin for decision — a margin in which people, leadership and events can arrive at concrete solutions in concrete cases. The Declaration of Independence and the Constitution wove individual freedom into our democratic fabric; Alexander Hamilton and Andrew Jackson added the conception of the positive state. The result has been our success in preserving a system where, except for the Civil War, neither majorities nor minorities have been thwarted to the point of resorting to revolution.

Our democratic tradition has been at its best an activist tradition. It has found its fulfillment, not in complaint or in escapism, but in responsibility and decision. In times of crisis, as I mentioned earlier, those who believe deeply in freedom and democracy have generally provided truly national leadership. The Jacksonians were only the first, and the New Dealers the most recent, of a number of rescue parties which radicals have launched to save a beleaguered capitalism. At its best, our left has provided superb political leadership and broadly effective administrative management. It has twice led the nation victoriously, for example, through that most exacting of all tests, twentieth-century war.

Yet the very existence of this activist capacity — this appetite for decision and responsibility — has tended to split the left between those, like Jackson and Roosevelt, who regard liberalism as a practical program to be put into effect; and those, like the Doughface progressives, who use liberalism as an outlet for private grievances and frustrations. On the one hand are the politicians, the administrators, the doers; on the other, the sentimentalists, the utopians, the wailers. For the doer, the essential form of democratic education is the taking of great decisions under the burden of civic responsibility. For the wailer, liberalism is the mass expiatory ritual by which the individual relieves himself of responsibility for his government's behavior.

This split goes to the very heart of the liberal predicament. Where the doer is determined to do what he can

to save free society, the wailer, by rejecting practical responsibility, serves the purpose of those who wish free
society to fail — which is why the Doughface so often ends
up as the willing accomplice of Communism. A liberalism
which purports to shape a real world must first accept the
limitations and possibilities of that world. It must reconcile itself to a tedious study of detail — less gratifying perhaps than the emotional orgasm of passing resolutions
against Franco, monopoly or sin, but probably more likely
to bring about actual results. It must recognize that the
great decisions of public policy are not actor's poses, struck
with gestures for purposes of dramatic effect; they are
decisions made in practical circumstances with real consequences which cannot be separated from the meaning of
the decision. Life, in short, is not a form of political soap
opera: it is sometimes more complicated than one would
gather from the liberal weeklies.

We may feel the conflict between doer and wailer, New
Dealer and Doughface, to be relatively new. It is a conflict within each of us; and it is true that only recently have
we been forced to choose one side or the other; only recently has the rise of Communism transformed the wailer
from a harmless and often beguiling character to a poten-
tially sinister one. But the conflict is an old one — as real
in Jackson's day, for example, as in our own. It goes to
the essential question of different attitudes toward human
nature. For the Jackson-Roosevelt tradition of liberal
activism had its roots in a set of assumptions, conscious
and unconscious, about man; and these assumptions are
flatly denied or ignored by the Doughface progressive.

A century ago in America, men of good will, indifferent
to political and economic reform in the real world, dis-

dainful of pragmatic compromise, sought to transform society by fleeing from it into model communities. The Utopians believed man to be perfectible; and that radiant belief permitted some of them to slide over into the inevitable next step — that is, to believe that they, at least, were already perfect. Men in a conviction of infallibility can sacrifice humanity without compunction on the altar of some abstract and special good.

That tough-minded Jacksonian, Nathaniel Hawthorne, spent a few months at Brook Farm, the showpiece of the Utopians. After his departure he wrote *The Blithedale Romance*, perhaps the most brilliant of American political novels. Into this book he poured the invincible repugnance which a Jacksonian cannot but feel toward a Utopian, a New Dealer toward a Doughface. In Hollingsworth, the Utopian reformer, Hawthorne with the artist's prescience glimpsed the ultimate possibilities of a belief in perfectibility. He created a figure which the twentieth century recognizes more quickly than the nineteenth; we know him well from the pages of Koestler and the transcripts of the Moscow Trials.

Hollingsworth, Hawthorne wrote, had "a stern and dreadful peculiarity"; while avowing his love for humanity, he did not seem himself entirely human. "This is always true of those men who have surrendered themselves to an overruling purpose. It does not so much impel them from without, nor even operate as a motive power within, but grows incorporate with all that they think and feel, and finally converts them into little else save that one principle." When that happens, warns Hawthorne, avoid them like the plague. "They have no heart, no sympathy, no reason, no conscience. They will keep no friend, unless he make himself the mirror of their purpose; they will smite and slay you, and trample your dead corpse under foot, all the more readily, if you take the first step with them and cannot take the second, and the third, and every other step of their terribly strait path."

"They have an idol," Hawthorne continued, "to which they consecrate themselves high-priest, and deem it holy work to offer sacrifices of whatever is most precious; and never once seem to suspect — so cunning has the Devil been with them — that this false deity, in whose iron features, immitigable to all the rest of mankind, they see only benignity and love, is but a spectrum of the very priest himself, projected upon the surrounding darkness. And the higher and purer the original object, and the more unselfishly it may have been taken up, the slighter is the probability that they can be led to recognize the process by which godlike benevolence has been debased into all-devouring egotism." [2]

With his intense conviction of the weakness of man before the temptations of pride and power, Hawthorne extrapolated unerringly from the pretty charades of Brook Farm to the essence of totalitarian man. Yet during the next century the serene course of progress seemed to give little warrant to the violence of Hawthorne's political imagination. The insights into the egotism of power consequently vanished from the mind of the liberal intellectual.

In the placid years before the First War, sin was fading fast into the world of myth. "He moved with such assurance in the realms of light," Louis Jaffe has written of Louis D. Brandeis, "that darkness had ceased for him to be a living reality. The demonic depths and vast violence of men's souls were part of the historical past rather than the smouldering basis of the present. . . . Nothing in his system prepared Brandeis for Hitler." [3] Vernon L. Parrington, turning to *The Blithedale Romance*, found its sharp probings "thin and unreal"; "the figure of Hollingsworth," Parrington could remark with sarcasm, "is Hawthorne's reply to the summons of the social conscience of the times." [4]

Parrington evidently thought that in Hollingsworth Hawthorne was portraying a George Norris or a Bob LaFollette. We know today that he was portraying a Zhdanov. And if the Brandeises and the Parringtons were caught off guard, if nothing in their system prepared them for totalitarianism, how much more unprepared were the readers of the liberal weeklies, the great thinkers who sought to combat Nazism by peace strikes, the Oxford oath and disarmament, the ever hopeful who saw in Soviet Communism merely the lengthened shadow of Brook Farm! . . . This was in a real sense a *trahison des clercs*. For the politicians themselves retained an instinctive and hardy skepticism. Even the most guileless of our democratic leaders have had in their heart a searching doubt about human perfectibility — a conviction that every form of human power requires relentless correction. This, indeed, is the gusto of democracy, the underlying sense of comedy which brooks no worship of authority because it knows that no man is that good.

Communism has been the greatest threat, because Communism draped itself so carefully in the cast-off clothes of a liberalism grown fat and complacent, and because the disguise took in so many of the intellectuals. But John Taylor of Caroline had defined long ago the corrosive

skepticism of the American radical who will not be taken
in: "The hooks of fraud and tyranny are universally
baited with melodious words. . . . There is edification and
safety in challenging political words and phrases as traitors
and trying them rigorously by principles, before we allow
them the smallest degree of confidence. As the servants
of principles, they gain admission into the family, and
thus acquire the best opportunities of assassinating their
masters." [5] While the radical intellectual dallied with
Communism, the radical politician remained faithful to
democracy.

Eugene Debs, for example, had no use for the Communist Party, nor had Bob LaFollette. "I have not
sought, I do not seek, I repudiate the support of any advocate of Communism," cried Franklin D. Roosevelt at the
height of the period when Communists sought to trap
liberals in the steel embrace of the united front. "The
Soviet Union," he said, a few years later, "as a matter of
practical fact . . . is a dictatorship as absolute as any other
dictatorship in the world." [6] No important New Dealer,
except Wallace himself, was involved in the Wallace
movement. *

---

* With the partial exception of Mr. Tugwell, who appeared at the
Philadelphia convention, expressed himself unhappily afterward, and then
relapsed into silence. He took no active part in the campaign. He differed
from the Progressive Party on such crucial issues as the Marshall Plan;
and had long opposed the machinations of the Communists. When a
Puerto Rican political leader briefly collaborated with the Communists,
Tugwell accused him of extending "a dangerous tolerance . . . forgetting
that they had no directed interest in Puerto Rico but were only using
independence as a means of causing trouble for another 'capitalist' nation.
. . . In typical communist fashion they worked night and day, admitted
no scruples in making decisions and conducted themselves in ways which
indicated their contempt for such bourgeois concepts as promises and
contracts. . . . It was obvious that the *comunistas* were getting ready for

Today, finally and tardily, the skeptical insights are in process of restoration to the liberal mind. The psychology of Freud has renewed the intellectual's belief in the dark, slumbering forces of the will. The theology of Barth and Niebuhr has given new power to the old and chastening truths of Christianity. More than anything else, the rise of Hitler and Stalin has revealed in terms no one can deny the awful reality of the human impulses toward aggrandizement and destruction — impulses for which the liberal intellectual had left no room in his philosophy. The conceptions of the intellectual are at last beginning to catch up with the instincts of the democratic politician.

When the challenge of Communism finally forced American liberals to take inventory of their moral resources, the inventory resulted in the clear decision that freedom had values which could not be compromised in deals with totalitarianism. Thus America found itself reaching much the same conclusion as the non-Communist left of Europe. In the years after the Second War Americans began to rediscover the great tradition of liberalism — the tradition of Jackson and Hawthorne, the tradition of a reasonable responsibility about politics and a moderate pessimism about man. In January, 1947, New Dealers

the day when the party line of international communism would diverge from policies of the United States. In this there could be no doubt that we were developing a dangerous vulnerability." *The Stricken Land,* New York, 1946, pp. 568, 570. Yet, after the party line of international Communism had diverged from U.S. policies, Tugwell evidently allowed his old friend Henry Wallace to persuade him into lending a kind of support to the Progressives. Apparently Tugwell came himself to feel that Wallace was extending a "dangerous tolerance" and expressed fears that the "wrong people," might get control of the Progressive Party. When asked to identify the "wrong people," he replied enigmatically, "I certainly don't know whether they are Communists but they certainly act like them." *New York Times,* August 11, 1948.

like Eleanor Roosevelt, Wilson Wyatt, Leon Henderson
and Paul Porter united with moderate pessimists like
Reinhold Niebuhr, Elmer Davis and Marquis Childs to
form Americans for Democratic Action (ADA), a new
liberal organization, excluding Communists and dedicated to democratic objectives. The formation of ADA
marks perhaps as much as anything the watershed at
which American liberalism began to base itself once again
on a solid conception of man and of history.

The very necessities of foreign policy — the growing
necessity of checking Communism by developing some
constructive alternative — speeded the clarification of liberal ideas in 1947 and 1948. For the only realistic hope
for a bulwark against Communism in Europe lay in the
strengthening of the democratic socialists — a program
which could not but rouse the bitter opposition of the
Communists. Intelligent State Department officials saw
the point and were prepared to take the risk at a time
when too many liberals were still deluding themselves
with talk of Big Three unity. The State Department, indeed, was changing fast from the stodgy and inefficient
department of the thirties, which Americans had reason-
ably regarded as a refuge for effete and conventional men
who adored countesses, pushed cookies and wore hand-
kerchiefs in their sleeves. Even in the age of Cordell Hull
a new breed of American foreign servant had been in the
making — the modern professional diplomat, a close student of history and politics, convinced that the desire of
men for freedom and economic security may be as legitimate a factor in foreign affairs as strategic bases or the
investments of Standard Oil. The leader of this group

was Hull's highly able undersecretary, Sumner Welles —
a man who could regret that Rosa Luxemburg's friend
Karl Liebknecht had not been given the chance to organize
Germany, who regarded our attitude toward the Spanish
Civil War as "disastrous," and who was to be in private
life an influential supporter of the conception of the
Third Force.[7]

The mountaineer vindictiveness of Mr. Hull hampered
Welles's efforts and eventually drove him from the Department. But Welles was only the most prominent of a
new generation of foreign service officers. When James F.
Byrnes began to rid the Department of the hacks, the
bright younger men assumed new prominence. Byrnes,
Dean Acheson, his able undersecretary, and Benjamin V.
Cohen, the wise counselor of the Department, were quick
to grasp the character of the European problem and to
throw United States support to the forces of the center
and the non-Communist left. Byrnes was succeeded by
George C. Marshall, who had learned from bitter experience in China that United States interests could expect
very little more support from the reactionaries than from
the Communists. Marshall gave two of the ablest foreign-
service officers new positions of authority. Charles E.
Bohlen, a brilliant student of Russia, became counselor;
George Kennan headed the State Department's Policy
Planning Group.

Under Byrnes and Marshall the State Department began to understand the significance of the non-Communist
left. The very phrase, indeed, was reduced in the Washington manner to its initials; and the cryptic designation
"NCL" was constantly to be heard in Georgetown draw-

ing rooms.* The return to Washington of Averell Harriman as Secretary of Commerce strengthened the support for this approach: successive appointments in Moscow and London had fully educated Harriman to the difference between socialism and Communism. By 1948 the State Department could tell Congress that the socialists were "among the strongest bulwarks in Europe against Communism." [8]

This quiet revolution in the attitudes of the State Department was carried out in great part under the guns of the reactionary 80th Congress. It did not affect all State Department officials, especially some serving overseas; and it had no perceptible impact at all on the Department of Defense, which remained a citadel of the non-Communist right. But the State Department of 1949 had changed impressively from Hull's croquet-playing set of a decade earlier.

The emergence of the non-Communist left in Europe eventually had its effect even on the American labor movement. The American Federation of Labor, it is true, under the spur of David Dubinsky, had given generous help to the Socialist parties and free trade-union federations of Europe. But, at a time when young men in the State Department were puzzling how best to support the Third Force, the Congress of Industrial Organizations across the street in Lafayette Place remained apparently indifferent. Men like Walter Reuther and James B. Carey were trying to rally the CIO in support of European democracy, but their efforts for a long time ran head on into the Communist bloc. Indeed the success in immo-

---

* A full history of the NCL movement would have to include the key rôle of a brilliant Oxford don, Isaiah Berlin.

bilizing the CIO for three crucial years was one of the few Communist triumphs in post-war America. In the end, the successful fight against Communist influence, culminating in Reuther's victory in the United Auto Works and the discharge of Lee Pressman as CIO general counsel, brought the CIO side by side with the AF of L, ADA and the NCL group in the State Department in support of the Third Force in Europe.

The election of 1948 came as a culmination of these various tendencies in domestic and foreign policy. The American people voted with some definiteness against the restoration to power of the business community; at the same time, they repudiated the Wallace movement. America, in other words, was going left — but it was categorically a non-Communist left. The job of liberalism, in other words, was to devote itself to the maintenance of individual liberties and to the democratic control of economic life — and to brook no compromise, at home or abroad, on either of these two central tenets. The American liberal concluded by 1948 that man, being neither perfect morally nor perfect intellectually, cannot be trusted to use absolute power, public or private, either with virtue or with wisdom.

Some perceive dangers in these new directions of liberalism. It is argued that the abandonment of the old faith in the full rationality of man leaves no foothold short of authoritarianism. Yet is it not rather the belief in the perfectibility of man which encourages the belief that a small group of men are already perfect and hence may exercise total power without taint or corruption? It is a moderate pessimism about man which truly fortifies society against authoritarianism — because such pessimism must apply far more strongly to a special élite or a single party, exposed to the temptations of pride and power, than it does to the people in general. "Sometimes it is said that man cannot be trusted with the government of himself," Jefferson once wrote. "Can he, then, be trusted with the government of others? Or have we found angels in the forms of kings to govern him?" [9] We have found no angels, whether in form of kings, gauleiters or commissars; and we know too well what happens when mere humans claim angelic infallibility. Despotism is never so much to be dreaded as when it pretends to do good: who would act the angel acts the brute.

The people as a whole are not perfect; but no special group of the people is more perfect: that is the moral and rationale of democracy. Consistent pessimism about man, far from promoting authoritarianism, alone can inoculate the democratic faith against it. "Man's capacity for justice makes democracy possible," Niebuhr has written in his remarkable book on democratic theory; "but man's inclination to injustice makes democracy necessary." [10]

The image of democratic man emerges from the experience of democracy; man is a creature capable of reason and of purpose, of great loyalty and of great virtue, yet also he is vulnerable to material power and to spiritual pride. In our democratic tradition, the excessive self-love which transforms power into tyranny is the greatest of all dangers. But the self-love which transforms radicalism from an instrument of action into an expression of neurosis is almost as great a danger. If irresponsible power is the source of evil, and irresponsible impotence, the source of decadence, then responsible power —

power held for limited terms under conditions of strict accountability — is the source of wisdom.

It is in this spirit that American democracy faces the future. For the 1948 election solved nothing: it simply gave liberalism a new lease on power. The great challenge still lies ahead. Our industrial organization, as we have seen, overpowers man, unnerves him, demoralizes him. The problem remains of ordering society so that it will subdue the tendencies of industrial organization, produce a wide amount of basic satisfaction and preserve a substantial degree of individual freedom.

The campaign against social anxiety has just begun. Before American radicalism prosecutes it any further, it must come to terms with the two problems which have dogged and perplexed it throughout its history: the problem of the rôle of classes in politics; and the problem of the rôle of government in social planning.

In spite of the current myth that class conflicts in America were a fiendish invention of Franklin D. Roosevelt, classes have, in fact, played a basic part in American political life from the beginning. The founders of the republic construed politics automatically in terms of classes. No more magistral summation of the economic interpretation of politics exists than James Madison's celebrated Tenth Federalist Paper. "The most common and durable source of factions," Madison wrote, "has been the various and unequal distribution of property. . . . The regulation of these various and interfering interests forms the principal task of modern legislation." [11] The Founding Fathers disagreed, not over the reality of class conflict, but over its origin: whether, as Hamilton and John Adams claimed, it was the inevitable result of natural differences in the talents of man, or, as Jefferson and John Taylor of Caroline claimed, it was the result of unnatural tyrannies, imposed by fraud and maintained by force.

The extension of the franchise expelled class conflict as an element in conservative oratory, since there ceased to be political profit in proclaiming the exclusive virtues of a class which was an electoral minority. But the tradition of Jefferson and Jackson firmly anchored class conflict in radical democratic thought. "It is to be regretted, that the rich and powerful too often bend the acts of Government to their selfish purposes," said Jackson, " . . . when the laws undertake . . . to make the rich richer and the potent more powerful, the humble members of society — the farmers, mechanics, and laborers — who have neither the time nor the means of securing like favors to themselves, have a right to complain of the injustice of their Government." [12]

The fight on the part of the "humble members of society" against business domination has been the consistent motive of American liberalism. Far from importing subversive European ideas when he renewed this theme, Franklin Roosevelt was only returning to the political doctrine of the hallowed past. Nor is there anything specifically Marxist about class conflict. "As far as I am concerned," Marx himself wrote, "the honour does not belong to me for having discovered the existence either of classes in modern society or of the struggle between the classes. Bourgeois historians a long time before me expounded the historical development of this class struggle." "To limit Marxism to the teaching of the class struggle," added Lenin, "means to curtail Marxism — to distort it,

to reduce it to something which is acceptable to the bourgeoisie. A Marxist is one who *extends* the acceptance of
the class struggle to the acceptance of the *dictatorship of
the proletariat.*" [13] It is precisely this extension which
American radicalism has refused to make.

The problem of classes is this: Economic conflict is
essential if freedom is to be preserved, because it is the
only barrier against class domination; yet economic conflict, pursued to excess, may well destroy the underlying
fabric of common principle which sustains free society.

I cannot imagine a free society which has eliminated
conflict. So long as there is inequality in the distribution of property and variety in the nature of economic
interests, so long will politics center on economic issues;
and so long the insurgency of the discontented will
provide the best guarantee against the tyranny of the
possessors.

Yet this conflict must be kept within bounds, if freedom itself is to survive. The differences among classes in
a capitalist democracy are often wide and bitter; but they
are much less impassable than the differences between
capitalist democracy and authoritarianism; and sometimes
in the heat of the battle the warring classes tend to forget
their family relationship. It is perhaps fortunate for the
continuity of the American development that the Civil
War came along to heal the social wounds opened up in
the age of Jackson; that one world war closed the rifts
created by the New Freedom and another those of the
New Deal. But external war is an expensive means of
making antagonistic classes suddenly realize how much
their agreement outweighs their differences.

Britain has been more successful than the United States

in domesticating the class struggle. The British tradition of responsible conservatism has prevented the possessing classes from seeing national disaster in every trifling social reform; while British labor has itself developed a profound sense of national responsibility; and class conflict has consequently become more an instrument of national progress than one of national disruption. We desperately need in this country the revival of responsibility on the right — the development of a non-fascist right to work with the non-Communist left in the expansion of free society. Conservatism, if it is wise, will see in legitimate social protest, not the gratuitous mischief of agitators, but the sign of an evil to be corrected. "The more we condemn unadulterated Marxian Socialism," Theodore Roosevelt used to say, "the stouter should be our insistence on thoroughgoing social reforms." [14]

This means, in part, that a sense of humility is indispensable to democratic politics. The conservative must not identify a particular *status quo* with the survival of civilization; and the radical equally must recognize that his protests are likely to be as much the expressions of his own self-interest as they are of some infallible dogma about society. People who know they alone are right find it hard to compromise; and compromise is the strategy of democracy. The protagonists in the class conflict must be honest, responsible and, above all, humble, or at least liable to moods of humility.

In the last analysis, however, the best way to prevent class conflict from tearing society apart is to prevent classes themselves from rigidifying into castes. In the past our free economic system has kept our class structure relatively loose. Depressions have been the great leveler;

and shirtsleeves have often returned to shirtsleeves by the third generation. But the rise of corporate bigness has tended to give classes a greater fixity. Today we have ruled out depression as a proper means of speeding the circulation of the élites. It may well be that such present expedients as the widening of educational opportunity and the opening up of places for talent in such new industries as government and Hollywood will not be enough to stop the hardening into caste.

Here is one field which calls for bold and imaginative action. President Conant of Harvard has suggested that a genuine American radical "would use the power of government to reorder the 'haves and have nots' every generation to give flux to our social order." Why, for example, should the ownership of industry be passed on by nepotism or patronage and not according to managerial ability? The American radical, says Conant, "will be resolute in his demand to confiscate (by constitutional methods) all property once a generation. He will demand really effective inheritance and gift taxes and the breaking up of trust funds and estates. And this point cannot be lightly pushed aside, for it is the kernel of his radical philosophy." [15]

President Conant's proposal of government intervention to limit the right of inheritance places squarely before the radical his second problem: the rôle of the state. American democracy emerged in an age which had conquered freedom by limiting the power of the government; American radicalism itself was born in a specific revolt against arbitrary government. This experience had a traumatic effect on the early radicals. The state had given them, so to speak, a prenatal fright, and they never quite recovered. The Jeffersonians concluded with real feeling that the government was best which governed least.

The administration of Andrew Jackson was the first one to govern energetically in the interests of the people. But, in order to combat the power of concentrated wealth, Jackson was obliged to enlarge the power of the state. He was using these enlarged powers, he believed, to restore America to that condition of pristine innocence where Jeffersonian maxims would once more be dominant; but the effect of his administration was less to break up concentrated wealth than it was to strengthen government. Under the banner of anti-statism, Jackson made the state stronger than ever before.

He had no alternative. American anti-statism was the function of a particular economic order. Jefferson had dreamed of a nation of small freeholders and virtuous artisans, united by sturdy independence, mutual respect and the ownership of property. Obviously, strong government would be superfluous in Arcadia. But the Industrial Revolution changed all that. The corporation began to impersonalize the economic order. It removed the economy, in other words, from the control of a personal code and delivered it to agencies with neither bodies to be kicked nor souls to be damned. Impersonality produced an irresponsibility which was chilling the lifeblood of society. The state consequently had to expand its authority in order to preserve the ties which hold society together. The history of governmental intervention has been the history of the growing ineffectiveness of the private conscience as a means of social control. The only alternative is the growth of the public conscience, whose natural expression is the democratic government.

Alexander Hamilton and John Quincy Adams had conceived of the national government as a purposeful instrument of social progress. But the Whigs and Republicans of the middle period lacked the vision of their Federalist predecessors. The Democrats, for their part, remained under the spell of the Jeffersonian dream. Salvation continued to lie for them in the atomization of economic power, the reduction of government and the return to a self-winding economy. And, in the meantime, the social pressures for affirmative government, accumulating throughout the nation, placed politics in a state of precarious tension.

Theodore Roosevelt was the first modern statesman to note the spirit of irresponsibility which was suffusing industrial society and to call upon positive government to redress the balance. In so doing, he invoked the dream of the benevolent state; and he raised in opposition the last serious resurgence of Jeffersonianism. The campaign of 1912 set the Hamiltonian and Jeffersonian solutions of the social question in vivid contrast. The debate between the New Nationalism of Theodore Roosevelt and the New Freedom of Woodrow Wilson was conducted with uncommon brilliance. American radicals have never been able to decide which side was right.

Theodore Roosevelt, supported by Herbert Croly and Walter Lippmann, spoke for what he called the socialization of democracy. The Socialists, Roosevelt said, were right in regarding trusts as an inevitable stage in the history of capitalism. The competitive era had gone for good; and the only answer, Roosevelt felt, was an expansion of the powers of government to convert business consolidation into a force for the public welfare. Trust-

busting, T. R. said, is "madness. As a matter of fact, it is
futile madness. . . . It is preposterous to abandon all that
has been wrought in the application of the cooperative
idea in business and to return to the era of cut-throat
competition." As Croly put it, the philosophy of the
Sherman Anti-Trust Act operated as a "fatal bar" to effective national planning. [16]

The New Nationalism was a philosophy of limited collectivism. "Its advocates," said Croly, "are committed to
a drastic reorganization of the American political and economic system, to the substitution of a frank social policy
for the individualism of the past, and to the realization of
this policy, if necessary, by the use of efficient government
instruments." [17] The state should incorporate large corporations, regulate them by means of federal commis-
sions, tax their excessive profits and eventually move
toward public ownership of natural monopolies.

Against the New Nationalism, Woodrow Wilson un-
furled the Jeffersonian standard of the New Freedom.
Backed by Louis D. Brandeis and Robert M. LaFollette,
Wilson denied that trusts were inevitable or desirable;
bigness, as Brandeis said, was a curse; and the solution
lay in an unsparing policy of breaking up huge combinations. Wilson had no faith in the positive enlargement of
governmental functions. The rôle of government intervention was, not to plan for the general welfare, but to
roll back the trend of economic development from consolidation to competition.

Wilson's profound instinct for social freedom gave
emotional cogency to what was only a superficial economic
case against the trusts. Much of the corporate combina-

tion of the day, it is true, was produced, not by the technical necessities of large-scale production, but by the legerdemain of the bankers. Yet Roosevelt was surely right on the long-run tendencies. Large-scale business enterprise, for all its defects, has played an indispensable part in enabling capitalism to achieve its productive miracles. When Wilson was forced to suspend the anti-trust act in order to increase war production in 1917, Roosevelt could exult with some justice, "If the Sherman Law hurts our production and business efficiency in war time, it hurts it also in peace time, for the problems of boring for oil, of producing steel, manufacturing and selling agricultural implements, are no different." [18]

Still, a healthy political impulse underlay Wilson's opposition to the New Nationalism. The Wilsonians simply could not see how the enlarged state was to be kept out of the hands of the interests it was supposed to control; and they were at war with those interests. The basic contrast between Wilson and Roosevelt, indeed, was that Wilson's policies were *politically* the more radical, Roosevelt's *economically* the more radical.

Wilson contemplated what was in effect a crusade against big business on behalf of small business and labor. A Jacobin in his politics, he was prepared to whip up emotions against the existing order, but he had no notion of basic social change. He aimed at little except increased opportunities for the small entrepreneur. Roosevelt, on the other hand, contemplated an enormous increase in the power of the state over an increasingly centralized economy. He was laying the foundations for central economic planning and for the welfare state, and he hoped to maintain political freedom by such extreme devices as the recall of judges. But he relied too much on the painless conversion of the great capitalists to his program, overinfluenced perhaps by the dubious example of George W. Perkins. He was unwilling to stir up the anti-business emotions which alone would prevent his planned economic order from turning into a dictatorship of the trusts. To economic radicalism Roosevelt added political conservatism — a conservatism inadequately concealed by the apparent leftism of some of his political devices. To economic conservatism Wilson added political radicalism; and neither combination could solve the large questions of economic policy.

The New Deal drew from both the New Nationalism and the New Freedom. The National Recovery Administration period, for example, was straight out of Roosevelt and Croly, just as the Temporary National Economic Commission period was pure Wilson and Brandeis. Again each tactic demonstrated its limitations. NRA revealed the incredible difficulties of national regulation of business under capitalism. So long as a sense of emergency gave the public interest a chance to win out over special interests, NRA worked fairly well (as the War Production Board would work well a decade later). But, as the conviction of crisis receded, NRA was placed in an intolerable dilemma. The businessmen who staffed it tended increasingly to resolve their doubts in favor of business: and a business-dominated NRA looked more and more like the road to the corporate state. If, on the other hand, the New Dealers had made NRA decisions against the business community, a political storm would either have overthrown NRA or have forced the Government itself in self-defense to march even faster in the direction of statism.

The failure of NRA drove Franklin Roosevelt to the strategy of the New Freedom. If he could not socialize the spirit of business, then he would isolate business and frighten it into good behavior. It was a pragmatist's answer to an almost insoluble dilemma. If you permit business to combine, how can you prevent it from eventually taking over the government agencies set up to regulate the combination? And, if you try to break business down into competitive units, are you not trying to reverse an irreversible economic process? Roosevelt's solution was the TNEC tactic of using trust-busting not so much as an economic solution as a means of keeping big business off binges of restriction. At best, this program could not abolish monopoly but only persuade businessmen, if not to stay on the water-wagon, at least to restrain themselves to about a 3.2 per cent indulgence in monopolistic practices.

Both the New Nationalism and the New Freedom, it should be noted, enhanced the power of the state, the one by rolling out the carpet for new governmental functions, the other by letting them sneak in the back door. The New Deal completed the exorcism of Jeffersonian inhibitions about strong government, committing liberals ever after to the Hamilton-T. R. faith in the state as a necessary instrument of the social welfare. Yet the very growth of government contained dangers. As Franklin Roosevelt himself pointed out, "We have built up new instruments of public power. In the hands of a people's government this power is wholesome and proper. But in the hands of political puppets of an economic autocracy such power would provide shackles for the liberty of the people." [19]

But what alternative was there to the expansion of the state? The free market has been decreasingly the main theater of economic decisions. We are changing from a market society to an administrative society; and the problem is which set of administrators is to rule. If the basic decisions are to be made either in a directors' boardroom or in a government agency, then the political process permits us a measure of access, at least, to a government agency. Big government, for all its dangers, remains democracy's only effective response to big business — especially when big business behaves with such political recklessness as it has behaved in the United States.

Yet experience imposes very definite cautions with respect to the expansion of governmental power. The record of democratic socialism, for example, has already caused a retreat from the notion of government as a play-by-play planner — not only because of the temptations this rôle presents to a bureaucracy, but because total planners do not have the information or the wisdom to plan successfully. Socialist Britain, someone observed, is more planned against than planning. The consequence has been a revulsion against pinpoint planning, against direct, physical controls and detailed intervention in business decisions (save when emergency conditions, such as war or forced reconstruction, permit no alternative).

The lesson of the experiments with democratic socialism is plainly that the state should aim at establishing conditions for economic decisions, not at making all the decisions itself. It should create an economic environment favorable to private business policies which increase production; and then let the free market carry the ball as far as it can. * Keynes, not Marx, is the prophet of the new radicalism.

The function of the state, in other words, it to define the ground rules of the game; not to pitch, catch, hit homers or (just as likely) pop up or throw to the wrong base. The state may acquire total economic power for the most benevolent of motives; but benevolence is no guarantee of wisdom. The danger of the total planner is, first, that his almost inevitable blunders may convulse the entire economy, and, second, that in a panic-stricken effort to cover up his blunders he may multiply his controls till they destroy the initiative and free movement of men and finally the free play of political criticism.

The state can do a great deal to set the level of economic activity by policies which at once will be stable enough to create an atmosphere favorable to private investment and adequate consumption and effective enough to prevent economic breakdown. Keynes and his followers have pointed out the great resources of fiscal and monetary policy. When a sag in spending or in demand threatens the economy, then the government through tax reduction and compensatory spending can maintain high levels of employment and production. Taxation and subsidies can be potent means of directing private investment to under-developed industries and regions; and a whole range of general incentives can be used to draw labor and capital into socially beneficial undertakings.

In some cases, as in Britain, the state may well wish to take over basic industries in order to insure that enough

* "A Socialist Government cannot do everything. What it leaves to private enterprise should not be grudged and sabotaged, but encouraged and aided to reach the highest possible efficiency." G. Bernard Shaw, London *Times,* January 19, 1948.

steel, coal or power will flow to the economy. The United
States wisely nationalized the production of atomic energy;
President Truman has suggested the possibility of govern-
ment-owned steel mills; and the public interest is obviously paramount in such areas as conservation and river
development. The public sector of the economy through
the use of uniform accounting procedures can serve as a
competitive spur to the private sector (and vice versa).
And anti-trust action may still have its rôle: some British
Socialists today appear to be turning to it, not in the New
Freedom spirit of reversing the trend toward concentration, but in the New Deal spirit of scaring businessmen
out of the restrictive practices which often (but not always) accompany monopoly.*

In the meantime, society itself must be safeguarded
against the internal evils which would otherwise disrupt
it. Legislation has already imposed essential standards
for working conditions, wages and hours, the employment
of women and children, and so on. Another kind of legislation provides for insurance in case of accidents, sickness, unemployment or old age. We have far to go in the
direction of meeting equivalent standards in education,
housing and medical care; and the Government must step
in to make sure that these standards are high enough for

* The Union for Democratic Action London Letter, October 15, 1948,
quotes a Labour M.P. as saying, "We agree that the effect of trust-busting
in America isn't permanent. Broken apart, business interests tend to
combine again in other forms. It's like painting the Firth of Forth
bridge; no sooner do you finish at one end than you have to start again
at the other. But it's a lot worse not to paint the bridge at all. British
industry would be in a far healthier state today if there had been a
constant barrage of government prosecution and public condemnation of
trusts and combinations. Price rings and gentlemen's agreements have put
British industry to sleep. It's high time we woke it up."

a free people. This drive toward "social security" cannot, of course, be the heart of a radical program. Indeed, an obsession with security may well contain dangers for economic progress. Monopoly, for example, tends to sacrifice production to a sure profit margin; labor, by overdoing seniority rights and apprenticeship, can block the rise of talent; and excessive security for all, in the sense of the provision of comforts without work, may well result in social stagnation. Yet we are far indeed today from risking that result. It is hard to see that a federal program of hot lunches for school children or of medical aid for sick people is going to remove all incentives to economic progress. No one should be allowed to starve for lack of food, or die for lack of doctors; all children should be well and amply fed and educated: when we reach this stage of social security, then we can consider how much farther it is safe to go.

But the state must *not* place its main reliance on a static program of welfare subsidies. Nor should it put much stock in the interminable enterprise of government regulation — an enterprise which only intoxicates the bureaucrat, paralyzes the businessman, and too often ends in the capture of the regulatory agency by the interests to be regulated. The state should expend its main strength (1) in determining the broad level and conditions of economic activity through indirect means and (2) in making a success of projects clearly its own responsibility.

If the state must have the powers to avert economic collapse, where should they be located? Excessive centralization is obviously the great evil (next to giving the state no powers at all); the instruments of public power must not all be collected in a single hand. David Lilien-

thal's argument for the independence of the Tennessee
Valley Authority put the case for decentralization in
classic terms. The fact is that government ownership and
control can take many forms. Federal ownership can be
direct or (preferably) in the form of the independent
public corporation like TVA; and state and municipal
ownership can exist alongside it. The co-operative movement can be greatly expanded. And private ownership
will have an indispensable rôle: we talk at present about
setting up public plants to provide yardsticks for the
efficiency of private management, but in the future we
may wish to use the private plants as the yardstick. The
more varieties of ownership in the economy, the better.
Liberty gets more fresh air and sunlight through the inter-
stices of a diversified society than through the iron cur-
tain of totalitarianism. The recipe for retaining liberty
is not doing everything in one fine logical sweep, but
muddling through — a secret long known to the British
who, as D. W. Brogan has put it, "change anything except
the appearance of things." [20]

It would be imprudent for a non-economist to talk
about the details of economic policy. But there seems to
be no reason to despair over our technical capacity to stay
on an even keel. *Saving American Capitalism* (New York,
1948), a collection of essays edited by Professor Seymour
Harris, gives an exciting impression of the vitality of our
economy and of the strength and variety of tools in our
economic kit.

What is equally (or more) important is the vitality of
our political leadership. The Democratic Party has performed in recent years the astonishing feat of rejuvenating
itself while still in power. Ordinarily power chokes up

the paths of advancement within a party and causes an organizational hardening of the arteries. The Republican Party, when it went out of power in 1932, had such a bad case of arteriosclerosis that it did not begin to produce able younger leadership until 1938 — the year when Robert A. Taft was elected senator from Ohio, Harold Stassen became governor of Minnesota and Thomas E. Dewey had his first try for the governorship of New York.

But the Democratic Party in 1949 has not only its quota of New Deal veterans — such men as Leon Henderson, W. Averell Harriman, Benjamin V. Cohen, Dean Acheson, William O. Douglas, Adolf A. Berle, Jr. It also had a new generation of younger men, who either played minor rôles in the original New Deal or were unknown to Washington in those years and have risen to prominence since — Wilson Wyatt, Adlai Stevenson, Paul Porter, Hubert Humphrey, Chester Bowles, Mike Monroney, Paul Douglas, Clark Clifford. All this constitutes a reservoir of vigor and talent which is quite remarkable for a party in power as long as the current Democratic Party.

In addition, the rise of the politicalized labor leader introduces a new and possibly valuable element in American politics. Walter Reuther, the extraordinarily able and intelligent leader of the United Auto Workers, may well become in another decade the most powerful man in American politics. Yet political power will impose grave responsibilities on the trade-union movement. If labor uses power as unwisely as the business community has used it, its claims to political leadership will be rejected as firmly by the American people. But if labor accepts

the rôle of partnership in government and subordinates
its sectional demands to the public welfare, it may become as politically significant as the British Labour Party.
The great dilemma will come when irresponsible labor
leaders, like John L. Lewis, and the Communists whip up
the sectional demands against the national interest in
order to entice away the rank-and-file from the responsible leaders. This dilemma will put to test both the skill
and capacity of the Reuthers, Dubinskys, Murrays and
Rieves, and the maturity of the union member. It will
also test the responsibility of the business community;
for, if it can restrain itself from forcing the dilemma as
part of its own anti-union tactics, it will contribute in the
long run to the strength and stability of free society.

Our problem is not resources or leadership. It is primarily one of faith and time: faith in the value of our
own freedoms, and time to do the necessary things to save
them. To achieve the fullness of faith, we must renew
the traditional sources of American radicalism and seek
out ways to maintain our belief at a high pitch of vibra-
tion. To achieve a sufficiency of time, we must ward off
the totalitarian threat to free society — and do so without
permitting ourselves to become the slaves of Stalinism, as
any man may become the slave of the things he hates.

IX

The Techniques of Freedom

Free society cannot survive unless it defeats the problems of economic stagnation and collapse. But economic success can only create the conditions for the survival of freedom; it can make no guarantees. The preservation of freedom requires a positive and continuing commitment. Specifically the maintenance of the United States as a free society confronts the American people with an immediate responsibility in two areas in particular: civil rights and civil liberties.

The distinction between the two areas is worth understanding. "Civil rights" refers to issues of racial and religious discrimination. The federal civil rights acts after the Civil War defined the field, and the report of the President's Committee on Civil Rights has given this generation a clear and eloquent statement of our present achievements and obligations. It is an area, on the whole, better understood than that of "civil liberties" — a term which refers primarily to the freedoms of conscience and expression.

Most Americans accept, at least in principle, the obligations spelled out in the Civil Rights report. The strengthened civil rights plank in the Democratic platform helped President Truman win the election. Popular fiction and the movies, with *Kingsblood Royal* and *Gentleman's Agreement,* have enlisted in the battle against racism. Even the revolt of the southern governors against President Truman's request for civil rights legislation, if one is to judge by the subsequent election returns, signified temper tantrums rather than a cry of conscience against civil rights; for, where Truman and the neo-Confederate Thurmond were on the same ticket, Truman ran ahead almost two to one. This result suggests that the South on the whole accepts the objectives of the civil rights program as legitimate, even though it may have serious and intelligible reservations about timing and method.

The sin of racial pride still represents the most basic challenge to the American conscience. We cannot dodge this challenge without renouncing our highest moral pretensions. John Quincy Adams one hundred and thirty years ago called Negro slavery "the great and foul stain upon the North American Union." [1] We have freed the slaves; but we have not freed Negroes, Jews and Asiatics of the stigmata of slavery. While we may not be able to repeal prejudice by law, yet law is an essential part of the enterprise of education which alone can end prejudice. It may be foolish to think that we can transform folkways and eradicate bigotry overnight. But it is fatal not to maintain an unrelenting attack on all forms of racial discrimination.

For most Americans, certainly, the basic principles of civil rights are now clearly defined. The basic principles of civil liberties require equally clear definition — and they require, in addition, a considered redefinition in terms of the threats to free society presented by fascism and Communism.

First we must answer the question: what is our traditional doctrine of civil liberties? Too many Americans are indifferent to the very bases of our libertarian faith. In 1944, when the National Opinion Research Center asked Americans about the Bill of Rights, one out of four queried had never heard of this keystone of our freedoms and two of the other three could not identify it.

We had known better in 1789. With one war against arbitrary government fresh in memory, the American people could not see their way to accepting a new government without safeguards against despotism. So they insisted on a Bill of Rights — ten amendments defining their freedom against the state — as the price of ratifying the Constitution.

The first of these amendments set forth the fundamental liberties of conscience and expression in language no American should ever have forgotten: "Congress shall make no law respecting an establishment of religion, or prohibiting the free exercise thereof; or abridging the freedom of speech, or of the press; or the right of the people peaceably to assemble, and to petition the government for a redress of grievance." Other articles of the Bill of Rights laid down guarantees against indiscriminate arrest, drumhead trial and military rule. Three

amendments adopted after the Civil War completed the
constitutional basis for our liberties: the Thirteenth,
abolishing slavery; the Fourteenth, forbidding states to
deprive persons of life, liberty or property "without due
process of law"; and the Fifteenth, affirming the right to
vote regardless of race, color or previous condition of
servitude.

Building on these constitutional foundations, the
American people have erected through the years a structure of freedom. It has not been so much our idealism
which has given that structure strength as it has been the
remorse which has followed our occasional betrayal of
idealism. For we have committed in our history many
crimes against freedom. There may always have seemed
good reason at the time for these crimes; but after a
while the reasons have faded away, and in their place has
come a deep sense of guilt. The result of each crime
against freedom has been to make it harder for the people
to destroy freedom in the next age of fright and hysteria.

The first cold war in our history produced the first
excesses and the first repentance. In the wake of the unde-
clared hostilities against France in 1798 came the notorious
Alien and Sedition Acts.* The Alien Act gave the Federalist administration power to deport foreigners considered dangerous to national security. The Sedition Act
punished persons who published writings with the intention of defaming the executive or Congress. Many citizens
were arrested under the second act, and ten were actually
convicted. A New Jersey editor, for example, was fined

---

* Professor Zechariah Chafee's great book *Free Speech in the United States*, Cambridge, 1941, is the fundamental source for any discussion of this question. For the Alien and Sedition Acts, see pp. 27 ff.

$100 for hoping in print that the wad of a cannon fired in a presidential salute might hit President John Adams on the seat of his pants. A Vermont Jeffersonian, who accused the President in a campaign speech of "unbounded thirst for ridiculous pomp, foolish adulation, and a selfish avarice," received a thousand dollar fine and four months in jail. A free people obviously could not long endure such laws, and Adams was beaten in the next election.

Each new martyr to freedom increased the national determination to protect nonconformity in the future. Often martyrdom came in a fight against respectability, very often in a fight against the business community. Yet subsequent generations tended to honor the victim and not the mob. Elijah Lovejoy, a humble printer of Alton, Illinois, affronted the conservative opinion of his day by advocating the abolition of slavery. Twice pro-slavery gangs destroyed his printing presses; and each time the Ohio Anti-Slavery Society sent another. When a third press was smashed, Lovejoy resolved that he would defend the next one to the end. On the night of November 7, 1837, pro-slavery toughs rushed the warehouse where Lovejoy's new press lay under abolitionist guard. Someone put a torch to the warehouse. Lovejoy, running to put the fire out, was shot down in his tracks.

Lovejoy was not the first or last American to be murdered for the crime of unpopular opinions. In 1886 someone, never identified, threw a bomb at a phalanx of policemen who were breaking up an orderly strike meeting in Haymarket Square, Chicago. Seven local anarchists were promptly arrested, though not one could be shown to have had any connection with the bomb and some were not even in the square at the time. All were sentenced to death. One killed himself, and four were hanged. Governor Altgeld of Illinois a few years later pardoned the two remaining in face of a storm of public disapproval. But by 1948 even Republican Governor Dwight Green of Illinois would be among those who gathered to do Altgeld honor.

The great national nightmare — the one from which the American people woke up with the deepest sense of horror — was the witch-hunt staged by Attorney General A. Mitchell Palmer after the First War. The Espionage Act of 1917 and the Alien Act of 1918 had given the Government broad powers to arrest persons whose offenses might range all the way from treason down to grumbling. During the war these laws were applied, to put it mildly, with sternness. Rose Pastor Stokes, for example, received a ten-year jail sentence for writing in a letter, "I am for the people, and the government is for the profiteers." [2] Men were thrown in jail for hot words overheard in trains, in hotel lobbies or even around the dinner table in the boarding house.

But the forces of repression were just warming up. By 1919, with the war over, A. Mitchell Palmer saw the opportunity of making a political career out of post-war anxieties. While Wilson lay ill in the White House, Palmer detonated the famous Red Scare. As the Attorney General, struggling in the grip of metaphor, described the situation a few months later, "Like a prairie-fire, the blaze of revolution was sweeping over every American institution of law and order a year ago. It was eating its way into the homes of the American workman, its sharp tongues of revolutionary heat were licking the altars of the churches, leaping into the belfry of the school bell, crawl-

ing into the sacred corners of American homes, seeking
to replace marriage vows with libertine laws, burning up
the foundations of society."

It is hard to do justice in brief space to the permutations
and vagaries of the Palmer terror. He liked to work in
large magnitudes, and scorned what he called the "nice
distinctions drawn between the theoretical ideals of the
radicals and their actual violations of our national laws." [3]
Unpopular ideas were his target, not illegal acts. At one
moment in 1919, he herded together 249 aliens, without
benefit of court trial, and shipped them off summarily to
Russia. On New Year's Day, 1920, he conducted simul-
taneous raids on radical centers through the country, sent
his agents into homes, with or without warrants, to seize
persons and property, and crowded the jails with the desperate characters trapped in his dragnet.

The mass raid hardly lived up to advance notices.
Palmer captured over four thousand presumably sinister
individuals, but only three revolvers and no dynamite at
all — not quite the raw material for the great conspiracy.
Yet his alarming noises did succeed in spreading a con-
tagion of fear. In Hartford, Connecticut, for example,
all visitors at the jail inquiring after friends caught in the
raid were themselves arrested on the ground that this
solicitude was prima facie evidence of Communist affilia-
tion. The result through the country was the rise of
vigilantism — that is, of minor officials or private persons
bent on assuming for themselves the prerogatives of trying,
convicting and punishing unpopular characters. In the
trail of Palmer came months of panic, intolerance and
repression.

A week after Palmer's raid, the speaker of the New York

State Assembly urged his colleagues to expel its five
Socialist members. The Socialist Party had opposed the
war, it should be noted, but no one had objected to ten
Socialists sitting in the Assembly in 1918. Moreover, these
men were Socialists, not Communists, and included such
bitter anti-Communists as Louis Waldman, the New York
labor lawyer. Yet, over the indignant and shocked protests of such conservatives as Charles Evans Hughes, the
Assembly actually purged itself of the wicked five.

A lingering death spasm of the Palmer hysteria caught
two more anarchists in Massachusetts. Sacco and Vanzetti,
shoemaker and fish-peddler, falling afoul of a prejudiced
judge and an inflamed public opinion, were assassinated
by the Commonwealth with solemn legal trappings. Governor Robert Bradford, lacking the courage of an Altgeld
or even of a Dwight Green, rejected in 1947 a memorial
plaque for Sacco and Vanzetti; some future governor will
repair his error.

Sanity eventually returned. President Harding freed
Eugene Debs, who had been condemned to Atlanta for ten
years for violating the Sedition Act. Second-class mailing
privileges were restored to left-wing magazines. After a
period dissent was able to raise its head again in the
United States. Americans, as usual, hated themselves in
the morning and looked back to A. Mitchell Palmer with
shame and incredulity.

This has been the historical pattern: hysteria, repression
and remorse. It is this experience which, crystallized by
the Supreme Court, has issued in our principles of civil
freedom. For in our system it is the Supreme Court which
must finally draw the line between the conflicting claims
of free speech and of public security — to determine who

should receive the protection of the First Amendment, when and why. A man was once arrested, according to a favorite civil liberties story, for swinging his arms and hitting another man in the nose. He asked the judge if he did not have a right to swing his arms in a free country. "Your right to swing your arms ends," said the judge, "where the other man's nose begins." The problem of judicial determination is always delicate and always in terms of specific cases; but the broad lines of judicial principle have great influence on society.

Thus decisions of the Supreme Court have marked the great advances — and the great setbacks — in the struggle for freedom. It was the Supreme Court which after the Civil War eviscerated the Fourteenth Amendment, struck down the basic civil rights statute and helped make America safe for Jim Crow. And it was the Supreme Court too which immeasurably strengthened the Bill of Rights half a century later by ruling that the First Amendment restrained, not just the federal Government, but the states also from curtailing civil liberties; such liberties, the Court said, were part of the "due process of law" imposed on state governments by the Fourteenth Amendment.

The first test in the Supreme Court's attitude toward curtailment of free speech is consequently that of "due process of law" — the guarantee, that is, of substantive legal rights and of fair and orderly judicial procedure. This requirement assures each individual of the full support of the Anglo-Saxon tradition of *personal* justice. It is of the essence of the institutions of liberty, as Charles Evans Hughes declared in comment on the New York Socialist case, that "guilt is personal and cannot be attributed to the holding of opinion or to mere intent in the absence of overt acts." [4]

The second requirement emerged in 1919, when the Court considered the case of a man named Schenck who had distributed circulars urging resistance to the draft. Justice Oliver Wendell Holmes, regarding Schenck's act as a direct provocation to disobey the law, sustained the conviction for a unanimous court. But in the course of his opinion he strove to set some limits on repressive action. The right to free speech in the First Amendment, he said, was not absolute. The most stringent protection would not protect a man who shouted fire in a crowded theater. Yet the test always had to be whether the words created "a clear and present danger" — a danger, that is, of bringing about overt acts in violation of law.

The Court did not immediately accept Holmes's test. But in a series of great dissents, which have since become majority doctrine, Holmes and Justice Louis D. Brandeis clarified the meaning of clear and present danger. "Those who won our independence," wrote Brandeis in his eloquent concurrence in *Whitney vs. California*, " . . . believed that freedom to think as you will and to speak as you think are means indispensable to the discovery and spread of political truth; that without free speech and assembly discussion would be futile; that with them, discussion affords ordinarily adequate protection against the dissemination of noxious doctrine. . . . If there be times to expose through discussion the falsehoods and fallacies, to avert the evil by the processes of education, the remedy to be applied is more speech, not enforced silence. Only an emergency can justify repression." [5] When Charles Evans Hughes became Chief Justice, the Court went over to the "clear and present danger" doctrine. It has remained there ever since.

What does "clear and present danger" mean? It does not mean the clear and present danger of a minority's persuading the nation of evil views through the democratic process. "Congress certainly cannot forbid all effort to change the mind of the country," said Holmes.[6] The danger was the danger of what Holmes called "substantive evils" — that is, of *acts* in violation of law, and especially acts which will destroy the whole climate of reason and discussion. Hence the example of shouting fire in a crowded theater: the state of tension is such that no one will wait quietly in his seat to hear those who would argue that, on the contrary, there is no fire.

Acts, not *thoughts.* "The wide difference between advocacy and incitement, between preparation and attempt, between assembling and conspiracy, must be borne in mind," warned Brandeis. "In order to support a finding of clear and present danger it must be shown either that immediate serious violence was to be expected or was advocated, or that the past conduct furnished reason to believe that such advocacy was then contemplated." [7]

We must tolerate dangerous opinions, Holmes and Brandeis were saying, even when their eventual tendency, should they win out by democratic methods, would be to extinguish freedom. But we must draw the line at opinion which results in the immediate and violent obliteration of the conditions of subsequent free discussion.

This is the traditional American answer to those who say that people who would destroy liberty for others should have none of their own. This tolerance does not come, I believe, from foolishness or decadence. It comes partly from our conviction that a free people will never vote for totalitarianism — that, so long as the climate of freedom is preserved, we do not need to worry about totalitarian ideas winning out by democratic methods. And it comes partly too from a hardboiled reading of our own experience: the curtailment of civil liberties in advance of any "clear and present danger" has simply given overwhelming power to the champions of the existing order — whether the cop on the corner, the local businessman or political boss, or the Attorney General of the United States.

New ideas may become the next generation's platitudes, but they always strike someone as dangerous at the time. This is particularly true in a country where the intellectual atmosphere of conservatism is dominated by a plutocracy. It was the shock that sheer novelty has for the American reactionary which provoked Justice Holmes's classic reminder: "It is only the present danger of immediate evil or an intent to bring it about that warrants Congress in setting a limit to the expression of opinion. . . . When men have realized that time has upset many fighting faiths, they may come to believe even more than they believe the very foundations of their own conduct that the ultimate good desired is better reached by free trade in ideas — that the best test of truth is the power of the thought to get itself accepted in the competition of the market, and that truth is the only ground upon which their wishes safely can be carried out. That, at any rate is the theory of our Constitution."

This theory, Holmes conceded, was an experiment, as all life was an experiment. Every year we wager our salvation upon some prophecy based on imperfect knowledge. But "while that experiment is part of our system I think that we should be eternally vigilant against attempts to

check the expression of opinions that we loathe and believe to be fraught with death, unless they so imminently
threaten immediate interference with the lawful and
pressing purposes of the law that an immediate check is
required to save the country." [8]

Due process of law and *the clear and present danger*
test thus constitute the framework of freedom secured by
our ancestors and ratified by the Supreme Court. This
framework has been adequate for past problems of civil
liberties. But today the rise of fascism and of Communism
has given the issue of civil liberties a new and difficult
form. We are not just confronted with unpopular
opinions, with eccentrics, zealots or bigots, with the
fantasies of A. Mitchell Palmer's deranged imagination. We are confronted with the spread of a ruthless totalitarianism abroad and with the propagation
of opinions at home which may well undermine our
own faith and sap our capacity to resist foreign tyranny.
A fanatical minority is engaged in a cruel conspiracy to
end forever the whole conception of a society based on
free discussion. Is there not some point in advance of
"clear and present danger" where free society must draw
the line if it is to preserve its own inner moral strength?

This condition gave rise a few years ago to an attempt
to overhaul the traditional civil liberty doctrine. Some
leading liberals were in the forefront of the enterprise; and
they concentrated on reversing both items in the traditional framework of freedom. O. John Rogge led the
attack on the doctrine of personal guilt, demanding in its
place a much extended doctrine of conspiracy in which
guilt by association would play a conspicuous rôle. Max
Lerner led the attack on the Holmes-Brandeis test of

"clear and present danger." These critics argued that in an age of fifth columns, psychological war and mass espionage, the traditional civil liberty doctrine only tied the hands of democracy. "It is becoming increasingly clear," Lerner wrote, "that the government which waits until propaganda has reached the point of clearly threatening the immediate survival of the nation is likely to wait until it is too late, and will probably never have the strength to strike when the time comes." The methods of totalitarianism had rendered the traditional doctrines of free society obsolete. "I am increasingly convinced," observed Lerner in concluding a powerful assault on the Holmes-Brandeis doctrine, "that a realistic legal policy would modify the 'clear and present danger' doctrine in the direction of an 'intellectual trading with the enemy' standard, which sought to find substantial propaganda connections with the enemy and the existence of an actual intent to play the enemies' propaganda game." [9] As a writer in the *Nation* recently summed up the new philosophy: "The classic view that traitorous conduct consists chiefly in selling military secrets to the enemy is philosophically, morally and legally inadequate." [10]

Clearly the neo-liberal critics of Holmes were demanding a basic reformulation of our civil liberties policy. The reformulation was precipitated, of course, by the threat of Nazism. Yet consistency required that it apply to all forms of totalitarianism. Under its influence, liberals sat by and applauded while a wildly expanded doctrine of conspiracy ran beserk under Rogge's guidance in the fantastic mass sedition trial of 1944–45. A few years later, the Department of Justice, preparing its brief against the Joint Anti-Fascist Refugee Committee for its refusal to open its records to the Un-American Activities Committee, would cite Lerner among its authorities. Indeed, a more unscrupulous régime might achieve interesting results by employing Rogge's 1944 methods against his present associates.

What have been the consequences in a time like the present of replacing "personal guilt" by "guilt by association" and of letting the "clear and present danger" test retreat before an "intellectual trading with the enemy" standard? * Our age combines the differing anxieties which produced the respective excesses of 1798 and 1920; we suffer from the hangover of a hot war, while we are presently engaged in a cold war, and the toll on the nerves is tremendous. We stand, in other words, in the precise situation where excess has led to repentance before; and the departure from "personal guilt" and "clear and present danger" invites excess today.

The immediate result, of course, has been to transfer attention from *acts* to *thoughts*. Unpopular ideas and organizations become the quarry. People who hounded the intellectual fellow travelers of fascism must not be surprised to find other people invoking their same principles in order to hound the intellectual fellow travelers of Communism. The consequent uproar darkens the whole climate of free discussion — that climate which a democracy requires for responsible decision.

* I do not mean, of course, to blame Lerner and Rogge for the present-day excesses of the anti-liberal witch-hunters. Mr. Lerner, for example, has made abundantly clear his essential devotion to the "clear and present danger" doctrine. But the critics of this doctrine have certainly contributed to the popular confusion over the basic civil liberties principles. The attempt to suspend our traditional guarantees in dealing with the fascists, however commendable in motive, has resulted in a dilution of our libertarian philosophy.

The performance of the House Committee on Un-American Activities, for example, has shown clearly the dangers to civil freedom of a promiscuous and unprincipled attack on radicalism. The fact that late in 1948, after sowing confusion and slander for more than a decade, the Committee finally found some valuable information in a pumpkin should blind no one to the reckless accusations and appalling procedures which have characterized its career,* nor to the unlovely progeny it has spawned in the form of similar local committees in California, Washington, Michigan and other states.

* I am not, of course, questioning congressional rights of investigation and exposure; but the abuse of these rights by the Un-American Activities Committee has done much to discredit one of democracy's most valuable instruments. It is hard to decide which of the many wretched acts committed by this committee and its various chairmen has been most shocking. The moral presumption of J. Parnell Thomas is exceedingly hard to take; after many months of hectoring witnesses, and, in one case, helping to precipitate a fatal heart attack, Thomas was finally indicted for a particularly mean and nasty attempt to defraud the federal government. But the most extravagant act was probably the one committed by Representative Karl Mundt of South Dakota. A few hours after the death of Laurence Duggan by a fall from a skyscraper window, Mundt called a midnight press conference and declared that Isaac Don Levine had quoted Whittaker Chambers as charging that Duggan, a former State Department official, had given him secret documents. When asked whether he planned to release the names of other officials accused of espionage, Mundt made the reply, "We will give out the other names as they jump out of windows." (*Christian Science Monitor,* December 22, 1948.)

Mundt apparently did nothing to check Levine's alleged statement with Chambers before smearing a dead man. He might have had to miss the morning editions. The next day Chambers denied ever having received papers from Duggan. Levine subsequently stated, "I never reported Mr. Chambers as having charged Mr. Duggan with transmitting confidential papers." (*Plain Talk,* February, 1949.) Mundt later said, "I do not regard this action as a blunder and I have no regrets." (*New York Herald Tribune,* December 23, 1948.)

The impact of these committees and of their amateur imitators can be seen most clearly in the field of education, which is one of the weakest links in the defense of free discussion. The press, on the whole, can take care of its own freedom. Freedom of assembly can be denied ordinarily only at the cost of publicity and scandal (though insignificant minorities are sometimes solicitously denied facilities by local authorities because of fire hazards and the like — even if, as Professor Chafee has observed, it might seem "more natural to protect one's friends from conflagrations and collapsing floors than one's enemies"). Attacks on academic freedom, however, rouse no well-organized pressure group; the teachers themselves, who are too impotent to win their profession a living wage, can be kicked around with impunity.

As a consequence, some universities have been increasingly hard put to defend the right of professors to hold unpopular ideas. The Universities of Wyoming, Texas and Washington and Olivet College, for example, have all recently suffered crude investigations by ill-informed trustees or bullheaded legislators, who wish to subject the teaching staff to political saliva tests. Even in Massachusetts, a Republican attorney-general named Clarence Barnes, a kind of road-company A. Mitchell Palmer, was able to propose repressive legislation of a vicious type which it required the considerable efforts of President Conant of Harvard and President Karl Compton of Massachusetts Institute of Technology to defeat. And colleges and universities are in a better position to defend themselves, of course, than the secondary and elementary schools.

Once the atmosphere of hysteria is ignited, the most

dubious creatures rush to exploit the honest fears of decent Americans. The recent textbook witch-hunt provides an edifying example. In August, 1947, on the letterhead of an organization calling itself the National Economic Council, Inc., a man named Merwin K. Hart wrote to every member of the boards of trustees of colleges using *Elements of Economics,* an economic text written by Professor Lorie Tarshis of Stanford University. An enclosed review denounced the book for its exposition of the doctrines of Lord Keynes and identified Keynesianism as a form of Marxism.

Hart's letter had an immediate effect. Organizations of small businessmen passed resolutions in his support. Trustees and alumni wrote outraged letters to college presidents. Yet who was Merwin K. Hart? His record had long been known to students of the American proto-fascist demi-monde. He revealed his own notions of Americanism some months later when, in a speech before Harvard's Free Enterprise Society, he inveighed against the Marshall Plan and "the international Jewish group which controls our foreign policy." [11] And, at the height of Hart's campaign, the ideas of Keynes were under equally brutal and ignorant attack from another source: that is, from the Communists themselves. "Keynesism," wrote William Z. Foster, "collides with Marxism at every point." [12] Foster and Hart, in fact, agreed in objecting not only to Keynes but to such proposals as the Marshall Plan as well; by the kind of reasoning Hart uses on other people, he should have had to classify himself as a Moscow agent.

Fortunately enough college presidents knew Hart's record to stand up courageously to the uproar. Dr. A. I. Strand of Oregon State College wrote bluntly to Hart:

"Your hands are dirty and you smell of foul associations, and now you have the effrontery to set yourself up as the protector of American youth! A greater insult to education has never come to my attention." The American Economic Association eventually appointed a special committee to deal with the attacks on the Tarshis book and on other economic texts.[13]

The issue is more fundamental than simply the fatuousness of mistaking Keynes for Karl Marx. If all Communism meant was deficit financing, then it would be hard to persuade anyone that it was very terrible. A genuinely Communistic textbook would be unacceptable for its distortions of fact, as a Communist teacher, who imported his party views into the classroom, would be an incompetent teacher. The deeper issue is the freedom of the teacher to teach his subject according to his most responsible understanding of it, and not according to the ukase of a board of trustees, a legislature, a political party or a foreign country.

President Conant has well said that unmolested inquiry is essential: "on this point there can be no compromise even in days of an armed truce." The fight to maintain freedom of discussion, Conant adds, will not be easy. "Reactionaries are going to use the tensions inherent in our armed truce as an excuse for attacking a wide group of radical ideas and even some which are in the middle of the road." But a free society must dedicate itself to the protection of the unpopular view. "Those who worry about radicalism in our schools and colleges are often either reactionaries who themselves do not bear allegiance to the traditional American principles or defeatists who despair of the success of our own philosophy in an open competition." They fail to recognize, Conant observes, "that diversity of opinion within the framework of loyalty to our free society is not only basic to a university but to the entire nation. For in a democracy with our traditions only those reasoned convictions which emerge from diversity of opinion can lead to that unity and national solidarity so essential for the welfare of our country." [14]

Conant makes here, I believe, the basic point. Popular ignorance about civil liberties is jeopardizing free discussion for everybody. It is threatening to turn us all into frightened conformists; and conformity can lead only to stagnation. We need courageous men to help us recapture a sense of the indispensability of dissent, and we need dissent if we are to make up our minds equably and intelligently. For freedom of discussion is an organic part of the process by which a democracy wins consent for its great decisions. No surgery can amputate it without crippling the system.

Hysteria is thus a useful secret weapon for the enemies of free society. That is why the Communists in America sought the passage of the Mundt-Nixon bill. That is why they are doing all they can to exacerbate public opinion, to prefabricate martyrs, and to inflame the atmosphere to the boiling point. That is why, too, all believers in free society must unite in vigorous support of free speech. On the old Court, Holmes, the Yankee aristocrat who believed that man should be free to act as foolishly as he could, and Brandeis, the Jewish crusader who believed that man should be free to act as wisely as he might, stood shoulder to shoulder in this issue. The responsible conservatism of Holmes, Hughes and Stimson must be reaffirmed against the corrupt conservatism of the Mundts and Thomases;

just as the principled liberalism of Brandeis, of the American Civil Liberties Union and Americans for Democratic Action, must be reaffirmed against the corrupt liberalism which favors freedom only for its friends.* The non-Communist left and the non-fascist right must collaborate to keep free society truly free.

* Mr. Wallace's design for liberty emerges from his public statements with rather disturbing clarity. Free speech evidently means to him his own right to denounce all who disagree with him as warmongers or fascists; Mrs. Roosevelt, for example, can be called by innuendo a spiritual descendant of the Cliveden set. But "red-baiting" — i.e., criticism of Communists — Wallace has declared to be a "criminal" practice (in his article "What is Liberalism?" *New York Times,* April 18, 1948) — which can only mean that he believes red-baiting should be punished as a crime. How then does Wallace's conception of free speech differ from that of Dimitrov or Stalin? Indeed, one can well imagine what kind of "sedition trial" O. John Rogge might be conducting today if fortune had made him Wallace's attorney general.

As for the American Communists, they, like their comrades everywhere in the world, seem to have dedicated themselves to the extinction of free discussion *to the limits of their power.* Where their power is limited, as in the United States, they are compelled to restrict their repression to their own party and fellow traveler circles and to a few rare public occasions when they think they will have opinion on their side (as in the Communist-inspired raid on a Gerald L. K. Smith meeting in Boston in the summer of 1947). Does anyone except Mr. Wallace believe that, if the Communists had the power, they would not extend their Boston tactics and smash all opposition?

The concern of the CPUSA for "free speech" is, of course, a concern for their own continued power to agitate. American Communists heartily supported the Smith Act when it was used against Trotskyites and against Nazi sympathizers; now that the same act is being turned against themselves, they suddenly discover it to be unconstitutional. In making this discovery, they commit themselves to views of democracy which reveal their utter cynicism. "In order to realize democracy," the Communists say, "it is essential that the minds of the people remain wholly independent of the government itself. For if the government can direct or control or, by coercive methods, influence the popular judgment, ultimate political power has in essence been transferred from the people themselves to the government . . . and the essential basis of democracy has thus been lost." ("From the Briefs on the Unconstitutionality of the Smith Act," *Political Affairs,* November, 1948.) Has the author of these stirring lines ever tried to apply them to the Soviet Union?

In the long run, hysteria will be fatal to the vitality of our free institutions. The theory of American society has been the theory of ever-expanding opportunity — opportunity for new men, new enterprise, new ideas. If we limit that opportunity, we may kill off those traits of daring and initiative which have made our nation great. Our personal freedoms are the lifeblood of free society. Cut off the flow, and the organism cannot function. That is the price we would pay for a course of repression.

Need we pay that price? Would the revival of personal guilt and of the "clear and present danger test" in full force expose the nation to grave harm? Is there anything to justify those who have lost faith in the methods of freedom? Quite the contrary. It was plainly demonstrated in the United States between 1946 and 1948 that the Communists could be whipped — in the labor movement, in the liberal movement, in the veterans' movement, in the political world — by the traditional democratic methods of debate, identification and exposure. If we can defeat Communism as a political force within the framework of civil liberties, why abandon that framework? There is no "clear and present danger" resulting from the political agitation of Communism which cannot be handled by constitutional methods. And there is a "clear and present danger" that anti-Communist feeling will boil over into a vicious and unconstitutional attack on nonconformists in general and thereby endanger the sources of our democratic strength.

We must not underestimate the awful potentialities of totalitarian conspiracy. We must be prepared to recognize the stage of "clear and present danger"; we must act swiftly if that stage should come. But here again the

Holmes-Brandeis test supplies the safest answer. A democracy in punishing efforts at persuasion punishes itself. But a democracy has the obligation to protect itself against hostile acts — against "substantive evils," whether espionage, violence or incitement, and against the individuals who contrive these evils.

Mr. Wallace and the Communists, for example, had every right to agitate against the Marshall Plan. But, now that it is enacted, attempts to obstruct its working must be punished. Mr. Wallace and the Communists had every right to oppose the restoration of selective service, along with many thousands of non-Communist Americans. But, when Congress restored it, those who urged specific resistance to the draft were liable to arrest. The third party and the Communists had the right of political action; but if the CPUSA organizes action committees which roam the streets on the model of eastern Europe, breaking up non-Communist meetings and beating up non-Communists, the Government must act vigorously in defense of the civil liberties of others.

We should stick to the last possible moment to the traditional Anglo-Saxon view that guilt is personal and not by association. But the First Amendment does not bestow upon the Communist Party the constitutional right, for example, to be a clandestine network for purposes of espionage or subversion. It would not justify Mr. Dennis in organizing a party militia. If such acts become really threatening and the party apparatus can be shown to be involved, the existence of the Communist Party itself may become a source of clear and present danger. Then it could be outlawed.

We must not be restrained by weakness when the

moment of crisis arrives. It may well be, for example, that the Communist parties of France and Italy are already committing a multitude of overt acts which would justify their suppression today. But we have plainly not reached that point in the United States. Until the Party is outlawed, its members are entitled to the protection of American laws — and are liable to prosecution for breaking those laws — just as any other citizens are.

I have been talking thus far about the right of political agitation in a free society. That general right must be energetically maintained for all, I believe, up to the point where the speech produces illegal acts. But the conflict between civil liberty and national security comes to a sharper focus on the narrower question: the problem of loyalty in government service. This narrower question has produced considerable anxiety in the last few years. What are the Government's rights and obligations in connection with the politics of government workers?

We have agreed that Americanism is not a totalitarian faith, imposing a single economic or political dogma or requiring a uniformity in observance from all its devotees. Yet is it not equally true that a serious problem has been created for our national security by the presence in the Government of sympathizers with those who reject all American interests in favor of those of the Soviet Union?

There can be no longer any question, for example, that the national Communist parties play an important rôle in Soviet espionage and have underground arms for that purpose. The report of the Canadian Royal Commission gave a vivid picture of the technique of employing study groups, ostensibly dedicated to the theory of Marx or to cultural affairs, as recruiting centers for agents. A shrewd

MGB man, observing a collection of intellectuals, scientists and professional workers united by left-wing political sympathies, could very soon pick out the espionage possibilities. Then it would become a matter of playing upon their social susceptibilities and grievances, feeling out their readiness to co-operate, involving them in a conspiratorial atmosphere and finally implicating them in the actual delivery of documents. The revelations of Whittaker Chambers show that much the same thing went on in the United States.

There can be no serious question that the USSR, through the MGB, the American Communist Party and the Communist front organizations, has commissioned agents to penetrate the "sensitive" branches of the Government, such as the State Department, the Department of National Defense and the Atomic Energy Commission. The conspiratorial character of the Party insures that some of the most dangerous agents will have no Party cards or even overt Party associations. What is the Government to do?

We must first understand that the right to work for the Government is not clearly a part of the civil liberties of a citizen — a point liberals were quite ready to perceive when it was a question of bringing pressure on the Government to discharge George Deatherage because he held pro-fascist political opinions. "The petitioner may have a constitutional right to talk politics," remarked Oliver Wendell Holmes in deciding the case of a policeman who lost his job for political reasons, "but he has no constitutional right to be a policeman." [15] An American citizen must be protected in his right to think and speak freely — as a Communist, a fascist or whatever; but it is hard to see that any rule of the Constitution or of common sense requires the State Department to hire him. The state has an obvious right to impose reasonable conditions on those who occupy its key positions; government must be conceded, in other words, the right of self-protection.

Certainly the first condition to be imposed is loyalty to the government. As Roger Baldwin, head of the American Civil Liberties Union, has clearly put it, "A superior loyalty to a foreign government disqualifies a citizen for service to ours." [16] Yet positive determinations of loyalty are very hard to make. There seems therefore no alternative in the case of a security agency except to construe substantial doubt in favor of the agency. Few Americans have shown more devotion to the cause of civil freedom than Benjamin V. Cohen; and his conclusions on this point seem to me unarguable. "Where the security of the United States is really concerned any reasonable doubt ought to be resolved in a way that will protect the integrity of the government service. . . . There may be cases even where the responsible head of a department or the department's loyalty board is convinced of the trustworthiness of an individual and still the cloud of substantial suspicion that hovers about the individual makes it highly inexpedient to continue that individual in a strategic security position." [17] Discharge in advance of an overt act may seem a rough policy. Yet the failure to discharge suspicious persons may well imperil national security; it certainly would compel the development of a comprehensive system of detection and counterespionage which would bring the police state much nearer. Let us recall for a moment the situation in 1938. Obviously Nazis, their conscious fellow travelers and soft-headed

Americans who conceived Hitler's Germany to be a much misunderstood nation, had no business in the State Department; and liberals were correct in demanding their dismissal in advance of overt acts. I cannot see why this same principle does not apply today to the fellow travelers of a rival totalitarianism.

Yet the attempt to safeguard the Government cannot be allowed to degenerate into a means of purging the Government of all liberals or nonconformists. Under the pressure of the witch-hunters in the Eightieth Congress, the executive branch was stampeded into a series of dismissals which ignored customary procedural protections and stigmatized persons with an odor of guilt which had never been established (or even charged) in a court of law.

A first constructive step would be to say that the only evidence relevant to questions of loyalty is evidence of connections with another government. To fire a member of the deeply anti-Soviet Socialist Workers Party from a clerical job in the Veterans' Administration — as was done in the case of the legless war veteran, James Kutcher — is to reduce the loyalty check to fatuity. *

Secondly, the security agencies must be distinguished, not only from the citizenry at large, but from the routine services of the government. In a doubtful case, as we have seen, the security agency rather than the individual must receive the benefit of the doubt. But it would be fantastic

---

* Kutcher's legs were amputated after a battle at San Pietro, Italy, in 1943. Learning to walk on artificial limbs, he went to work for the Veterans' Administration in Newark, New Jersey. In August, 1948, he was dismissed for membership in the Socialist Workers Party. Since the SWP is fiercely anti-Soviet, Kutcher's only crime would seem to be his opposition to capitalism. In view of his conduct at San Pietro, it would be hard to challenge his patriotism.

to apply this principle to postmen, laborers on reclamation projects, or barbers in veterans' hospitals.

Thirdly, the process of dismissal from security agencies must be hedged around with firm procedural safeguards. The State Department, for example, must be able to terminate employment upon reasonable suspicion; but it cannot be allowed to stigmatize individuals and wreck lives on suspicion. Unless there is enough evidence of disloyalty to justify prosecution, individuals must be allowed to resign without prejudice.

Fourthly, where individuals do not wish to avail themselves of the right of resignation, they must be granted full right to a hearing and appeal. At some point in the administrative process, full power to summon witnesses and to weigh evidence must be concentrated. That point plainly must be, not the investigative agency, but a Government review board to which all persons dismissed on security grounds can appeal. That board must acquaint the accused with the charges and permit him the protection of counsel. It must be able to obtain from the FBI full data concerning the reliability of the evidence; the situation is intolerable where the review board must decide on the basis of statements from informants identified only by letters, numbers or FBI code names.

The board must have the further power to interrogate these informants. The problem of permitting the accused to confront the informants is not, of course, so simple as it sounds. Espionage breeds counterespionage; and Government counterespionage agencies simply cannot be expected to unveil their agents at every demand of a defense attorney. Where the evidence by itself is substantial, the review board cannot be expected to require confrontation. But, where the evidence is tenuous, the board must have the power of confronting the accused with the accuser. If the FBI does not think the case important enough to risk blowing a counterespionage chain, it must choose between the chain and the conviction.

Such a set-up must seek to strengthen administrators in the fight to prevent witch-hunting from spreading any further through the executive branches the black taint of fear which discourages independence and originality of thought. It must just as resolutely reject the curious Doughface doctrine that prosecution of Communists or fellow travelers in any circumstances is a violation of civil liberties.

The success of any administrative mechanism is dependent in last resort on the atmosphere in which it operates. The final safeguard against injustice lies in the appeal to public opinion. Newspapers like the *Washington Post*, lawyers like Paul Porter, Joseph Rauh, and John Lord O'Brian, public figures like Dwight D. Eisenhower and James B. Conant must be supported in their effort to keep feelings calm on this subject. There are spies, and there are also victims of gross injustice: the problem is to preserve an atmosphere in which effective judicial determinations as to which is which can be made. Liberals, it should be added, often contribute as much to hysteria as reactionaries. When they denounce the Un-American Activities Committee for failing to distinguish between liberals and Communists, they should remember how long it took them before they started making that distinction themselves.

There is no easy answer to this conflict of principles between civil liberty and national security in the field of government employment. The practical results thus must depend too much for comfort upon the restraint and wisdom of individuals. This responsibility becomes only one aspect of the great moral challenge which confronts us. If we cannot handle this conflict of principle soberly and responsibly, if we cannot rise to the world crisis, then we lack the qualities of greatness as a nation, and we can expect to pay the price of hysteria or of paralysis.

So far as the broader field of political liberty is concerned, we can still afford to play from strength, not from weakness. In the absence of convincing proof of clear and present danger, we must maintain our libertarian principles. In a world under the shadow of the police state, we only strengthen our claim to moral leadership by creating here an environment for free and responsible discussion.

Yet, if the moment should come when Communist activities do present, not just a potential threat, but a clear and present menace, if there be not time, in Brandeis's words, "to avert the evil by the processes of education," then we must act swiftly in defense of freedom. Civil liberties do not deny society its right of self-protection. They only make sure that this right is used, not to punish dissenters or to flail at nightmares, but to ward off real dangers to the commonwealth.

X

Freedom in the World

Hᴉsᴛᴏʀʏ has thrust a world destiny on the United States. No nation, perhaps, has become a more reluctant great power. Not conquest but homesickness moved the men of Bradley and Stilwell; Frankfurt or Tokyo were but way-stations on the road back to Gopher Prairie. Our businessmen, instead of welcoming the opportunities of empire, spend their time resisting its responsibilities. The pro-consul is such a rare American type that we become dependent on the few we have simply because we cannot replace them.

Yet we are in the great world to stay; and two world wars have made us accept this fact with a sad sense of irrevocability. No one need argue the interventionist-isolationist debate any more. With the death of Professor Beard, isolationism lost its last trace of intellectual respectability. As Max Ascoli has pointed out, an isolationist today is simply a man who wants to help some other continent than the one currently under discussion. We are condemned to think in global terms even to justify non-global policies.

World destiny has belatedly thrust upon the United States the necessity for having a real foreign policy — a policy, that is, which exists in terms of day-to-day operations, not in terms of Fourth of July oratory. Webster's reply to Hülsemann served too long as the model for American diplomacy: "The power of this republic at the present moment is . . . of an extent in comparison with which the possessions of the House of Hapsburg are but as a patch on the earth's surface." Americans today, both conservative and liberal, still tend to think of foreign policy in terms of such ringing defiances of European tyrants — foreign policy as a means of expressing sentiments, in other words, not of influencing events.

For the sentimentalist in foreign policy, the most important thing in the world is to discover an outlet for his moral indignation, at whatever cost to the world. The sentimental conservative, for example, would "show" the USSR by withdrawing the American ambassador, as if this gesture could have effect on anything except ourselves; while the sentimental liberal, who was asserting a few years ago the absurdity of non-recognition as an instrument of pressure when Coolidge and Hoover applied it to the USSR, now proposes to use this same weapon to strike down Franco or Peron. The foreign policy sentimentalist, in short, retains certain of the irresponsibilities of the isolationist in a world where isolationism is no longer possible.

The object of foreign policy, it must be constantly repeated, is not to ventilate our grievances; it is to produce real changes in a real world. Refusing to recognize an existing régime may soothe our own damaged nerves; but it is not ordinarily an effective means of overthrowing an established government. International denunciation on an official level may give us a pleasing sense of virtue, but it is quite likely to rebound against our interests: Mr. Braden's compaign against Peron won the State Department more votes in the offices of the liberal weeklies than it did in Argentina.

Let us agree, for example, that the Peron régime or, say, the Rakosi régime in Hungary are entirely repugnant to the friend of free society.* The responsible diplomat will share this repugnance; yet he is compelled to calculate coolly the consequences of a diplomatic campaign against them. Neither nation is accessible to economic pressure; we have no intention of attempting military intervention. In such a situation, indiscriminate political warfare will only excite our friends into premature exposure while rallying the great mass behind our enemies. A policy of cold correctness, on the other hand, provides us with intelligence facilities, with opposition contacts, with great possibilities of pressure and propaganda. Why throw these advantages overboard in order to gratify our emotions?

Foreign policy is not a matter of expressing national

* Both régimes have done much for the common man in the two countries. Each has based itself on the trade-union movement and alienated the great landlords. Each has committed itself to ambitious programs of industrialization. Peron, for all his terror and repression, rates better than Rakosi from the viewpoint of civil liberties. The Communist Party, for example, is legal and active in Argentina, while all non-Communist parties have been subverted or destroyed in Hungary.

likes or dislikes. It is, at bottom, a matter of achieving
terms of survival in a complicated and diversified world.
Theodore Roosevelt was the first president to try to edu-
cate the nation to the worldwide terms of its existence.
But as late as Cordell Hull, a secretary of state could still
regard foreign policy as a sub-branch of rhetoric. One
factor in the conflict between Hull and Sumner Welles was
the inevitable friction between a man who thought of
foreign policy primarily in terms of words and one who
thought of it primarily in terms of operations. Today our
Department of State is finally adjusting itself to a world
where the United States has continuing, far-flung and
incredibly complex responsibilities.

The beginnings of maturity in foreign policy lie in the
understanding that a nation has certain unalterable interests which no government can abandon. No responsible
American government, for example, could permit the
totalitarianization of Europe, or the destruction of freedom of the seas in the Atlantic or Pacific, or the loss of
Hawaii. It was this substratum of national interest which
provided the foundation for the bipartisan foreign policy
in the United States — a policy which began when
Franklin D. Roosevelt invited Henry L. Stimson and
Frank Knox to join his cabinet in 1940. Those who
attack the bipartisan foreign policy in this sense, as Lind-
bergh did in 1940 or as Wallace did in 1948, are simply
calling for the abandonment of what the tremendous
majority of Americans regard as vital national interests.
Nor should anyone have been surprised when a Socialist
government in Britain refrained from reversing in every
respect the foreign policy of Winston Churchill. Any
British government is constrained to defer to some very

concrete strategic and economic considerations; a government which ignored them would betray the security of its people.

Yet the existence of inalienable national interests does not solve all the questions of foreign policy. The British Socialists, for example, have changed British foreign policy in important respects, especially in the colonial field. Similarly, a Republican victory in 1948 would almost certainly have altered the political and economic direction of United States policy — away from support of the Third Force, toward support of de Gaulle, Franco, Peron and Chiang Kai-shek; away from liberal commercial policies, toward high tariffs and restrictions. Granted that any administration must defend certain primary national interests, there is always need for a legitimate and healthy debate, both over the definition of these interests, and over the best means of serving them. A bipartisan foreign policy, in other words, has a real meaning; but its existence certainly does not remove foreign affairs from political controversy.

American foreign policy is inevitably concentrated today on the problem of checking Soviet expansion. This policy, as it has gradually evolved since the end of the war, has two main parts. One is the policy of *containment*: that is, the prevention of overt Communist aggression against states not now under Communist domination. The other is *reconstruction*: that is, the removal in non-Communist states of the conditions of want and insecurity which invite the spread of Communism. The first is the policy of the Truman Doctrine and the North Atlantic Pact, the second the policy of the Marshall Plan.

Some observers have argued that the Truman Doctrine

and the Marshall Plan involved contradictory conceptions. The Truman Doctrine, it is true, was launched in ill-considered and somewhat inflammatory language under circumstances which gave the impression that the United States was offering a blank check to anti-Communist governments, however reactionary. But experience has shown that the Truman Doctrine, in fact, offered no such blank check. Indeed, the record on balance justifies the Administration's insistence that, far from being contradictory, the Truman Doctrine and the Marshall Plan are complementary. Each is essential to the success of the other.

Present Soviet policy can be roughly described as a policy of kicking at doors. If the doors fly open, the USSR moves in. But, if the doors are locked, the USSR does not break down the door because it does not want to get involved in a fight with the householder or his friends. The policy of the Truman Doctrine is a policy of locking doors against Soviet aggression. Our policy in Greece has not been a notable success; but at least it has discouraged the USSR from further employment of the guerrilla tactic as a means of concealed aggression. If we had reacted less swiftly, not only would Greece now be in the Soviet sphere, but the same tactics of sending armed guerrillas over the border would be in use at every soft point along the periphery of Soviet power.

The containment policy, it should be emphasized, is a policy of protection for non-Communist countries; it is not a policy of threatening Soviet interests in what has become the settled sphere of Soviet power. The function of the containment policy is to make reconstruction pos-

sible by guaranteeing the security of those who seek to
rebuild Europe in face of Communist disapproval. The
workers of Berlin would not continue their defiance if
they did not count upon the continued presence of the
US Army; nor perhaps would the free Socialists of Italy
invite the fate of the Bulgarian Socialist Kosta Lulchev or
of the Polish Socialist Kazimierz Puzak if they thought the
Russians could move into Italy with impunity tomorrow.

But the containment policy also aims to strengthen the
peace group, if one exists, in the Soviet Union. The history of appeasement shows that, while its intention is to
strengthen the moderates in the nation appeased, its effect
is to strengthen those who find in a soft answer arguments
for increased wrath. As Clemenceau observed of the policy
of perpetual concession, "There is no better means of
making the opposite party ask for more and more." [1] The
peace party in the Hitler régime, for example, sent messages to Downing Street in September, 1938, begging
Chamberlain not to give in. Munich destroyed the peace
party by disproving its prediction that German aggression
would provoke British resistance.* So today those in the
Kremlin who argue against expansion are made stronger
every time the West holds and weaker every time it yields.
In such a situation, the notion of concession as a means
of inspiring Soviet confidence in the good intentions of
the West becomes futile. "Instead of looking at it as a
gesture of good will," asserts Mrs. Roosevelt after months
of negotiation in the United Nations, "they look on it as

* As Karl Friedrich Goerdeler, who was executed by the Nazis in 1944
for his rôle in the anti-Hitler putsch, wrote to an American friend a few
weeks after Munich, "By shying away from a small risk Mr. Chamberlain
has made war inevitable." Dulles, *Germany's Underground*, p. 48.

a gesture of weakness." * The failure of the Wallace
campaign in 1948 clearly increased rather than lessened
the chances of peace. As Professor Laski has noted, a
large vote for Wallace "would have given strength to all
the forces in Russia which hinder a common move to
sensible understanding." [2]

Yet containment is not enough — locking the door is
not enough — as the case of Greece demonstrates so conclusively. If conditions inside the house are intolerable, if
a few people live in luxury while the rest scramble for table
leavings and sleep in the cellar, then eventually someone
will admit the Communists by stealth. So the locking of
the door must be accompanied by the cleaning up of the
house: our policy must secure the inhabitants against the
desperation which breeds totalitarianism by seeking to
restore them to a state of economic and political health.
Economic health means high levels of production and
employment; political health means free institutions
under law. This is the policy of the Marshall Plan.

Without the Marshall Plan, the Truman Doctrine
would become a program of resisting Communism by
sheer force — and would be doomed to failure. Without
the Doctrine and the Pact, the Marshall Plan would have no
means of warding off the ruthless Soviet campaign against
European recovery — and it would be doomed to failure
too. Some Americans say that you cannot fight ideas with
guns, which is true. But it is equally true that you can-

---

* "I don't think I'll ever again accept what I don't think is as good,"
Mrs. Roosevelt continued, "just in the hope of bringing the U.S.S.R. into
an agreement." *New York Times*, January 15, 1949. Mrs. Roosevelt later
in "My Day" defined the "usual U.S.S.R. idea of compromise. You give
up everything on your side and agree with the U.S.S.R. on all points and
then the compromise is accepted." *Boston Globe*, February 8, 1949.

not fight guns with ideas alone, as many Europeans have learned the hard way twice in this generation. The worst fallacy is to think that military force by itself constitutes a guarantee against totalitarian aggression. And the next worse fallacy is to believe that economic and political health by themselves constitute such a guarantee: that you can, for example, stop a Soviet-instigated civil war, as in Greece, by tractors and fertilizer. After all, was it internal economic failure which caused Czechoslovakia to succumb to totalitarianism twice within a single decade?

Our present policy for world peace has thus settled into the formula of reconstruction plus containment. The application of this formula to Europe since the war, it must be stated, has had its damaging passages of timidity and ambiguity. We should have committed ourselves much earlier, for example, to the policy of rebuilding western Europe; and we should have proclaimed from the start that we were looking for support, not to the representatives of a decrepit plutocracy or of a nascent fascism, but to the men of the center and the non-Communist left. Nothing is more superficially attractive than the notion that "hard" men, affirming their anti-communism day in and day out, provide, in the cant phrase, the best "bulwark against Communism." But a government is only as strong as the faith of its people; and right-wing dictatorships have always been marked by brittleness and instability. They look invincible until the day they are overthrown. In the long run, security lies with governments which do not fear to permit their people freedom of expression and choice. An American policy which would force the Europeans to select between one totalitarianism and another is not likely to inspire wild enthusiasm. Indeed, as good a way as any to expedite Communist expansion would be to provide unconditional backing to right-wing dictatorships. The far right and the far left have in common the desire to eliminate the democratic center. Each thinks that it will stand to gain if its polar rival is the only alternative. The men of the right think that, if the choice is between themselves and the Communists, the people will choose them; the men of the left think that, if the choice is between themselves and the oligarchy, the people will choose them. It is hard to see why it is in the interest of the United States to support either extreme.

Yet thus far United States policy, for all its intimations of schizophrenia, has remained basically anti-fascist as well as anti-Communist. The reconstruction/containment formula — the Marshall Plan plus the Truman Doctrine — gives every promise of repelling the Soviet threat to Europe. With another decade of peace, a democratic federation may well have brought lasting prosperity and strength to the free nations of Europe.

Europe, indeed, has characteristics which simplify the application of the reconstruction/containment formula: its people are relatively industrialized and literate, and they present no mass problems of racial discontent. Yet our natural and justified pre-occupation with Europe must not blind us to the fact that in other areas people are underindustrialized and illiterate and seethe with the aspirations and resentments of color; and that these areas, where we are presently fighting a losing battle, comprise most of the land and most of the people of the earth.

Most of this world is already in the throes of a social revolution — a revolution deriving its force from discontent on the land and having as its goal the assertion of national independence and the beginnings of industrialization. It is a revolt against the landlords, against the money-lenders, against foreign political domination, against foreign economic exploitation. It is taking place across the world from the paddyfields of China to the pampas of Argentina — in Burma, in India, in Indonesia, in the Middle East, and, in a somewhat different form, in the independent nations of Eastern Europe and Latin America. It is a revolution which has not reached its climax and which will not be checked by attempts to reinstate the past through main force. Its beneficiaries are Mao Tse-tung, Rakosi, Tito, Peron, Villareol; its beneficiaries are also Nehru, Soekarno, Betancourt, Haya de la Torre, Luis Muñoz-Marin. And in Africa, as to an extent in Latin America and Asia, the social revolution is given an edge of bitterness by the hatred of the colored races of the world for their white oppressors.

This revolution presents our foreign policy with problems distinct from the problems of Europe — problems requiring special consideration and special solutions. In competing for this revolution, in the first place, the Soviet Union enjoys advantages which it does not possess in a more developed society. In Europe Communism robs people of cherished freedom. But Asia and Africa have little freedom to lose. The Mongolian or Iranian who has never read a newspaper and cannot tell a habeas corpus from an eggbeater is not likely to regard the absence of a bill of rights as a major issue — especially when he compares it with the liberating effects of such concrete social changes as the ownership of land or the expulsion of the village usurer. The drastic Soviet techniques of execution and expropriation of class oppressors therefore strike far deeper chords among poverty-stricken and illiterate people than does the western concern for parliamentarianism and due process of law. The USSR is uniquely capable of the social ruthlessness which can accelerate and exploit the social revolution. Lacking colonies itself, it has nothing to lose and a world to gain by lighting nationalist fuses under the rickety structure of western imperialism.

In addition, the USSR claims to stand — and many thousands of individual Communists have stood honestly and courageously — for racial equality.* The racial cruelties in the United States or in most areas of western colonialism compare unfavorably with the Soviet nationalities policy (at least as described in Soviet propaganda) and with the long Russian traditions of racial assimilation. This fact gives Communism a special prestige for African or Asiatic intellectuals who have had to suffer under discriminations of color in the West. The western democrat sympathizes with this resentment, while at the same time he cannot but feel that it leads to a fatal misinterpretation of the great world conflict — to the feeling that Russian racial policies excuse the tyranny of Communism, and that western racial policies condemn the freedom of democracy. Yet we must understand that the prejudice of the West is still another source of Communist strength in the East.

The more we succeed in Europe, in other words, the more we divert Communism to the part of the world where, in a real if temporary sense, it may be thought to come, not as conqueror, but as liberator. How can we prevent the loss of Asia and Africa to the Soviet Union?

It seemed clear a few years ago that the first step must be the abandonment of the colonial imperialism which has

---

* [This was written before the flagrant revival of Russian anti-Semitism.]

mobilized the Asiatic masses against us. For that first step, the United States was not ill prepared. The unimperialist state-of-mind which culminated in the relinquishment of the Philippines, the anti-imperialist emotions of the second Roosevelt and most of our leading politicians, conservative and liberal, all made it easy for Americans to view with equanimity the break-up of British, French and Dutch colonial empires.

Yet we are discovering that an anti-imperialist frame of mind is no longer enough. The break-up of a colonial system leaves a vacuum; and the first power to rush into that vacuum is likely to be Communism. Must we therefore subsidize the old imperialism or its native equivalent lest the disappearance of authority expose the subject peoples to Communist aggression? or should we go full speed ahead on the creation of strong, progressive native governments which will themselves resist Communism? It is this conflict which has created the basic uncertainty in the heart of our present Asiatic policies.

A glance at recent developments shows, I believe, that our first impulse is still right — that imperialism and reaction remain Moscow's most reliable long-run allies in Asia. So long as the British were in India, for example, the Communists were influential in the nationalist movement. Only now that the British have left and that Communism has begun to reveal itself as a new species of foreign intervention has Communist political influence begun to wane. The same Nehru who worked with Communists in the days of British domination today throws them into prison. This pattern is continuous throughout liberated Asia. Free Burma has been plunged into chaos by Communist uprisings; the Indonesian Republic, in its few months of precarious independence, had to put down a Communist rebellion; and we may anticipate that Communist control in China will provoke a nationalistic reaction.

We can either strengthen democratic-minded native governments against Communism, or we can take advantage of the confusion to try to destroy the native governments and reinstall reaction or imperialism. The British followed the first course in India, the Dutch the second in Indonesia. The effect of British policy was to begin the construction of a group of progressive native régimes which would stand as bulwarks against Soviet expansion. The effect of Dutch policy has been to undo much of the British work in India and to strengthen the Communists throughout Asia; in particular, the Dutch policy restored the Communists to the place of influence in the Indonesian nationalist movement from which Soekarno had so laboriously driven them. In the same way, the French have strengthened the Communist Ho Chi Minh as the leader of Indo-Chinese nationalism.

Support for nationalist governments is thus necessary; but it will not be enough if all we do, as we did in China, is to back a native despot instead of a foreign one. We must encourage the native governments to evolve in a democratic direction; we must strengthen them internationally — for example, by welcoming the development of a South Asia regional system; and we must collaborate with such a federation in working out affirmative programs to meet the problems causing the surge of revolution — the problem of the remnants of colonialism, the problem of land, and the problem of industrialization.

Without American support no colonial empire can survive. But the abrupt end of empire may well have disastrous economic consequences for the colonizing power. American funds might well assist in the peaceful expropriation of the imperialists, helping tide both the colonies and their former possessors over the period of economic readjustment.

As for the land problem, the Communists solve it expeditiously by destroying the large landlords and parceling out the land to the peasants. We not only do not take happily to the methods involved, but we note that crude redistribution of land reduces production and may well, as in Russia itself, cause famine. Our own resources and imagination might well produce more effective solutions. American funds can buy out landlords; American methods of scientific farming and of land rehabilitation can increase production; American study of village sociology could help us to understand how we may most effectively release the energies so long pent up in the villages of Asia.

An even greater opportunity lies, as President Truman has pointed out, in our possible contribution to the industrialization of Asia. No people in the world approach the Americans in mastery of the new magic of science and technology. Our engineers can transform arid plains or poverty-stricken river valleys into wonderlands of vegetation and power. Our factories produce astonishing new machines, and the machines turn out a wondrous flow of tools and goods for every aspect of living. The Tennessee Valley Authority is a weapon which, if properly employed, might outbid all the social ruthlessness of the Communists for the support of the people of Asia.

We have, in other words, a technological dynamism to set against the political dynamism of the Russians. Few people have seen more clearly than Stalin himself the potential of this technological dynamism. Instructing the Russian people in the revolutionary fundamentals, Stalin actually pointed out that the "Russian revolutionary spirit" by itself was not enough for the Leninist "style in work"; it must be accompanied by "American efficiency." And American efficiency, wrote Stalin, means "that indomitable spirit that neither knows nor will be deterred by any obstacle, that plugs away with businesslike [*sic*] perseverance until every impediment has been removed, that simply must go through with a job once it has been tackled even if it be of minor importance." [3]

A little American efficiency, accompanied by a policy of support for native progressive movements, would go far to counter the appeal of the Russian revolutionary spirit in the undeveloped areas. We have to accept the fact that we must apply this efficiency selectively in Asia. The reconstruction/containment formula stretches our resources in Europe alone, and we can hardly undertake a program of comparable scope for all the peoples of Asia and Africa. We must choose our spots — Japan, perhaps, the Philippines, Indonesia, India, Israel, Turkey — concentrate on exporting technology rather than commodities, and seek to make those nations the leaders of a progressive Asian civilization along democratic lines. A confused and mistaken policy has lost us the battle in China. But, if we learn from the Chinese failure, we may be able to help build a pro-democratic alternative to Communism in the other crucial areas of the Orient. We must pursue our Asian objectives with as much determination as we have pursued our objectives in Europe. Europe's mighty industrial capacity undoubtedly gives it top priority in the Soviet plan of expansion; but, in the long run, the loss of either Europe or Asia would be fatal to the democratic position.

The present design of our foreign policy, then, is to carry out the reconstruction/containment policy in Europe and to develop some more complex and limited equivalent in the underdeveloped lands. These policies cannot succeed, however, unless the United States itself does things we have not done in the past. First, we must stay out of a depression and thereby show the world that our strength is solid and stable. Second, we must revise our commercial expectations, reduce our tariffs and open our gates wide to foreign goods. Our efforts to increase production through the world will have little effect in ending the dollar gap unless we are willing to accept foreign goods in exchange for our own. Third, we must reform our own racial practices — not only repeal such insulting symbols as the Oriental exclusion laws, but demonstrate a deep and effective concern with the racial inequities within the United States. Fourth, we must not succumb to demands for an anti-Soviet crusade or a preventive war, nor permit reactionaries in the buffer states to precipitate conflicts in defense of their own obsolete prerogatives.

Suppose we can carry out our own part of the task, suppose our foreign policies succeed in stabilizing the non-Communist world, what hope is there then of peace?

It is idle, I believe, to delude ourselves into thinking that totalitarianism and democracy can live together happily ever after. Until Russian public opinion can control its rulers, and not be controlled by them, we are not dealing with a nation in any intelligible sense; we are dealing with a group of men whose objective is the retention of power and who will sacrifice anything to that objective.

The problem of world peace, in other words, is to get some element of popular control into the Soviet system.

This system, as we have seen, is essentially a system of tension. Its internal character renders highly unlikely the voluntary relinquishment by the rulers of their absolute power. On the contrary, the interests of the ruling group require the maintenance of this tension at all costs: once it breaks down in one area, it will tend to break down everywhere, and the rulers will perish in the resultant convulsion. So they must strive endlessly, by the use of terror internally and by the invocation of monstrous enemies abroad, to keep the tension at a high pitch.

The threat of fascism gave Soviet tension a legitimate basis and enabled the Communists to relax their centripetal compulsions: hence the moderation of Soviet tactics in the decade after 1935. So today a policy of western intimidation, with the flourish of guided missiles and atomic bombs, would give Soviet tension once again an objective basis and allow the Communist régime to hide its totalitarian purposes behind a cloak of self-defense. A policy of western appeasement, on the other hand, would only persuade the Soviet rulers that aggression pays.

The containment policy, however, avoids the extremes of intimidation or appeasement. It is based on the conviction that the internal contradictions of democratic capitalism, though acute and troubling, are far less urgent than the internal contradictions of Communism. By refraining from supplying Communism with any legitimate basis for tension (or for hope of democratic surrender), the containment policy prevents the USSR from concealing its own monolithic compulsions under the mantle of external crisis or triumph. The Soviet Union is forced, in other words, to resort to artificial devices to maintain tension; it is forced to condemn people to forced-labor camps, to discipline intellectuals, to purge the national Communist parties, to rush the consolidation of Moscow's authority throughout the Soviet sphere — all without real external justification.

The longer the period of external stability, the more indefensible will be the Communist insistence on internal uniformity, and the more swiftly, in consequence, will Communism be impaled on its own internal contradictions. It is this context which gives the heresy of Tito its peculiar significance. During the war, the Soviet Union could accommodate itself to the ardent nationalism of the Yugoslav Partisans; but today the Soviet rulers, if they are to maintain their monolithic system, cannot permit the emergence of even a semi-independent center of power. A few years ago in a time of real crisis, Soviet spokesmen were able to proclaim that there were many roads to peace and prosperity. They cannot admit as much today without damaging their own claims to infallibility. "There is only one road," cried Vishinsky in his farewell appearance at Belgrade, "and that is the Stalin road which we have been following for thirty years." [4]

The doctrine of Soviet infallibility, in short, leaves no room for the impulses of native nationalism. Yet nationalism is an essential component in the worldwide social revolution which the USSR seeks to exploit. Where either western aggression or western appeasement — war or surrender — might have kept the conflict submerged, containment gave the latent incompatibilities between "the Stalin road" and the Yugoslav nationalism the chance to come into the open. The Yugoslav declaration of independence is thus the first important dividend of the containment policy.

The contradiction between Moscow and Tito is inherent in the international Communist movement. Tito alone has been able to make an open defiance, because he alone in eastern Europe came to power through his own (and Anglo-American *) efforts; he alone had his own army and secret police; he alone was separated geographically from Russia. But other eastern European Communists, like Gomulka in Poland and Patrascanu in Rumania, have fallen victim to the same nationalist infection. The bold and confident nationalism of the Chinese Communist movement, geographically isolated, economically independent, militarily strong, will put an even greater strain on Soviet uniformity. How will Vishinsky take to the emergence of "the Mao Tse-tung road"?

A period of world stabilization will open up these fissures within the Soviet sphere. In the meantime, as the Marshall Plan succeeds, an economically revivified Western Europe will exert a gravitational pull upon the "new democracies" in the throes of social revolution; for these young nations, intoxicated with dreams of industrialization, will increasingly seek in the West the machine tools they cannot get from the Soviet Union. It will also cause the Soviet régime to redouble its use of discipline and terror to nourish the monolith at home. But the more the Soviet régime seeks to tighten its controls, the more

* In particular the efforts of such stout British conservatives as Winston Churchill, Fitzroy MacLean, Randolph Churchill and Evelyn Waugh. Tito's break with Stalin suggests that one nationalist may be able to recognize another. In any case, it came just in time to spare Mr. Churchill from writing what would otherwise have been an embarrassing chapter in his memoirs.

narrow and bleak will be the basis of that power in popular consent, and the more ominous will become the
shadow of the Tito heresy.

An early Soviet response to these developments might
possibly be a change of tactics, in the hope that an appearance of moderation may lull the West into a relaxation of effort. Such a change of tactics must not be re-
buffed, particularly if it involves acts as well as words; but
neither must it be misunderstood. It would imply an
alteration, not in Soviet purposes, but in Soviet timing.
The USSR may well propose a formalization of the divided world, trusting to force to organize its own sphere,
and to capitalist incompetence and Communist subversion to bring down the West. We may wish to negotiate
on the basis of present divisions; but we must not abandon
the reconstruction/containment formula nor return native
Communists in the West to positions of confidence and
trust.

If the democratic world continues stable and prosper-
ous, the disintegration of Soviet power will accelerate;
and the Soviet rulers may finally be driven to desperate
measures to arrest that disintegration. The one measure
which would unite the weary, the sullen, and the halfhearted would be war. The Russian people would certainly rally to the defense of the Soviet régime as they have
rallied to the defense of every other despot in their tragic
past. The best way to deter the Politburo from so reckless
a course is to build up the military capabilities of the West
so that, at any given moment of decision, the Soviet General Staff will advise against war on the ground that Russia
will have no chance of winning.

Russia must become more democratic if we are to have

peace. But we cannot hurry the process by force. If we seek to intimidate the Soviet rulers, we will only unite the people behind the totalitarian régime. We must allow its own internal contradictions to take care of Russian totalitarianism, meanwhile keeping our own powder dry. The future is unpredictable. No one can forecast, for example, what will happen in the scramble for power after the death of Stalin. No one knows what effect more abundant consumers' goods and increased living standards will have on the Soviet system. But that system must lose its totalitarianism before the world can give up its preparations for war.

When Russia loosens the totalitarian grip, then the noble dream of world government will begin to make some contact with reality. In the long run, the supporters of world government are right; but in the short run, their efforts too often serve to distract men of good will from the urgent tasks of the moment. The theory that parchment can bridge the abysses opening up in a disintegrating world is false and deceptive. The tensions between Russia and the West, for example, are much too deep to be waved away by constitutional formulas, however learned and ingenious. We have strayed too far from the insights of Burke and de Maistre; we have forgotten that constitutions work only as they reflect an actual sense of community. Our own experience should remind us that, while constitutions may play a vital part in the process which creates community, they cannot create community by themselves: our national unity results less from the Constitution than from Civil War. The adoption of world government will not necessarily mean the end of war. It will only set up the framework within which world war will be, in fact, civil war and may have a better chance of producing genuine world unity. In the meantime, we had better do what we can to foster community where we can, through regional federations and through the United Nations, and not ignore these small gains in pursuit of a pot of legalisms at the end of a rainbow.*

Yet world government, in a sense, cannot emerge too soon; for the people of the world cannot long afford to expend their energies in squabbling with each other. The human race may shortly be confronted by an entirely new range of problems — problems of naked subsistence whose solution will require the combined efforts of all people if the race is to survive. We have raped the earth too long, and we are paying the price today in the decline of fertility. Industrial society has disturbed the balance of nature, and no one can estimate the consequences. "Mankind," writes William Vogt, "has backed itself into an ecological trap." [5] Vogt, Fairfield Osborn, Sir John Boyd Orr have described some of the dilemmas awaiting us as the world population presses hard upon our vanishing agricultural and mineral resources. The results of industrialization and introduction of public health standards in Asia, for example, may well be calamitous, unless they are accompanied by vigorous birth-control policies and by expanded programs of land care and conservation.

In the light of this epic struggle to restore man to his

* A penetrating statement of the case against immediate agitation for world government is to be found in an article by Reinhold Niebuhr, "The Illusion of World Government," *Foreign Affairs*, April, 1949. For an historian's well-documented doubts, see Crane Brinton, *From Many One*, Cambridge, 1948.

foundations in nature, the political conflicts which obsess us today seem puny and flickering. Unless we are soon able to make the world safe for democracy, we may commit ourselves too late to the great and final struggle to make the world safe for humanity.

XI

Freedom: A Fighting Faith

Industrialism is the benefactor and the villain of our time: it has burned up the mortgage, but at the same time sealed us in a subtler slavery. It has created wealth and comfort in undreamed-of abundance. But in the wake of its incomparable economic achievement it has left the thin, deadly trail of anxiety. The connecting fluids of industrial society begin to dry up; the seams harden and crack; and society is transformed into a parched desert, "a heap of broken images, where the sun beats, and the dead tree gives no shelter, the cricket no relief, and the dry stone no sound of water" — that state of social purgatory which Durkheim called "anomie" and where Eliot saw fear in a handful of dust.

Under industrialism the social order ceases to be society in faith and brotherhood. It becomes the waste land, "asocial society," in Alex Comfort's phrase — "a society of

onlookers, congested but lonely, technically advanced but
utterly insecure, subject to a complicated mechanism of
order but individually irresponsible." [1] We live on from
day to day, persisting mechanically in the routine of a
morality and a social pattern which has been switched off
but which continues to run from its earlier momentum.
Our lives are empty of belief. They are lives of quiet
desperation.

Who can live without desperation in a society turned
asocial — in a social system which represents organized
frustration instead of organized fulfillment? Freedom has
lost its foundation in community and become a torment;
"individualism" strips the individual of layer after layer
of protective tissue. Reduced to panic, industrial man
joins the lemming migration, the convulsive mass escape
from freedom to totalitarianism, hurling himself from the
bleak and rocky cliffs into the deep, womb-dark sea
below. In free society, as at present constituted, the
falcon cannot hear the falconer, the center cannot hold.
Anarchy is loosed upon the world, and, as in Yeats's terrible vision, some rough beast, its hour come round at
last, slouches toward Bethlehem to be born.

Through this century, free society has been on the de-
fensive, demoralized by the infection of anxiety, stagger-
ing under the body blows of fascism and Communism.
Free society alienates the lonely and uprooted masses;
while totalitarianism, building on their frustrations and
cravings, provides a structure of belief, men to worship
and men to hate and rites which guarantee salvation. The
crisis of free society has assumed the form of international
collisions between the democracies and the totalitarian
powers; but this fact should not blind us to the fact that
in its essence this crisis is internal.

Free society will survive, in the last resort, only if enough people believe in it deeply enough to die for it. However reluctant peace-loving people are to recognize that fact, history's warning is clear and cold; civilizations which cannot man their walls in times of alarm are doomed to destruction by the barbarians. We have deeply believed only when the issue of war has reduced our future to the stark problem of self-preservation. Franklin Roosevelt read the American people with his usual uncanny accuracy when he named the Second War, not the "war for freedom," but the "war for survival." Our democracy has still to generate a living emotional content, rich enough to overcome the anxieties incited by industrialism, deep enough to rally its members to battle for freedom — not just for self-preservation. Freedom must become, in Holmes's phrase, a "fighting faith."

Why does not democracy believe in itself with passion? Why is freedom not a fighting faith? In part because democracy, by its nature, dissipates rather than concentrates its internal moral force. The thrust of the democratic faith is away from fanaticism; it is toward compromise, persuasion and consent in politics, toward tolerance and diversity in society; its economic foundation lies in the easily frightened middle class. Its love of variety discourages dogmatism, and its love of skepticism discourages hero-worship. In place of theology and ritual, of hierarchy and demonology, it sets up a belief in intellectual freedom and unrestricted inquiry. The advocate of free society defines himself by telling what he is against: what he is for turns out to be certain *means* and he leaves other people to charge the means with content. Today democracy is paying the price for its systematic cultivation of the peaceful and rational virtues. "Many a man

will live and die upon a dogma; no man will be a martyr
for a conclusion." *

Democracy, moreover, has not worn too well as a philosophy of life in an industrial age. It seemed more solid
at the high noon of success than it does in the uncertain-
ties of falling dusk. In its traditional form, it has pre-
supposed emotional and psychological stability in the individual. It has assumed, much too confidently, that the
gnawing problems of doubt and anxiety would be banished by the advance of science or cured by a rise in the
standard of living. The spectacular reopening of these
problems in our time finds the democratic faith lacking
in the profounder emotional resources. Democracy has
no defense-in-depth against the neuroses of industrialism.
When philosophies of blood and violence arise to take up
the slack between democracy's thin optimism and the
bitter agonies of experience, democracy by comparison
appears pale and feeble.

Yet it seems doubtful whether democracy could itself
be transformed into a political religion, like totalitarianism, without losing its characteristic belief in individual dignity and freedom. Does this mean that democracy is destined to defeat, sooner or later, by one or another of the totalitarian sects?

The death pallor will indeed come over free society,
unless it can recharge the deepest sources of its moral
energy. And we cannot make democracy a fighting faith
merely by exhortation nor by self-flagellation; and certainly not by renouncing the values which distinguish

---

* J. H. Newman, *Grammar of Assent*, London, 1930, p. 93. This
neglected work remains one of the most valuable of all analyses of the
way in which man gives his assent.

free society from totalitarianism. Yet we must somehow dissolve the anxieties which drive people in free society to become traitors to freedom. We must somehow give the lonely masses a sense of individual human function, we must restore community to the industrial order.

There is on our side, of course, the long-run impossibility of totalitarianism. A totalitarian order offers no legitimate solution to the problem of freedom and anxiety. It does not restore basic securities; it does not create a world where men may expect lives of self-fulfillment. It enables man, not to face himself, but to flee himself by diving into the Party and the state. Only he cannot stay there; he must either come up for air or drown. Totalitarianism has scotched the snake of anxiety, but not killed it; and anxiety will be its undoing.

An enduring social order must base itself upon the emotional energies and needs of man. Totalitarianism thwarts and represses too much of man ever to become in any sense a "good society." Terror is the essence of totalitarianism; and normal man, in the long run, instinctively organizes himself against terror. This fact gives the champions of freedom their great opportunity. But let no one deceive himself about the short-run efficacy of totalitarian methods. Modern technology has placed in the hands of "totalitarian man" the power to accomplish most of his ends of human subjection. He may have no enduring solution, but neither, for example, did the Dark Ages. Yet the darkness lasted a longer time than the period which has elapsed since the discovery of America.

We cannot count upon totalitarian dynamism running down of its own accord in a single generation. Man is instinctively anti-totalitarian; but it is necessary for wise policies to mobilize these instincts early enough to do some good. Our problem is to make democracy the fighting faith, not of some future underground movement, but of us all here today in the middle of the twentieth century.

The essential strength of democracy as against totalitarianism lies in its startling insight into the value of the individual. Yet, as we have seen, this insight can become abstract and sterile; arrogant forms of individualism sometimes discredit the basic faith in the value of the individual. It is only so far as that insight can achieve a full social dimension, so far as individualism derives freely from community, that democracy will be immune to the virus of totalitarianism.

For all the magnificent triumphs of individualism, we survive only as we remain members of one another. The individual requires a social context, not one imposed by coercion, but one freely emerging in response to his own needs and initiatives. Industrialism has inflicted savage wounds on the human sensibility; the cuts and gashes are to be healed only by a conviction of trust and solidarity with other human beings.

It is in these fundamental terms that we must reconstruct our democracy. Optimism about man is not enough. The formalities of democracy are not enough. The fact that a man can cast a secret ballot or shop in Woolworth's rather than Kresge's is more important to those free from anxiety than it is to the casualties of the industrial order. And the casualties multiply: the possessors are corrupted by power, the middling undone by boredom, the dispossessed demoralized by fear. Chamber-of-commerce banalities will no longer console industrial man.

We require individualism which does not wall man off from community; we require community which sustains but does not suffocate the individual. The historic methods of free society are correct so far as they go; but they concentrate on the individual; they do not go far enough. It would be fatal to abandon Winston Churchill's seven tests of freedom. But these tests are inadequate to create free society because they define means, not ends. We know now that man is not sufficiently perfect to shape good means infallibly to good ends. So we no longer describe free society in terms of means alone: we must place ends as well in the forefront of our philosophy of democracy.

An adequate philosophy of free society would have to supplement the Churchill tests by such questions as these:

Do the people have a relative security against the ravages of hunger, sickness and want?

Do they freely unite in continuous and intimate association with like-minded people for common purposes?

Do they as individuals have a feeling of initiative, function and fulfillment in the social order?

It has become the duty of free society to answer these questions — and to answer them affirmatively if it would survive. The rise of the social-welfare state is an expression of that sense of duty. But the social welfare state is not enough. The sense of duty must be expressed specifically and passionately in the heart and will of men, in their daily decisions and their daily existence, if free men are to remain free.

The contemporary schism between the individual and the community has weakened the will of man. Social conditions cannot, of course, make moral decisions. But they can create conditions where moral decisions are more or less likely to be made. Some social arrangements bring out the evil in man more quickly than others. Slavery, as we knew well in America, corrupts the masters; totalitarian society, placing unbearable strains on man's self-restraint, produces the most violent reactions of fanaticism and hatred; the unchecked rule of the business community encourages greed and oppression. So the reform of institutions becomes an indispensable part of the enterprise of democracy. But the reform of institutions can never be a substitute for the reform of man.

The inadequacy of our institutions only intensifies the tribute that society levies from man: it but exacerbates the moral crisis. The rise of totalitarianism, in other words, signifies more than an internal crisis for democratic society. It signifies an internal crisis for democratic man. There is a Hitler, a Stalin in every breast. "Each of us has the plague within him," cries Tarrou in the Camus novel; "no one, no one on earth is free from it. And I know, too, that we must keep endless watch on ourselves lest in a careless moment we breathe in somebody's face and fasten the infection on him. What's natural is the microbe. All the rest — health, integrity, purity (if you like) — is a product of the human will, of a vigilance that must never falter." [2]

How to produce a vigilance that never falters? how to strengthen the human will? Walt Whitman in his later years grew obsessed with the moral indolence of democracy. Once he had hymned its possibilities with unequaled fervor. Now he looked about him and saw people "with hearts of rags and souls of chalk." As he pondered "the shallowness and miserable selfism of these crowds of men, with all their minds so blank of high humanity and aspiration," then came "the terrible query . . . Is not

Democracy of human rights humbug after all?" The expansion of the powers of government provided no solution. "I have little hope of any man or any community of men, that looks to some civil or military power to defend its vital rights. — If we have it not in ourselves to defend what belongs to us, then the citadel and heart of the towns are taken."

Wherein lies the hope? In "the exercise of Democracy," Whitman finally answered. " . . . to work for Democracy is good, the exercise is good — strength it makes and lessons it teaches." The hope for free society lies, in the last resort, in the kind of men it creates. "There is no week nor day nor hour," wrote Whitman, "when tyranny may not enter upon this country, if the people lose their supreme confidence in themselves, — and lose their roughness and spirit of defiance — Tyranny may always enter — there is no charm, no bar against it — the only bar against it is a large resolute breed of men." [3]

In times past, when freedom has been a fighting faith, producing a "large resolute breed of men," it has acquired its dynamism from communion in action. "The exercise of Democracy" has quickened the sense of the value of the individual; and, in that exercise, the individual has found a just and fruitful relation to the community. We require today exactly such a rededication to concrete democratic ends; so that the exercise of democracy can bring about a reconciliation between the individual and the community, a revival of the *élan* of democracy, and a resurgence of the democratic faith.

The expansion of the powers of government may often be an essential part of society's attack on evils of want and injustice. The industrial economy, for example, has become largely inaccessible to the control of the individual; and, even in the field of civil freedom, law is the means society has for registering its own best standards. Some of the democratic exhilaration consequently has to be revived by delegation: this is why we need the Franklin Roosevelts. Yet the expansion of the powers of government, the reliance on leadership, as Whitman perceived, have also become a means of dodging personal responsibility. This is the essential importance of the issues of civil rights and civil liberties. Every one of us has a direct, piercing and inescapable responsibility in our own lives on questions of racial discrimination, of political and intellectual freedom — not just to support legislative programs, but to extirpate the prejudices of bigotry in our environment, and, above all, in ourselves.

Through this joint democratic effort we can tap once again the spontaneous sources of community in our society. Industrialism has covered over the springs of social brotherhood by accelerating the speed and mobility of existence. Standardization, for example, while it has certainly raised levels not only of consumption but of culture, has at the same time cut the umbilical cord too early; it has reduced life to an anonymity of abundance which brings less personal fulfillment than people once got from labor in their own shop or garden. More people read and write; but what they read and write tends to have less connection with themselves. We have made culture available to all at the expense of making much of it the expression of a common fantasy rather than of a common experience. We desperately need a rich emotional life, reflecting actual relations between the individual and the community.

The cultural problem is but one aspect of the larger problem of the rôle of independent groups, of voluntary associations, in free society. There is an evident thinness in the texture of political democracy, a lack of appeal to those irrational sentiments once mobilized by religion and now by totalitarianism. Democracy, we have argued, is probably inherently incapable of satisfying those emotions in the apparatus of the state without losing its own character. Yet a democratic society, based on a genuine cultural pluralism, on widespread and spontaneous group activity, could go far to supply outlets for the variegated emotions of man, and thus to restore meaning to democratic life. It is the disappearance of effective group activity which leads toward emptiness in the individual, as it also compels the enlargement of the powers of the state.

People deprived of any meaningful rôle in society, lacking even their own groups to give them a sense of belonging, become cannon fodder for totalitarianism. And groups themselves, once long established, suffer inevitable tendencies toward exclusiveness and bureaucratization, forget their original purpose and contribute to the downfall of freedom. If the American Medical Association, for example, had given serious attention to the problem of meeting the medical needs of America today, Doctor Fishbein would not be dunning his membership for funds to support a lobby against national health insurance. In the short run, the failure of voluntary initiative invites the spread of state power. In the long run, the disappearance of voluntary association paves the way for the pulverization of the social structure essential to totalitarianism. By the revitalization of voluntary associations, we can siphon off emotions which might otherwise be driven to the solutions of despair. We can create strong bulwarks against the totalitarianization of society. [4]

Democracy requires unremitting action on many fronts. It is, in other words, a process, not a conclusion. However painful the thought, it must be recognized that its commitments are unending. The belief in the millennium has dominated our social thinking too long. Our utopian prophets have always supposed that a day would come when all who had not worshiped the beast nor received his mark on their foreheads would reign for a thousand years. "And God shall wipe away all tears from their eyes; and there shall be no more death, neither sorrow, nor crying, neither shall there be any more pain: for the former things are passed away."

But the Christian millennium calls for a catastrophic change in human nature. Let us not sentimentalize the millennium by believing we can attain it through scientific discovery or through the revision of our economic system. We must grow up now and forsake the millennial dream. We will not arise one morning to find all problems solved, all need for further strain and struggle ended, while we work two hours a day and spend our leisure eating milk and honey. Given human imperfection, society will continue imperfect. Problems will always torment us, because all important problems are insoluble: that is why they are important. The good comes from the continuing struggle to try and solve them, not from the vain hope of their solution.

This is just as true of the problems of international society. "What men call peace," Gilson has well said, "is never anything but a space between two wars; a precarious equilibrium that lasts as long as mutual fear prevents dissension from declaring itself. This parody of true peace, this armed fear . . . may very well support a kind of order, but never can it bring mankind anything of tranquillity. Not until the social order becomes the spontaneous expression of an interior peace in men's hearts shall we have tranquillity." [5] Does it seem likely (pending the millennium) that we shall ever have an interior peace in the hearts of enough men to transform the nature of human society? The pursuit of peace, Whitehead reminds us, easily passes into its bastard substitute, anesthesia.

So we are forced back on the reality of struggle. So long as society stays free, so long will it continue in its state of tension, breeding contradiction, breeding strife. But we betray ourselves if we accept contradiction and strife as the total meaning of conflict. For conflict is also the guarantee of freedom; it is the instrument of change; it is, above all, the source of discovery, the source of art, the source of love. The choice we face is not between progress with conflict and progress without conflict. The choice is between conflict and stagnation. You cannot expel conflict from society any more than you can from the human mind. When you attempt it, the psychic costs in schizophrenia or torpor are the same.

The totalitarians regard the toleration of conflict as our central weakness. So it may appear to be in an age of anxiety. But we know it to be basically our central strength. The new radicalism derives its power from an acceptance of conflict — an acceptance combined with a determination to create a social framework where conflict issues, not in excessive anxiety, but in creativity. The center is vital; the center must hold. The object of the

new radicalism is to restore the center, to reunite individual and community in fruitful union. The spirit of
the new radicalism is the spirit of the center — the spirit
of human decency, opposing the extremes of tyranny. Yet,
in a more fundamental sense, does not the center itself
represent one extreme? while, at the other, are grouped
the forces of corruption — men transformed by pride and
power into enemies of humanity.

The new radicalism, drawing strength from a realistic
conception of man, dedicates itself to problems as they
come, attacking them in terms which best advance the
humane and libertarian values, which best secure the
freedom and fulfillment of the individual. It believes in
attack — and out of attack will come passionate intensity.

Can we win the fight? We must commit ourselves to it
with all our vigor in all its dimensions: the struggle
within the world against Communism and fascism; the
struggle within our country against oppression and stagnation; the struggle within ourselves against pride and
corruption: nor can engagement in one dimension ex-
clude responsibility for another. Economic and political
action can help restore the balance between individual
and community and thereby reduce one great source of
anxiety. But even the most favorable social arrangements
cannot guarantee individual virtue; and we are far yet
from having solved the social problem.

The commitment is complex and rigorous. When has
it not been so? If democracy cannot produce the large
resolute breed of men capable of the climactic effort, it
will founder. Out of the effort, out of the struggle alone,
can come the high courage and faith which will preserve
freedom.

Acknowledgments

A book like this is in essence a collaboration. I owe a general debt to the many persons who have taken a part in the great enterprise of the revaluation of liberalism and whose achievements this book is largely concerned with reporting. I have sought to identify most of these people in the text.

I am under a special debt to some who helped me directly in this work. John E. Sawyer submitted the entire draft to keen and illuminating criticism. Anne Whyte read a large portion of the book at an early stage. Barbara Wendell Kerr read the book, and, as the researcher assigned to my *Life* articles on the American Communist Party and on civil liberties, contributed greatly to my knowledge of these subjects. The friends with whom I have worked so closely in Americans for Democratic Action — in particular, Joseph L. Rauh, Jr., James A. Wechsler and James Loeb, Jr. — though they may disagree with some of the ideas I have set forth, have helped to mold the general direction of my thinking and to renew in me the conviction that American liberalism has a bright future. My observations on civil liberties and the loyalties issue benefit much from the generous advice of Paul A. Porter and Nancy Wechsler. My father's absence from the country deprived me of the opportunity to consult him on specific points, but the general approach owes much to his wisdom on questions of politics and society. My wife Marian Cannon Schlesinger gave shape and character to the book by the ruthless application of her rigorous taste to the manuscript.

Some of the passages in this book have appeared in print before: in an article for *Life* magazine, "The American Communist Party"; in an article for the *Partisan Review*, "The Future of Socialism, III, The Perspective Now"; in an article for the *Nation*, "Political Culture in the United States"; and in two articles for the *New York Times Sunday Magazine*, "What is Loyalty?" and "Not Left, Not Right." I am grateful to the editors of the publications named for permission to reprint these passages. The poem in the front of the book is from W. B. Yeats: *Later Poems*, copyright, 1924, by The Macmillan Company, and used with their permission. I have also adapted certain sentences from material I contributed to the Americans for Democratic Action pamphlet on foreign policy, *Toward Total Peace*.

Notes

CHAPTER I

1. Peter C. Brooks to Edward Everett, July 15, 1845, Everett Papers, Massachusetts Historical Society.

2. William M. Gouge, *A Short History of Paper Money and Banking in the United States,* Philadelphia, 1833, Part I, p. 43.

3. Winston Churchill, London *Times,* August 29, 1944.

4. H. D. Thoreau, "Plea for Captain John Brown," *Works,* Boston, 1894, vol. iv, p. 429.

5. John C. Calhoun, *A Disquisition on Government,* New York, 1854, p. 90.

CHAPTER II

1. Georges Sorel, *Reflections on Violence,* London, 1925, p. 58.

2. *Nation,* March 13, 1943.

3. Sorel, *Reflections on Violence,* p. 72.

4. Matthew Josephson, *The President-Makers,* New York, 1940.

5. Charles Francis Adams, *An Autobiography,* Boston, 1916, p. 190.

6. Brooks Adams, "Natural Selection in Literature," *American Economic Supremacy,* New York, 1900, pp. 94, 111–113, 116.

7. H. C. Lodge to Theodore Roosevelt, October 20, 1902. *Selections from the Correspondence of Theodore Roosevelt and Henry Cabot Lodge,* 1889–1918, New York, 1925, p. 542.

8. Quoted by Richard Hofstadter, *The American Political Tradition,* New York, 1947, p. 217.

9. Theodore Roosevelt, "The Strenuous Life," *Works,* Memorial Edition, vol. XV, p. 281.

10. Theodore Roosevelt to Sir Edward Grey, November 15, 1913, *Works,* Memorial Edition, vol. XXIV, p. 409.

11. Theodore Roosevelt to T. C. Platt, Spring 1899, *Works,* Memorial Edition, vol. XXIII, p. 146.

12. Theodore Roosevelt, Osawatomie speech, August 31, 1910, *Works,* Memorial Edition, vol. XIX, p. 24.

13. Brooks Adams, *The Theory of Social Revolution,* New York, 1913, p. 33.

14. Herbert Hoover, *The New Day,* Stanford University, 1928, p. 16.

15. Raymond Moley, *After Seven Years,* New York, 1939, p. 160.

16. Joseph A. Schumpeter, *Capitalism, Socialism and Democracy,* New York, 1947, p. 142.

17. Schumpeter, *Capitalism, Socialism and Democracy,* p. 156.

18. Quoted by Joseph and Stewart Alsop, "Last Chance," *Atlantic Monthly,* January, 1947.

19. Robert A. Taft, "The Housing Problem," an address before the Cincinnati Chamber of Commerce, January 7, 1946, reprinted in the Congressional Record, January 17, 1946.

20. Harold Stassen, *Where I Stand!* New York, 1947, p. 205.

21. *New York Herald Tribune,* November 21, 1948.

CHAPTER III

1. D. W. Brogan, *Is Innocence Enough?,* London, 1941, p. 13.

2. Dwight Macdonald, *Henry Wallace: The Man and The Myth,* New York, 1948, p. 23.

3. Thomas Jefferson to John Adams, July 5, 1814, *Works of Thomas Jefferson,* Federal edition, XI, 394.

4. Reinhold Niebuhr, "The Sickness of American Culture," *Nation,* March 6, 1948.

5. Sigmund Freud, *Civilization and its Discontents,* New York, 1930, p. 89.

6. Marcel Proust, *Remembrance of Things Past,* New York, 1934, vol. I, p. 190.

CHAPTER IV

1. S. Kierkegaard, *Begriff der Angst,* 57, quoted Reinhold Niebuhr, *The Nature and Destiny of Man,* New York, 1941, vol. I, p. 252.

2. J. P. Sartre, *Existentialism,* New York, 1947, p. 27.

3. *Bay State Democrat,* Boston, January 15, 1844.

4. T. S. Eliot, *Four Quartets,* London, 1944, pp. 10–11.

5. F. Dostoievsky, *The Brothers Karamazov,* Bk. V, chap. 5.

6. Marshal Zhukov's remark is from his fascinating discussion with General Eisenhower. D. D. Eisenhower, *Crusade in Europe,* New York, 1948, p. 472. For Simonov, see his preface to *Soviet Writers' Reply to English Writers' Questions,* London, 1948, p. 10. Goebbels's statement is from *Michael,* p. 25, quoted by Erich Fromm, *Escape from Freedom,* New York, 1941, p. 233.

7. Elio Vittorini, in *Esprit,* January, 1948, reprinted *Modern Review,* June, 1948.

8. André Malraux, *Man's Hope,* New York, 1948, p. 153.

9. Quoted by Sir John Maynard, *Russia in Flux,* New York, 1948, p. 278.

10. E. H. Carr, *The Soviet Impact on the Western World,* New York, 1947, p. 85.

11. Arthur Koestler, *The Yogi and the Commissar,* London, 1945, p. 14.

12. Cf. especially preface to André Malraux, *Days of Wrath,* New York, 1936.

13. Quoted by Benjamin Gitlow, *I Confess!,* New York, 1940, p. 561.

14. Robert Lowell, "Mr. Edwards and the Spider," *Lord Weary's Castle,* New York, 1947, p. 58.

15. Arthur Koestler, *Darkness at Noon,* New York, 1941, p. 14.

16. *Report of Court Proceedings in the Case of the Anti-Soviet "Bloc of Rights and Trotskyites,"* Moscow, 1938, pp. 777, 778.

17. Herman Rauschning, *The Voice of Destruction,* New York, 1940, p. 131.

18. Christopher Burney, *The Dungeon Democracy,* New York, 1946, p. 156.

19. André Malraux and James Burnham, *The Case for De Gaulle,* New York, 1948, p. 62. See also Malraux's essay on Lawrence, " 'Was That All, Then?' " *Transition,* No. 2, 1948.

20. Hitler on July 13, 1934, quoted by H. B. Gisevius, *To the Bitter End,* Boston, 1947, p. 121.

21. Quoted by Konrad Heiden, *Der Fuehrer,* Boston, 1944, p. 751.

22. E. H. Carr, *The Romantic Exiles,* New York, 1933, 140. I am indebted to Malcolm Muggeridge for pointing this quotation out to me.

23. Lenin, *What Is to be Done?,* New York, 1929, p. 112.

24. A. W. Dulles, *Germany's Underground,* New York, 1947, p. 14.

CHAPTER V

1. Karl Marx and Friedrich Engels, *The Communist Manifesto,* New York, 1948, p. 22.

2. Joseph Stalin, "Lenin's Contribution to Marxism," interview with the American Labor Delegation, September 9, 1927, *On the Theory of Marxism,* Little Lenin Library, vol. xxxi, p. 31.

3. B. D. Wolfe, *Three Who Made a Revolution,* New York, 1938, pp. 293, 253.

4. L. Trotsky, *Dictatorship vs. Democracy,* New York, 1922, p. 63.

5. Quoted by Arthur Koestler, *The Yogi and The Commissar,* p. 188.

6. D. W. Brogan, *Is Innocence Enough?,* pp. 85–86.

7. Cf. the cogent analysis by Rudolf Hilferding, "State Capitalism or Totalitarian State Economy," *Modern Review,* June, 1947.

8. See "USSR Today — Documents," *Politics,* Spring, 1948; also *Newsweek,* April 4, 1949.

9. Molotov's speech of November 6, 1947, on the thirtieth anniversary of the Revolution. Reprinted in House Document 619, 80th Congress, *The Strategy and Tactics of World Communism,* Supplement I, p. 235.

10. A. Zhdanov on cultural policy, *Voks Bulletin No. 51.*

11. K. Simonov in *Litraturnaya Gazeta,* November 23, 1946, reprinted in *Strategy and Tactics of World Communism,* Supplement I, p. 181.

12. A. Fadeyev in *Izvestia,* quoted *Newsweek,* December 8, 1947.

13. André Malraux, "Man's Death is the Problem," *New Republic,* November 15, 1948.

14. Tikhon Khrennikov in *Soviet Art,* February 28, 1948, quoted by Nicholas Nabokov, "The Music Purge," *Politics,* Spring, 1948.

15. *Time,* May 17, 1948.

16. *New Statesman and Nation,* March 6, 1948.

17. *New York Herald Tribune,* April 27, 1948.

18. *New Statesman and Nation,* March 6, 1948.

19. Dostoievsky, *The Possessed,* Part II, chap. viii.

20. George Fitzhugh, *Sociology for the South, or the Failure of Free Society,* Richmond, 1854, pp. 67, 26, 251, 61, 70, 27–28, 49, 245.

21. André Malraux, *Man's Fate,* New York, 1934, 327.

22. Hannah Arendt, "The Concentration Camps," *Partisan Review,* July, 1948.

CHAPTER VI

1. William Z. Foster, *Marxism-Leninism vs. Revisionism,* New York, 1948, p. 11. See also Budenz, *This Is My Story,* p. 303.

2. James F. Byrnes, *Speaking Frankly,* New York, 1947, chap. 3.

3. Marx, "The Eastern Question," *New York Herald Tribune,* 1853, quoted by James F. Byrnes, *Speaking Frankly,* p. 282.

264   NOTES

. P. F. Iudin, *Socialism and Communism,* Moscow, 1946, p. 32; quoted in *Trends in Russian Foreign Policy Since World War I,* Library of Congress, Washington, 1947, p. 53.

5. *Literary Gazette,* No. 44, 1946, quoted by Harry Martin, *Guild Reporter,* May 28, 1948.

6. *New York Times,* September 24, 1948.

7. Edgar Snow, "Will Tito's Heretics Halt Russia?" *Saturday Evening Post,* December 18, 1948.

8. See the daily press, February–April, 1949.

9. "The Communist Party," *Fortune,* September, 1934.

10. Benjamin Gitlow, *The Whole of Their Lives,* New York, 1948, pp. 236–37.

11. J. H. Dolsen, testifying before the Committee on Un-American Activities, 76 Congress 3 session, *Hearings . . .* vol. XII, p. 7407.

12. Article ix, section 4, *Constitution of the Communist Party of the United States of America.*

13. *Political Affairs,* September, 1947.

14. *Daily Worker,* November 6, 1939.

15. Quoted by another Communist leader, Robert Thompson, *The Path of a Renegade,* New York, 1946, p. 17.

16. Eugene Dennis, *What America Faces,* New York, 1946, pp. 37–38.

17. See Alfred Friendly's interview with Quill, *Washington Post,* May 2, 1948; also *Newsweek,* September 27, 1948.

18. *New York Post,* December 31, 1947.

19. The best analysis of the campaign is Dwight Macdonald, "The Wallace Campaign: an Autopsy," *Politics,* Summer (i.e., late fall) , 1948. The best piece on Wallace himself during the campaign is James A. Wechsler's perceptive, "My Ten Months with Wallace," *The Progressive,* November, 1948. The most circumstantial analysis of the personnel of the Wallace movement is by Victor Lasky, "Who Runs Wallace?" *Plain Talk,* June, 1948. Indispensable documents for a study of the campaign are "Henry Wallace, the First Three Months" and "Henry A. Wallace, the Last Seven Months of his Presidential Campaign" — critical memoranda prepared by the anti-Com-

munist liberal organization, Americans for Democratic Action
(ADA).

20. Dwight Macdonald, *Henry Wallace,* pp. 177–181.

21. *New York Times,* May 29, 1924.

22. *New York Times,* July 26, 1948.

23. *New York Times,* September 26, 1948.

24. *New York World Telegram,* March 22, 1944.

25. Albert Maltz, "What Shall We Ask of Writers?", *New
Masses,* February 12, 1946.

26. Albert Maltz, "Moving Forward," *New Masses,* April 9,
1946. Cf. also James T. Farrell's brilliant "Stalinist Literary
Discussion," *New International,* April, 1946.

27. Harold J. Laski, *The Secret Battalion,* London, 1946,
pp. 15, 27, 14.

CHAPTER VII

1. Rosa Luxemburg, *Die Russische Revolution,* 113, quoted
by Paul Frölich, *Rosa Luxemburg,* London, 1940, 276–277.

2. Joseph Stalin, *Foundations of Leninism,* New York, 1932,
p. 18.

3. V. I. Lenin, *"Left Wing" Communism: An Infantile
Disorder,* London, 1934, pp. 54, 70.

4. William Z. Foster, *Toward Soviet America,* p. 177; O.
Kuusinen, *The Right-Wing Social-Democrats Today,* Moscow,
1948, p. 20.

5. Interview with Ray Josephs, *Washington Post,* October
14, 1947.

6. *New York Times,* July 1, 1946.

7. *New York Herald Tribune,* May 30, 1948.

8. *Washington Star,* January 3, 1947.

9. London *Times,* September 1, 1948.

10. *New York Herald Tribune,* April 14, 1948.

11. *New York World Telegram,* June 22, 1945.

12. Stalin, *Foundations of Leninism,* p. 103.

13. *Guild Reporter,* June 11, 1948. See also William S.
White's stories in the *New York Times,* June 2, 3, 1948.

14. *New York Times,* November 14, 1948.

15. Matthiessen, *From the Heart of Europe,* p. 167.

16. Gollancz, *The Betrayal of the Left,* p. 297.

17. W. C. Bruce, *John Randolph of Roanoke,* New York, 1922, vol. II, p. 211.

18. Marx and Engels, *The Communist Manifesto,* p. 11.

19. Engels to Conrad Schmidt, October 27, 1890, *On the Theory of Marxism,* Little Lenin Library, vol. xxxi, pp. 15, 16.

20. Frances Perkins, *The Roosevelt I Knew,* New York, 1946, p. 230.

21. Ignazio Silone, "Socialism and Marxist Ideology," *Modern Review,* January, 1948.

22. Pascal, *Pensées,* No. 358.

CHAPTER VIII

1. J. D. Richardson, ed., *Messages and Papers of the Presidents,* Washington, 1908, vol. I, pp. 322, 323.

2. Nathaniel Hawthorne, *The Blithedale Romance,* chap. ix. The same point could be made in terms of Herman Melville; see, for example, the illuminating essay by Richard Chase, "Melville's *Confidence Man,*" *Kenyon Review,* Winter, 1949.

3. Louis Jaffe, *University of Chicago Law Review,* April, 1947.

4. V. L. Parrington, *Main Currents in American Thought,* New York, 1927, vol. ii, p. 448.

5. John Taylor, *Inquiry into the Principles and Policy of the Government of the United States,* Fredericksburg, 1814, pp. 558–59.

6. F. D. Roosevelt, *Public Papers and Addresses,* New York, 1938–41, vol. v, p. 384; *New York Times,* February 11, 1940.

7. Sumner Welles, *The Time for Decision,* New York, 1944, pp. 16, 57.

8. *New York Herald Tribune,* January 15, 1948.

9. Richardson, ed., *Messages and Papers,* vol. I, p. 332.

10. Reinhold Niebuhr, *The Children of Light and the Children of Darkness,* New York, 1944, p. xi.

11. James Madison, *Federalist No. 10.*

12. Richardson, ed., *Messages and Papers,* Vol. II, p. 590.

13. Marx to Weydemeyer, March 5, 1852, V. I. Lenin, *State and Revolution,* New York, 1932, pp. 29, 30.

14. Theodore Roosevelt, *The Foes of Our Own Household,* New York, 1917, p. 177.

15. James B. Conant, "Wanted: American Radicals," *Atlantic Monthly,* May, 1943.

16. Theodore Roosevelt, introduction to S. J. Duncan-Clark, *The Progressive Movement,* Boston, 1913, p. xix; Herbert Croly, *The Promise of American Life,* New York, 1909, p. 274.

17. Herbert Croly, *Progressive Democracy,* New York, 1914, p. 15.

18. Theodore Roosevelt, *The Foes of Our Own Household,* p. 122.

19. Franklin D. Roosevelt, *Public Papers,* vol. v, p. 16.

20. D. W. Brogan, *The English People,* New York, 1943, p. 108.

CHAPTER IX

1. John Quincy Adams, *Memoirs,* vol. iv, p. 531.

2. Quoted by Chafee, *Free Speech,* p. 52.

3. Both Palmer quotations are from A. Mitchell Palmer, "The Case Against the 'Reds,'" *Forum,* February, 1920.

4. From Hughes's brief to the Judiciary Committee of the New York Assembly for the Bar Association of the City of New York (1921) on behalf of the Socialist assemblymen.

5. Alfred Lief, ed., *The Social and Economic Views of Mr. Justice Brandeis,* New York, 1920, pp. 261–62.

6. In Abrams v. the U.S. (1919), Alfred Lief, ed., *The Dissenting Opinion of Mr. Justice Holmes,* New York, 1929, p. 48.

7. Alfred Lief, ed., *The Social and Economic Views of Mr. Justice Brandeis,* p. 262.

8. Alfred Lief, ed., *The Dissenting Opinions of Mr. Justice Holmes,* p. 50.

9. Max Lerner, *The Mind and Faith of Justice Holmes,* New York, 1943, pp. 315, 316.

10. Gilbert Gordon, "Fascist Field Day in Chicago," *Nation,* January 24, 1948.

11. *Harvard Crimson,* February 6, 1948.

12. William Z. Foster in *Political Affairs,* January, 1948.

13. The documents in this controversy are in the files of the American Economic Association.

14. James B. Conant, *Education in a Divided World,* Cambridge, 1948, pp. 172, 178–79.

15. Holmes's opinion in McAuliffe v. the Mayor of New Bedford, 155 Mass. 216, 220, N.E. 517 (1892).

16. Letter to the editor, *Harper's,* November, 1947.

17. Letter to the editor, *New York Herald Tribune,* December 18, 1947.

CHAPTER X

1. *Aurore,* August 15, 1905, quoted Sorel, *Reflections on Violence,* p. 71.

2. Harold J. Laski, "Truman's Task in Europe," *New Republic,* December 20, 1948.

3. Stalin, *Foundations of Leninism,* p. 124.

4. London *Times,* September 8, 1948.

5. William Vogt, *Road to Survival,* New York, 1948, p. 284.

CHAPTER XI

1. Alex Comfort, *The Novel and Our Time,* London, 1948, p. 12.

2. Albert Camus, *The Plague,* New York, 1948, p. 229.

3. Walt Whitman, "Notes for Lecturers on Democracy and 'Adhesiveness,'" C. J. Furness, *Walt Whitman's Workshop,* Cambridge, 1928, pp. 57, 58.

4. For the rôle of private associations, see Alexis de Tocqueville, *Democracy in America,* Part I, chap. 12, Part II, bk. i, chaps. 5–7; and the essay, "Biography of a Nation of Joiners," Arthur M. Schlesinger, *Path to the Present,* New York, 1949.

5. Etienne Gilson, *The Spirit of Medieval Philosophy,* New York, 1936, p. 399.

INDEX

Gandhi, Mohandas K., 7
Gaulle, General Charles de, 61, 93, 223
Gentlemen's Agreement, 190
Germany, presumed peace negotiations with, 95
Gide, André, 147
Gil Robles, José María, 93
Gilson, Étienne, quoted, 254-255
Gitlow, Ben, 109, 114; quoted, 105
Goebbels, Joseph, 62; quoted, 54
Goerdeler, Karl Friedrich, 66; quoted, 225 n.
Goering, Hermann, 66
Gold, Mike, 124
Gollancz, Victor, 146
González Videla, Gabriel, quoted, 135
Gorky, Maxim, 57 n.
Government ownership, 155
Government service, loyalty in, 212-218
Gradualism, 134, 154-155
Great Britain, foreign policy, 14-15, 222-223, 232;
    Toryism, 15-16;
    Communist tactics against, 139-142;
    class struggle, 173-174;
    social planning, 182, 183-184
Greece, American policy toward, 224, 226, 227
Green, Dwight, 194
Hamilton, Alexander, 16, 17, 158, 171, 177
Hamsun, Knut, 61
Hanna, Mark, 21
Harding, Warren G., 24
Harriman, W. Averell, 168, 187
Harris, Seymour, 186
Hart, Merwin K., 206-207
Hawthorne, Nathaniel, 161-162, 163, 165
Haymarket riot, 193
Hemingway, Ernest, 45, 147
Henderson, Arthur, 133
Henderson, Leon, 166, 187
Herndon, Angelo, 121
Hicks, Granville, 106
History, conservative and plutocratic views, 20 n.
Hitler, Adolf, 14, 15, 49, 61-62, 66-67, 110, 139, 227; quoted, 60
Ho Chi Minh, 232
Hogg, Quintin, quoted, 16
Hollywood, influence of, on writers, 125
Holmes, Justice Oliver Wendell, 198, 208; quoted, 199, 200-201, 213
Homage to Catalonia (Orwell), 45
Hoover, Herbert C., 28, 29; quoted, 24
Hoover, J. Edgar, 129
Hughes, Charles Evans, 24, 196, 198, 208; quoted, 197
Hull, Cordell, 166, 167, 222
Humphrey, Hubert, 187
Ickes, Harold, 24, 136
Independent Citizens' Committee for

the Arts, Sciences and Professions, 115, 121, 136
India, 232
Individualism, 84-87, 244, 248-249
Indo-China, 232
Indonesian Republic, 231-232
Industrial Revolution, 4, 7, 15, 16, 20, 176
Industrialism, American, 44;
    influence of, on society, 4-6, 243-244, 252
Institute of World Economics, 82
Institutions, reform of, 250
Isolationism, 219-220
Italy, weakness of Socialism, 148
Iudin, P. F., quoted, 99

Jackson, Andrew, 18, 158, 165, 176; quoted, 172
Jaffe, Louis, quoted, 162
Jaurès, Jean, 47
Jefferson, Thomas, 16, 42, 172, 176; quoted, 42, 158, 170
Jews. *See* Anti-Semitism
Josephson, Matthew, quoted, 19
Judas Time, The (Schneider), 105
Juenger, Ernst, 61

Kamenev, Lev Borisovich, 63
Kapital, Das (Marx), 54
Kautskians, 133
Kautsky, Karl, 131-132, 143
Kemenov, Vladimir, quoted, 80
Kennan, George, 167
Keynes, John Maynard, 183, 206
Kierkegaard, Sören, 39; quoted, 52
Kingdon, Frank, quoted, 116
Kingsblood Royal, 190
Kirshon, Vladimir, 55
Knox, Frank, 24, 222
Koch, Erich, 62
Koestler, Arthur, 120, 147; quoted, 56
Kronstadt, uprising at, 69-70, 72
Kutcher, James, 215

Labor movement, American, 168-169, 187-188. *See also* Trade unions
La Follette, Robert M., 164, 178; quoted, 117
Land problem, in present-day social revolution, 233
Laski, Harold J., 12; quoted, 128, 226
Latin America, social revolution in, 229
Laval, Pierre, 60
Lawrence, T. E., 61
Lawson, John Howard, 125
Leclerc, General Jean, 61
Left, democratic, Communist tactics with, 131-143;
    rise of non-Communist, 143-148;
    rejection of totalitarianism, 149-153;
    economic policy, 153-154;
    outlook for, 154-156. *See also* Radicalism, American
Lenin, Nikolai, 47, 61, 63, 64, 66, 68-